Cold War Hot

Cold War Hot

Alternate Decisions
of the
Cold War

Edited by Peter G. Tsouras

Skyhorse Publishing

CONTENTS

ILLUSTRATIONS

MAPS

THE CONTRIBUTORS

JAMES R. ARNOLD is a professional writer who specializes in military history. He has published over 20 books roughly divided into three major topic areas: the Napoleonic era, the Civil War; and the modern period. His two most recent books are a Napoleonic campaign study, *Marengo and Hohenlinden: Napoleon's Rise to Power* and *JeffDavis's Own: Cavalry, Comanches, and the Battle for the Texas Frontier.* He has also contributed numerous essays to military journals, including the British *Journal of the Society for Army Historical Research* and the American journals *Army History, Army Magazine,* and *Navy History.* His chapter in this book reflects his interest in the influence of intelligence and espionage upon military events. Most recently he contributed to *Rising Sun Victorious: How the Japanese Won the Pacific War.*

JOHN D. BURTT is the editor of *Paper Wars* magazine, an independent review journal devoted to wargames. In his day job he is an advisory nuclear engineer consulting for the US Nuclear Regulatory Commission. However, his real love is military history. A former Marine sergeant and a veteran of Vietnam, he holds a master's degree in military history and is pursuing a PhD in the same field. He has written for *Command* magazine, *Strategy & Tactics,* and *The Wargamer,* and was the original editor of *Counter-Attack* magazine. He was also a contributor to *Rising Sun Victorious* and *Third Reich Victorious: How the Germans Won the War.*

WADE G. DUDLEY holds a master's degree in maritime history and nautical archaeology from East Carolina University (1997) and a doctorate in history from the University of Alabama (1999). He contributed chapters to *Rising Sun Victorious* and *Third Reich Victorious,* and is the author of *Drake: For God, Queen, and Plunder!* and *Splintering the Wooden Wall: The British Blockade of the United States, 1812–1815.* He is a visiting assistant professor at East Carolina University in Greenville, North Carolina.

PADDY GRIFFITH is a freelance military history author and publisher who first studied the Vietnam War for a part of his book *Forward Into Battle* (1981). Since then he has continued to write occasional articles on the subject, and in 1995 he edited Greg McCauley's *Buckle for* *your Dust* guide to Vietnam wargaming. He lectured on insurgency and counter-insurgency issues (among other things) at the Royal Military Academy, Sandhurst, in the 1970s and 1980s, and more recently at the University of Salford. He was also a contributor to *Rising Sun Victorious* and *Third Reich Victorious.*

MICHAEL R. HATHAWAY retired from the US federal civil service in 1999 and is currently a consultant living in Reston, Virginia. He earned a BA in Political Science, University of California at Berkeley, 1972; an MBA from Jacksonville State University, 1977; and a Juris Doctorate from Golden Gate University, 1981. He was commissioned second lieutenant in the US Army in 1972 and had three years active duty service in Military Intelligence. Civilian employment with the Social Security Administration and the Office of Naval Research followed. In 1981 he became the National Security Legislative Assistant to US Senator Alfonse D'Amato. In 1985 he was appointed Staff Director, Commission on Security and Cooperation in Europe and in 1987 Staff Counsel to the Minority, US Senate International Narcotics Control Caucus; in 1989 Professional Staff Member, US Senate Select Committee on Intelligence; in 1995 Deputy Chief of Staff, Commission on Security and Cooperation in Europe; and in 1997 Chief of Staff. He has contributed a chapter to *Just Cause: The US Intervention in Panama.*

DAVID C. ISBYhas written and edited 18 books and over 350 articles on national security and intelligence. He is the author of three books on Afghanistan (and many articles): *War In A Distant Country: Afghanistan, Invasion And Resistance; War In Afghanistan: The Soviet Empire At High Tide,* and *Russia's War In Afghanistan.* He was also a contributor to *Rising Sun Victorious* and *Third Reich Victorious.* A Washington-based attorney and consultant on national security issues, Mr Isby is a frequent visitor to south Asia. He has provided policy support for US government negotiations (bilateral and multilateral), and studies and advice for government departments and agencies. He has testified before congressional committees as an independent expert on Afghanistan. Mr Isby frequently appears in print and electronic media as an expert on national security issues. He was condemned by the Soviet government (pre-glasnost) as a "bourgeois falsifier of history" and "a CIA agent... with whom accounts will be settled" in recognition of his work on Afghanistan.

KEVIN F. KILEY is a former Marine Artillery officer who served in combat with the 10th Marine Regiment in Kuwait in 1991. A West Point graduate, he commanded two artillery batteries, and he now teaches middle school mathematics in Jacksonville, North Carolina.

An avid collector of toy and model soldiers, he is now working on his first book on Napoleonic artillery. He is married, and he and his wife, Daisy, have a young son, Michael, who is named after Kevin's brother, Captain Michael J. Kiley, who was killed in action in the Republic of Vietnam on November 19, 1967 in the Battle of Dak To while commander of A Company, 2nd Battalion, 503rd Infantry (Airborne). This is for all three of them—*Virtute et Valore.*

LT COLONEL FORREST R. LINDSEY, USMC (ret) served nearly 30 years in the US Marine Corps, including time in combat in Vietnam. He had a variety of assignments in his military career, including nuclear weapons testing with the Defense Nuclear Agency, service as a United Nations Truce Supervisor in Egypt, and as an arms control treaty Inspection Team Leader in the former Soviet Union with the On-Site Inspection Agency. Lt Col Lindsey was assigned several artillery duties during his career, and also served as a battalion operations officer, regimental logistics officer, and commanding officer of the 5th Battalion, 11th Marines. Upon retirement from active duty in 1996, Lt Col Lindsey continued work with the Marine Corps as Senior Engineer for the Marine Corps Warfighting Laboratory at Quantico, Virginia. He is responsible for weapons experimentation and precision targeting and led the design, development and testing of the 120mm Dragon Fire automated mortar. He has published several articles on professional military issues in the *Marine Corps Gazette* and has been an invited speaker for several military conferences, including the Jane's International conference on fire support in limited war in 1998. He has a Bachelor of Science degree from Old Dominion University, Norfolk, Virginia, and is presently pursuing a master's degree in Business Administration. Lt Col Lindsey also contributed to *Rising Sun Victorious* and *Third Reich Victorious.*

DR. SEAN MALONEY served as the historian for 4th Canadian Mechanized Brigade and wrote *War Without Battles: Canada's NATO Brigade in Germany 1951–1993* which detailed Canada's land commitment to NATO during the Cold War and its initial operations in Croatia and Bosnia with the UN. Considered to be Canada's leading military historian of the Cold War and post-Cold War periods, he currently teaches in the War Studies Programme at the Royal Military College of Canada and is the author of *Canada and UN Peacekeeping: Cold War by Other Means 1945–1970; Chances for Peace: The Canadians and UNPROFOR 1991–1995; Operation BOLSTER: Canada and the European Community Monitor Mission, 1991–1994; The Hindrance of Military Operations Ashore: Canadian Participation in Operation SHARP GUARD, 1993–1996; Securing Command of the Sea: NATO Naval Planning 1948–1954;*

and *Learning to Love The Bomb: Canada's Cold War Strategy and Nuclear Weapons, 1951–1968* (forthcoming). Dr Maloney has extensive field research experience throughout the Balkans and the Middle East and is currently writing a history of Canadian operations in Kosovo.

LT COLONEL PETER G. TSOURAS, USAR (ret) is a senior analyst with the Battelle Memorial Institute in Washington. Formerly he was a senior analyst at the US Army National Ground Intelligence Center. He served in the Army as an armor officer in the 1st Battalion, 64th Armor

Regiment in Germany and subsequently in Intelligence and Adjutant Generals Corps assignments. He retired from the Army Reserve in 1994 after serving in Civil Affairs. His assignments have taken him to Somalia, Russia, the Ukraine, and Japan. He is the author or editor of 22 books on international military themes, military history, and alternate history. His books include *Disaster at D-Day: The Germans Defeat the Allies; Gettysburg: An Alternate History; The Great Patriotic War; The Anvil of War; Fighting in Hell; The Greenhill Dictionary of Military Quotations; Panzers on the Eastern Front: General Erhard Raus and His Panzer Divisions in Russia;* and most recently *Rising Sun Victorious: The Alternate History of How the Japanese Won the Pacific War* and *Third Reich Victorious: How the Germans Won the War.* He has just begun work on *Dixie Victorious: Alternate Roads to Southern Independence.*

INTRODUCTION

The black seed of the Cold War grew long before the end of World War II. As far back as the 1920s Lenin had left his successors a powerful document, a blazing declaration of war to the death with the West. Within it, he presciently identified the United States as the core of the West's strength. Even then the moral exhaustion of Europe was evident, and his eye traveled across half the world to a country still in the throes of isolation after its disappointing experience in the First World War, to fix upon the West's still vibrant heart.

Stalin gladly enshrined Lenin's declaration into every fiber of the Evil Empire he fashioned with the flesh and blood of 30 million of his own people. Even as the Germans battered at the very gates of Moscow in the dread days of December 1941, Stalin pointedly warned his shaken General Staff that the *Wehrmacht* was only a temporary problem. Let no one forget, he thundered, that the United States was the main enemy, the *glavnii vragI*[1]

Four years later, in June 1945, he stood atop Lenin's polished red granite tomb to review the victory parade over that temporary enemy. As a phalanx of his helmeted officers hurled the banners of the broken German Army[2] onto its steps, his thoughts surely sped across continents and oceans to the ultimate struggle with the main enemy. Thus was the black seed, so carefully stored for 20 years, now planted.

It took three years from Stalin's very Roman victory parade for the United States to realize the nature of the new struggle as it tried to make sense of the postwar world. But once Stalin's enmity was unmistakable, the Americans boldly picked up the gauntlet. The result was an almost 50-year struggle quickly named the Cold War. It was clearly war, for no two systems could be more fundamentally opposed. It was clearly war, for one of those systems, at its very core, was dedicated to the destruction of the other. It was cold, in the sense that neither system would risk direct conflict with the other. Although Stalin, in one of his drunken banquets during the war had famously hitched up his pants like a man ready to fight and said: "The war will soon be over. We shall recover in 15 or 20 years and then we will have another go at it."[3]

The brake on the cycle of world wars was the atom bomb. Over the years the implications of the use of that ultimate weapon by both sides evolved into the concept of Mutually Assured Destruction or MAD. War between the two great powers was ultimately a suicide pact. But, especially for the Soviets, war was a supple instrument with many variations. The destruction of the West could be achieved short of unleashing the heat of the sun across the planet. It could be done on subtle battlefields of the mind in campaigns of propaganda and subversion. It could be fought safely by proxies whose victories would add to the ultimate victory of Soviet Power in small increments, the sum of which over time would be decisive.

Thus, until the fall of the Berlin Wall in 1989, the Cold War struggle smoldered and oft times burst out into local hot wars that both the Soviets and Americans stoked safely from a distance. On only one occasion did they directly confront each other—the Cuban Missile Crisis of 1962—and the world trembled on the edge of nuclear war. For that reason, neither side again allowed itself to come that close to the abyss. On only three occasions—Korea, Vietnam, and Afghanistan—did the two great powers become directly involved in hot wars, but then never in open conflict with each other, still preserving the rules of the game. The rules were very clear—no open, direct action against each other. Stalin and Kim II Sung had planned the Korean War, sure that the United States would not enter. When they were proven wrong, Stalin went to great pains to ensure that his aid to the North Koreans and Chinese was masked. Although it was evident that Soviet pilots were flying the MiGs that challenged America over Korean skies, he was loathe to let that aid become so blatant that it would force the Americans to act.[4]

Similarly, in Vietnam the Soviets limited their aid to equipment and advisors. Unlike North Korea, North Vietnam proved to have a mind of its own, an affordable conceit in the absence of a common border with the Soviet Union. It gladly took everything it could from the Soviets but determinedly kept the Soviets at arm's length. Thus the use of proxies in the Cold War often proved to be a two-edged sword. The proxies did not always take instruction well. Amazingly, they proved to have agendas of their own. In Vietnam and Afghanistan the two powers stumbled over another problem—they had backed the wrong horses. They had staked national reputation on incompetent proxies and could not summon the strategic clarity or political will to craft a way out of those impasses.

Even outside their direct involvement, the two powers found their proxies to be the source of often serious entanglements that threatened to drag them to that ultimate confrontation both dreaded. Thus Nasser's 1967 descent into feckless miscalculation triggered a major war that drew the sponsors of both the Arabs and the Israelis to their support, transforming their local interests into great power interests. The Cold War was not supposed to work that way. The men in the Kremlin and the White House may have thought they dominated the region, but it was the charismatic but incompetent Egyptian who truly pulled the strings that brought the powers into confrontation. Even more in the 1973 Arab–Israeli War did the actions of clients and proxies drag in the Soviets and Americans and make their strategic interests dance at the end of strings pulled from Cairo, Damascus, and Jerusalem.

Webs of alliances drew both sides into regional conflicts that increased the risks of ultimate confrontation on wider scales. Schisms within the two blocs each side managed added further layers of complication to the Cold War. The greatest of these schisms was the Sino-Soviet split into competing camps for the damned soul of international communism. This rivalry led to a dangerous subset of the Cold War in which the Soviets and Chinese, both mortal enemies of the West, still competed for allies on the world stage. The cockpit of this rivalry was the Indian subcontinent where each found difficult allies in India and Pakistan. It was a competition that came dangerously close to major war between two nuclear-equipped states. Perhaps it rivaled the Cuban Missile Crisis in the danger of unleashing nuclear war on the world.

If the Soviets had to contend with the Chinese in marshaling their forces for the Cold War, the United States had a similar if ultimately less serious problem with France. French unwillingness to harness itself with the other members of NATO against the common threat was more than a case of national egotism. It deprived NATO of strategic depth in Europe and ran competing policies, more appropriate to the petty nation-state mentality of the era of Louis XIV than the epic struggle against an Evil Empire. French policy of defense "in all directions" was a slap in the face against Allies who had bled so profusely on French soil in two world wars. The French attitude seemed to be epitomized by de Gaulle's order to remove all Allied troops and facilities from France. Charged by President Johnson with briefing de Gaulle on the plan to evacuate French bases, Secretary of State Dean Rusk asked the French president if he wanted the United States to remove the bodies of its war dead as well from their cemeteries. For once de Gaulle was left speechless and simply showed Rusk the door. He was not as reticent during a state visit to Canada in 1968 when he exclaimed to a crowd in Quebec City: "Vive Quebec Libre"— "Long live Free Quebec." It was a gross provocation of a friendly NATO ally whose armies had lost 80,000 dead on French battlefields. The support for Quebec's secession was an unprecedented attack on the territorial integrity of a friendly country.[5]

Such were the battlefields of the Cold War. They flared across the planet in hot wars that often risked the involvement of the United States and the Soviet Union. Where the great hosts of these two powers faced each other in their might, across the European Iron Curtain, was the coldest, most inert theater of all. Yet, the Cold War was like no other war, or like no other long-term confrontation of great powers, in its potential for sudden instability. Always there was the possibility for miscalculation. Despite this very real danger, the world survived the Cold War through a combination of sheer luck and sometimes inspired leadership.

This book, by a team of British, Canadian, and American military historians, explores the alternatives to such a fortunate outcome. History does not run along a well-worn groove. It is a continuously shifting synthesis of chance, design, character, accident, and luck both good and bad. History is a constantly shifting array of decision nodes—the ultimate game of choice and chance based on strategy and guessing in the dark. Here in the dark recesses of bypassed decisions lurk different worlds, different outcomes of a war more nuanced and complicated than any in mankind's long pact with strife.

Clarifications

The ten chapters in this book do not form a continuous thread or single plot line. Rather they are the stories woven by ten authors each charged with examining a different period or episode of the Cold War in light of the very real potential for different outcomes. Each is self-contained within its own alternate reality.

Our historical accounts of this alternate reality naturally need their own explanatory references, which appear in the footnotes at the end of each chapter. The use of these "alternate reality" notes, of course, poses a risk to the unwary reader who may make strenuous efforts to acquire a new and fascinating source. To avoid an epidemic of frustrating and futile searches, the "alternate notes" are indicated with an asterisk (*) before the number. All works appearing in the bibliographies included separately in each chapter are, however, "real".

Also, to assist the reader, the names of Western military units are given in roman type and Soviet and client state units are given in *italics* (with the exception of those names that are invariably italicized such as those of ships—these are *italicized* for all nations). In Chapter 6 Soviet forces are *italicized* and Chinese forces are in roman type.

The Chapters

The chapters are presented in chronological order. Thus the story of the Berlin Blockade— "First Blood: Berlin, 1948," by Michael Hathaway leads off with the first snarling spilling of Soviet and American blood in the skies over the former capital of the Reich. It was the first confrontation of the war and the last serious confrontation in Europe, despite the crisis over Berlin in 1962. The action shifts halfway around the world to James Arnold's "The Pusan Disaster, 1950" in which the Soviet gamble to engage on the periphery of Western power pays off.

The book lingers in Asia where, in Paddy Griffith's "Vietnam: The War That Nobody Noticed," the United States backs the advice of the British counter-insurgency expert, Sir Robert Thompson, to deliver an altogether different ending to the war that in reality consumed almost 60,000 US and well over a million Vietnamese lives.

The next three chapters take place in 1967–68, probably one of the most dangerous periods of the entire Cold War. They concentrate on events in the Middle East, North America, and East Asia. Chapter 4 is located in the Middle East and the 1967 War. John Burtt's "To the Brink" brings out the layered miscalculations that led to the festering misery we now see in Israel and Palestine but shows how events could have spun even more disastrously out of control. Chapter 5: "Another Savage War of Peace: Quebec, 1968" by Sean Maloney, Canada's foremost military historian, paints the picture of Canadian civil war based upon serious outside subversion and support of the separatists in Quebec. Forrest Lindsey draws the horrors of war over mastery of the international communist movement in "A Fraternal War: The Sino-Soviet Disaster" in Chapter 6, when the nuclear genie is uncorked and spreads the dust of his deadly wishes across the planet.

The 1970s open with Kevin Kiley's depiction of a successful American invasion of North Vietnam in 1970. This chapter forms the perfect bookend to Paddy Griffith's chapter and represents the ultimate escalation of the war. Chapter 8, Wade Dudley's "Fire and Ice: Sixth Fleet versus *Fifth Eskadra*" lays out the events that led to the unprecedented advance to DEFCON 3 during the 1973 War, the highest state of war alert ever ordered by a President of the United States, and then goes a chilling step further. Chapter 9 by David Isby: "Afghanistan: The Soviet Victory," is a masterpiece of political and foreign policy analysis of how the impotence of the Carter administration could have led to a major war on the Indian subcontinent.

Finally, Chapter 10 attempts something altogether different in the alternate history genre—to use a lighter touch, that of humor, to describe the defeat of the Soviet Theater Strategic Operation (TSO) against NATO in 1987. This story points out the missed opportunities for the strategy of the indirect approach employing the subtle human factors in war as the two massive mechanized, high-tech hosts of the Warsaw Pact and NATO faced each other in Europe.

Peter G. Tsouras
Alexandria, Virginia 2003

Notes

1. *Glavnii vrag* ("the main enemy") became the common synonym for the Unites States in Soviet usage.
2. Those banners, magnificently embroidered in gold and silver thread on black, red, gold, blue, and green cloth, are still exhibited in the Armed Forces Museum in Moscow, under glass on the floor level to give the same impression of their moment of humiliation as they fell upon the steps of Lenin's Tomb.
3. M. Djilas, *Conversations With Stalin* (Rupert Hart-Davis, London, 1962), p. 106.
4. Soviet rules of conduct in that war required their pilots to wear Chinese uniforms and speak in basic Chinese during flight operations, though that unworkable nonsense was observed more in the breach than in fact.
5. Thus the English speaking world can understand how the Royal Navy was able to retain a weekly toast in use until only recently: "Damn the French."

1
FIRST BLOOD
Berlin, 1948

Michael R. Hathaway

Frankfurt-Berlin Air Corridor: 1100, October 18,1948
"Bogies, 12 o'clock low!" Lieutenant Russell Brown, USAF, watched the Soviet Yak-9s roll in from 20,000 feet, then make a diving head-on pass at the C-54 Skymaster. He was flying combat air patrol, leading the three other F-80s of Blue flight at 30,000 feet over the transport stream in the Frankfurt-Berlin air corridor.

Lieutenant Charlie "Boots" McCoy's Texas drawl came through Brown's headset. "Looks like Ivan's in the mood to..." McCoy never finished his sentence. Bright sparks appeared on the C-54, then its left wing exploded into flames and snapped off, throwing the plane into a dive.

The Yaks split. The lead element, the one that fired on the C-54, pulled up and to the left of the descending F-80s. The trail element continued diving past the falling, spinning C-54, then started to pull up to the right.

Brown and McCoy, his wingman, went after the lead element, rolling left and diving. The F-80s were coming out of the sun. Before the Yaks realized they were there, Brown got off a 45 degree deflection shot at a closing velocity of around 900 knots. He knew it was not a high-percentage shot, but took it anyway, and so did McCoy.

The two Yaks were cold meat. They were watching the C-54 go in—there were no parachutes—and were not paying attention. Brown got the lead and McCoy got the wingman. Brown saw the engine of the leader burp a ball of flame as he shot past. McCoy saw the canopy come off the wingman. They zoomed back up. Over the radio, Blue 3 called: "Bandits 4 o'clock low, running for it." Blue 3 was Lieutenant Ralph Gibson, Brown's second element leader. He had been keeping track of the other Yaks, who had seen Brown and McCoy bounce their buddies and were now diving for the deck and running for the edge of the corridor.

Brown rolled inverted and started to go down after them, when he heard the call from the GCI (Ground Controlled Intercept) Fighter Controler: "Blue flight—break off! Break off!"

"Home Plate—they've splashed a C-54!"

GCI came back: "Break off, that's an order!"

Reluctantly, Brown pulled up and continued around to the right, climbing back to 30,000 feet, and led Blue flight on to Berlin.

An hour later, Brown, McCoy, and the rest of Blue flight stood at attention in front of the desk of Colonel Royal N. Baker, commander of the 36th Fighter Group. Brown finished his report: "Those Yaks are supposed to be tough from behind, sir, but they're not so tough from ahead." He paused, then added: "We could have knocked down more."

Colonel Baker looked hard at the lieutenant. "It's a good thing you didn't, that wasn't just my order, it was General LeMay's. And I have another order for you—from even higher up. Everything you just told me is secret. In fact, it's beyond secret," he continued. "Neither you nor Lieutenant McCoy can claim a kill. No press release, no stories at the Club—not a word, not to anyone, maybe not ever. Do you read me?"

Brown and the rest of Blue flight knew there was only one answer to that question, and it was a smart "Yes, Sir!" Softening, Baker continued: "Don't worry, the Air Force knows what you did, and that's going to have to be enough. Dismissed!"[1]

With that, a disappointed yet relieved Lieutenant Brown and his Blue flight officers saluted and left his Group Commander's office, silenced by an official order that would remain in force until the end of the Cold War.[2]

It may have been bad luck or it may have been plain stupidity, but the action of that Yak pilot on a bright October day in 1948, caused a ripple effect that went thousands of miles beyond Berlin. A spark had been tossed into the powder magazine that was occupied Germany. The undeclared Cold War had just gone hot.

Berlin 1945–48

The Allied Control Council (ACC) had been established by the European Advisory Committee during World War II to be in charge of the occupation of Germany. Originally, the USSR, the USA, and Britain were to have been members, but France was added at the Potsdam Summit. Each occupying power was to designate an ACC member and, at the outset, these were the commanders of the respective Allied forces.[3] For the US, General of the Army Dwight D. Eisenhower was quickly succeeded by General Joseph T. McNarney, who was in turn succeeded by Lieutenant General Lucius Clay in March, 1947. But in fact, Clay acted as Military Governor of the US Zone from the outset, and was officially head of the Office of Military Government for Germany (US) (known as OMGUS) before becoming Commander of US Forces Europe and titular Military Governor.[4]

The blockade of Berlin actually began on March 27, 1948, when Marshal Vassily Danilovich Sokolovsky, the Soviet Military Governor and Commander of Soviet Forces in Germany, issued an order imposing new traffic regulations. This was the first step in the Soviet plan to force the USA, Britain, and France to abandon Berlin.[5]

On March 31, General Clay sent a telegram to General Omar Bradley, who had succeeded General Eisenhower as US Army Chief of Staff. In this telegram, Clay told Bradley about the new Soviet restrictions on rail travel to and from Berlin that would go into force in 24 hours and would affect both military and civilian personnel and freight. He advised that he intended to order US soldiers guarding the trains to open fire on any Soviet personnel attempting to board the trains without permission. Washington responded with approval of Clay's stance, but also with an order not to open fire unless fired upon.[6]

The Soviets stopped trains at the zonal border crossing point at Marienborn. The French allowed the Soviets to board their train, check documents, and arrest and remove 67 German passengers, after which the French train was allowed to proceed to Berlin. The British did not allow the Soviets aboard, and their train was not allowed to proceed. The US had three trains stopped. Clay cancelled American rail services to Berlin following this border confrontation, not desiring a daily repetition of these disruptions.[7]

What later became known as the "baby lift" began on a very small scale in response to the effective termination of the official rail service from the British and American Zones of Occupation to Berlin (civilian rail traffic was still permitted at this stage, and a Soviet train continued to run across the interzonal boundary). Both the British and the Americans began flying priority passengers and freight into Berlin.[8]

In fact, the Soviet approach to the blockade followed a two-steps-forward, one-back tactic. After the initial confrontation, train traffic was allowed to resume, but barge traffic was impeded. Road traffic was continued, but two British and American way stations along the route to Berlin were closed, and civilian trucks were sometimes refused passage because they did not have the correct permits. Official allied road transport was not interfered with.[9]

But signs of worse to come were visible. On April 5, a Soviet Yak fighter buzzed a civilian British Viking airliner about two miles from touchdown at Gatow airport, and had a midair collision with it, killing all aboard both aircraft. Clay and his British counterpart, Lieutenant-General Sir Brian Robertson, immediately ordered fighter protection for allied aircraft in the three air corridors from the western zones of occupation to Berlin. Robertson sought an urgent meeting with Sokolovsky. After some delay, they met. The marshal claimed the British airliner had caused the crash by "ramming" the Soviet fighter. But aside from this ridiculous assertion, the Soviet assurance that the incident had been unintentional was taken at face value. Clay and Robertson accordingly cancelled the first order for fighter cover for the transports.[10]

In London, a conference of Western powers was under way to make decisions on Germany and the defense of the west. On June 1, the representatives reached agreement on the introduction of a new currency in the western zones of Germany. The Reichsmark had continued in circulation after the war, but was of decreasing value. The Soviets had been printing unknown quantities of it in a Leipzig plant and using this money to purchase goods. Inflation was gaining strength and the availability of goods and services in return for payment in Reichsmarks was rapidly declining. Cigarettes had become the standard currency of exchange.[11]

Just as important as currency reform, the London conference had instructed the Allied military governors to call upon the heads of the German states located in the western zones to convene a constituent assembly by September 1 to begin drafting a constitution for a federal state in the territories under Allied occupation.[12]

The combination of economic and political reform in the western zones of occupation was the trigger for the final two steps forward in the Soviet Berlin operation. On June 24, the Soviets closed all road, rail, and water access to the western sectors of Berlin to both civilian and official Allied traffic. This is generally accepted as the formal beginning of the Berlin blockade. The Soviets asserted "technical difficulties" as the cause for the interruption of rail traffic, and gave no explanations for their other moves.[13]

Clay was determined. He and his State Department advisor, Ambassador Robert Murphy, advocated immediate dispatch of an armed convoy from the American Zone to Berlin.[14] Washington's response to that idea was frosty.

In contrast to Teddy Roosevelt's foreign policy dictum that the United States should "talk softly but carry a big stick," following the post-World War II demobilization (described by some as more of a "rout") the United States was perilously weak. General Omar Bradley, who had taken over as Army Chief of Staff on February 7, stated that: "the Army of 1948 couldn't fight its way out of a paper bag."[15]

In Germany, the forces directly available to General Clay were also quite weak, in comparison to Soviet forces. In Berlin itself, Clay had the 3rd Battalion of the 16th Infantry Regiment, the 16th Constabulary Squadron (Sep), and the 759th Military Police Battalion, totaling 4,677 personnel. ("Constabulary" units were light infantry assigned to police duties.)

Outside Berlin, in the rest of Germany, Clay had the 1st Infantry Division, and the 1st and 2nd Constabulary Brigades. The 1st Constabulary Brigade had been fleshed out by the addition of the 18th Regimental Combat Team from the 1st Infantry Division, so the division was a regiment short.

As for combat air strength, the US Air Force Europe, under the command of Lieutenant General Curtis LeMay, had no bombers assigned and only two fighter groups, totaling 75 F-80 jet fighters in the 36th

Fighter Group based at Furstenfeldbruck and 75 P-47s in the 86th Fighter Group at Neubiberg. (Two B-29 squadrons later sent to Germany remained under Strategic Air Command control.)

There were also major British and French military units involved in the occupation, but unified Allied military command had been dissolved shortly after the end of World War II, and NATO had not yet been created. While their respective commanders and staffs coordinated operations to the degree their national command authorities allowed, they had neither a unified chain of command nor a common plan to conduct the defense of Western Europe.

This aggregation of forces faced a Soviet garrison in Germany estimated at 273,000 ground troops with 4,000–5,000 tanks and 1,400 combat aircraft.[16]

To counterbalance the Soviet conventional predominance, the United States had the atomic bomb. But what it did not have until just about the start of the Berlin Blockade was a war plan for using the bomb. James Y Forrestal, the first US Secretary of Defense, convened a meeting with the Joint Chiefs of Staff at Truman's "Little White House" at the naval base at Key West, Florida, in early March 1948. The purpose of the meeting was to draw up a unified short-range emergency war plan and the first unified military budget. The war plan was called "Halfmoon."[17]

General Bradley described the plan as follows:

"This was the first formal and comprehensive enunciation of what later became known as a strategy of nuclear 'massive retaliation.' If Russia launched an all-out war, its huge Army overrunning Western Europe (as we assumed), we would respond by dropping atomic bombs on the Soviet homeland—mainly population centers—with the aim of destroying the Soviet government and breaking the Kremlin's will to wage war. The bombs would be carried to Soviet targets by our B-29 and B-50 heavy bombers, staging from bases in England and Egypt, and in the Far East, Okinawa. Air Force studies had suggested that 133 atomic bombs dropped on seventy Soviet cities would be required. Since we then had only about fifty bombs, the plan was to launch the strategic air attack against Russia on D plus 9 with twenty-five bombs, follow up with another twenty-five, then continue the attack with bombs coming right off the production line."[18]

While well aware of this weakness, the United States determined to stay in Berlin. Following a series of meetings in Washington, the President met with senior leaders on June 28 and decided "we would stay period."[19] Truman also approved the dispatch of two wings of B-29s to Britain and two squadrons of B-29s to Germany.[20]

In Germany, Clay had already taken steps to make sure the US could stay. On June 26, he called General LeMay and asked that all available

transport aircraft be used to supply Berlin. This was the formal beginning of the Berlin Airlift. The first aircraft landed in Berlin later that day,
delivering 80 tons of milk, flour, and medicine.[21]

On the diplomatic front, the Allies concluded that the Soviet game was
to offer to trade, lifting the Berlin blockade in return for a suspension of the
London initiative to create a government in the western occupied zones of
Germany. The Soviets wanted a meeting of the Council of Foreign Ministers to discuss the German problem. Neither Washington nor London was
willing to agree to that proposal while the blockade was in force.[22]

But the US Air Force and the British Royal Air Force began to
rewrite the script as they worked out the ways and means to supply
not just the Allied garrisons in Berlin, but the citizens, too. By the end
of July, the USAFE and RAF were averaging 2,500 tons a day against
a target of 2,000 tons of food for both the city and the garrison. With
more aircraft, they were confident they could get to 3,500 tons a day.
But while that would sustain the city during the summer, it would not
meet the winter needs for coal.[23]

There was a solution to the problem. This had several component
parts. First, use more large aircraft by phasing out the twin-engined C-47s
in favor of an all four-engined C-54 force. Second, open more capacity to
receive aircraft in Berlin. And finally, reorganize the airbases from which
the transports were launched in the western zones.

As the Soviets saw the airlift become better organized and more
successful, they began taking steps to put pressure on it. However, unlike
for the ground access routes, there had been a written four-power agreement to establish and operate the air corridors. This agreement, concluded
by the ACC on October 25, 1946, put the Soviets in the position of having
to violate an arrangement to which they were a party if they wanted to
disrupt the airlift.[24]

In the case of Clay's armed convoy proposal, Soviet interference with
the convoy could place Allied troops in the position of having to fire the
first shot on Soviet Zone territory, thus arguably placing the responsibility
for any subsequent war on the Allied powers. In the case of supply by
air, to halt the airlift the Soviets would have to be the first to use armed
force, in violation of an international agreement to which they were a
party, placing on them the responsibility for starting the war.[25]

Harassment by the Soviets began to grow. They conducted aerial
maneuvers in the corridors, sending bombers through in formation or
fighters to buzz the airlifters. They fired anti-aircraft artillery at targets
towed behind their own planes so shells would burst in the corridors.
They fired ground flares up into the corridors. On 55 occasions ground
fire was found to have hit airlift aircraft.[26]

The crisis built to its peak in October. Apparently fearing that weather
alone (November is the worst month for flying weather in Germany)

would not halt the airlift, the Soviets increased military incursions into the corridors; there had been two in August and seven in September, but three occurred during the first ten days of October alone.[27]

Berlin: October 13,1948

On Wednesday, October 13, there occurred another midair collision, this time between a buzzing Soviet fighter and a C-54 from the US 61st Troop Carrier Wing.[28] Once again, all aboard both aircraft were killed.

Clay received an eye-witness report of the incident. Having taken over command of the airlift on July 29, Brigadier General William Tunner had established a three-minute interval between transport aircraft in the stream in the Berlin corridor.[29] Thus, when the Soviet fighter collided with the C-54, the crew of the following C-54, the *Mary Jane,* saw the whole event unfold ahead of and 1,000 feet above them.[30]

Colonel Lawrence Richmond, Clay's Air Staff Officer, brought into Clay's office two of the *Mary Jane's* crew and Sergeant Burt Haskins, the radar operator who had been on duty in the Berlin Air Safety Center covering that part of the corridor at the time of the accident. Returning their salutes and telling them to take seats, Clay asked: "Larry, what happened out there this morning?"

Richmond replied: "It's April 5th all over again. Just like the British Viking, a Soviet fighter buzzed a C-54 from the 61st and managed to hit it at 6,000 feet about 15 miles out from Tempelhof. Both aircraft went down, no parachutes were seen. It happened in the left half of the corridor."

Clay asked: "And these men witnessed the collision?"

Richmond said: "Captain Black and Lieutenant Fiorino were pilot and co-pilot of the C-54 right behind the aircraft that was involved in the collision. Sergeant Haskins was sitting at the radar screen in Berlin Air Safety Center and watched it happen on radar."

Clay asked Black: "What did you see, son?"

Captain Roger Black replied: "It was a normal flight, cloudy but with some breaks in the deck above us at 10,000 feet. We were at 5,000 feet, right on schedule three minutes behind the C-54 ahead of us. We've been here since August, so we're used to seeing Soviet aircraft in the corridor. We heard a warning over the radio from Berlin Air Safety Center—I know now that it was Sergeant Haskins speaking—that unknown high-speed aircraft were operating in the corridor above the cloud deck at about 20,000 feet, and they were changing headings, speeds, and altitudes without warning. We thought: 'Oh no, here they come again,' and just after the warning, here come several fighters diving down through a hole in the clouds."

"Then what happened?" Clay asked.

Black continued: "We counted four Yaks coming toward us, and two split to the left of our heading and dove down toward the deck, and two pulled up and broke to their left, our right, into level flight just below the cloud deck. Then the pair that had gone low pulled up in front of us, behind and below the C-54 ahead of us, while the pair under the cloud deck did a roll reversal and headed down at the C-54 from above and behind. I think they were intending to startle the crew by passing just above and in front of that aircraft in a dive, but one of them miscalculated, and cut it too close. He struck the right inboard engine with his wingtip. His wing snapped, and so did the 54's, and they both cartwheeled down. We saw no parachutes from either plane."

Clay asked: "What did the other Yaks do then?"

Black responded: "They rejoined in a three-plane formation and circled the crash site at low altitude—we passed to the right of them and lost sight of them as we called in the collision to Tempelhof and to Group back at Rhein-Main."

Clay said: "Lieutenant Fiorino, that's what you saw, too?" Fiorino responded: "Yes, sir."

"And you were in the corridor at the time of the collision?"

Black responded: "Yes, sir. We were maybe a little left of the center line, because there was a southeast wind blowing and we were trimmed into it, but we could see the ground and we were okay."

Clay then turned to Sergeant Haskins, asking: "Was the collision in the corridor?"

Haskins, sitting on the edge of his chair and working his hat with both hands, responded: "Yes, sir. Impact was about six miles north of the centerline, still four miles inside the corridor. Sir, those Yaks were dancing in and out of the cloud deck for 20 minutes before the collision. I asked Captain Jefforts, my shift commander, to take it up with the Soviet liaison, Captain Zorchenko, but he was nowhere to be found. Jefforts told me to make repeated radio announcements to our aircraft as long as the Yaks were there."

"And where did our aircraft come down?" asked Clay.

Black said: "He went down to our left, more toward the edge of the corridor, but still in it, I'm sure." Haskins added: "Yes, sir, he was still about three miles inside the corridor when I lost him off the scope."

Turning to Colonel Richmond, Clay said: "Get me General LeMay on the horn. Then write up a report on the collision and send it to Washington. The Air Force will send one in from the 61st, but I want one to Bradley ASAP!"

Richmond left with the witnesses, and had the call placed to LeMay. Buzzed by his secretary, Clay picked up the phone.

"Curt, it's the Soviets again. This time we've lost a C-54 to a midair. I'm going to see Sokolovsky, but I want fighter cover for our airlifters in the corridor as soon as you can do it."

LeMay replied: "General, you know we're short on fighters, but we'll do it. I'll have the first flights up later today."[31]

LeMay, notoriously a man of few words, was concerned that if things were going to get out of hand, his only fighter force would be strung out from Frankfurt to Berlin and back again through the central corridor, in penny-packet-sized groups that would be easy prey for massed Soviet fighters.

"'I decided the best way to do this was to put the F-80s from the 36th Fighter Group into top cover by flights. We only had 75, and usually only around 60 were flight worthy at any time—something we'd have to improve upon and quick. In the 86th Fighter Group, all we had were P-47s—outclassed by the front line Soviet fighters, but maybe useful. I decided to run the 75 P-47s also as flights, but between the F-80s and the transport stream. That way, the fast jets would be high, and the medium speed P-47s would be close to but always above the slower transports. The Soviets, even with radar, would have trouble fitting any more of their games into our transport stream without some of our fighters being near. Yeah, I know that's not how my B-17s were covered by P-51s during the war, but these weren't bombers, and this wasn't war—at least not yet.'"[32]

After giving instructions to LeMay, Clay called Sokolovsky, with whom he had believed he had a friendly relationship.[33] It took until the next day to arrange the meeting. Sokolovsky demanded that Clay come to his headquarters at the Soviet Military Administration in Karlshorst.

Berlin: October 14,1948
Clay was escorted into Sokolovsky's office, in the former German military cadet school's officers' club. Clay did not speak Russian, nor did Sokolovsky speak English, so each had an interpreter present.

"Good morning, Marshal, how are you today?" Clay greeted Sokolovsky. Sokolovsky responded: "General, I am well." Skipping the normal pleasantries, he continued: "I understand you urgently requested this meeting. What do you wish to discuss?" Clay stiffened, then referred to a paper his staff had prepared and which he had cleared with Washington.

"Marshal, yesterday at about 1015 hours, one of your fighters was performing aerobatic maneuvers in the Frankfurt–Berlin air corridor, about 15 miles southwest of Berlin, in violation of the 'Flight Rules for Aircraft Flying in Air Corridors in Germany and Berlin Control Zone,' and without prior notification to the Berlin Air Safety Center. As a result of these maneuvers, in violation of paragraph 20 of the Flight Rules which specifically ban aerobatic flying that endangers other air traffic, your aircraft collided with a US C-54 transport aircraft that was in straight and level flight within the designated corridor on a mission that had been properly notified to the Berlin Air Safety Center."

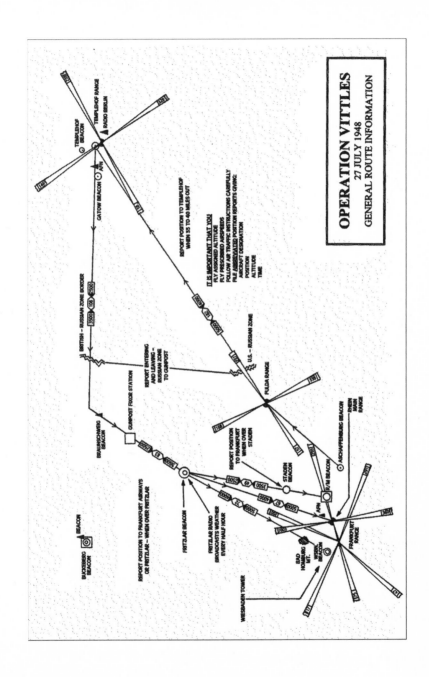

Clay continued grimly: "The United States first strongly protests this violation by Soviet forces of the Flight Rules which the Allied Control Council, including Marshal Zhukov, approved on October 25, 1946, and demands that such violations cease immediately. The United States also requests access for its crash investigators and graves registration personnel to the crashed C-54 and the remains of its crew of three."

Sokolovsky, stone faced, responded through his interpreter: "General, according to my information, that US aircraft was not in the proper flight corridor at the time of the accident. In fact, the US aircraft was conducting a provocation, flying into an air exercise area where one of our fighter regiments was conducting air-to-air combat training. Since the collision occurred outside of the area covered by the 'Flight Rules,' a fact that can easily be determined from the location of the crash site, your protest of a 'violation' is inadmissible. Moreover, as the Soviet representative to the Berlin Air Safety Center has made clear, repeated flagrant violations of these 'Flight Rules' by US aircraft have rendered that agreement void. I have instructions to present to you, the United States Military Governor, a strong protest of this deliberate violation of the Soviet Zone of Occupation in contravention of the Potsdam agreement, and to demand compensation for the loss of a Soviet pilot and his aircraft. In addition, the crash site of the aircraft conducting the provocation is in a restricted military zone. I have had no instructions from my government to permit foreign military personnel to enter the restricted zone. That is all I have to say on this subject."

Clay listened to the translation of Sokolovsky's remarks, and responded: "Marshal, my government's position is clear. The accident happened in the corridor and was caused by the Soviet fighter's prohibited aerobatics. Accordingly, I cannot participate in any discussion of compensation. I do once again repeat my request, on humanitarian grounds, for crash site access at least to recover the remains of the deceased flight crew."

Sokolovsky, unmoved, responded: "General, I am awaiting instructions. Until I receive those instructions, I cannot act on your request."

With that, Sokolovsky closed the short meeting, and Clay was escorted out.[34]

Clay called LeMay again when he reached his headquarters: "Curt, you're going to have to keep up the escorts. I'm calling Robertson now to get the BAFO [British Air Forces of the Occupation} to put up cover in the northern corridor. This time, Sokolovsky didn't say it was an accident, and charged that we caused it as a 'provocation.'"

LeMay said: "General, you know I'm going to have to get more help from the States if this keeps up. I'm also moving the fighters from Fursten-feldbruck and Neubiberg up to Wiesbaden, so they have a shorter flight time to Berlin. But I backed you on the convoy, and I'm backing you on this, too. If we stand tall, the Russians will back down."[35]

Clay then had a "telecon"[36] with Secretary of the Army Royall and Army Chief of Staff General Bradley. He had already cabled to them the facts of the midair collision, his order that USAFE fly cover for the transports, and the proposed text for his meeting with Sokolovsky, which had been approved. Now, he wanted to talk strategy.

Bradley wrote: "We're not in any condition to go to war with the Soviets. As you know, we only have an emergency short-term war plan, with nothing agreed with the Allies."

Clay responded: "Yes, that's so, but if we back down now, we will have to shut down the airlift, and that means we have to leave Berlin. You have a copy of our 30 Aug 48 plan for an orderly evacuation of Berlin. We have to move a minimum of 8,378 people, military and US civilians out of our sector alone, not counting the French, who would depend on us for their transportation, and any German civilians we want to protect from Soviet reprisals. Our people, their hand baggage, and light household goods require 546 C-54 loads and 91 C-47 loads alone, and that is before we add air transportable government property and records, which more than double that requirement. In short, it would take us three days in perfect weather without Soviet disruption or civil unrest in our sector to do the job. And I would not want to be on the last plane out."[37]

Bradley responded: "We don't have direction from the President or the NSC, beyond staying in Berlin. That we will do until forced out."[38]

Clay wrote: "As you know, with the British and French we've looked at what we would do if war broke out. The conclusion was, and I quote: 'Wargaming of the defense of the Rhine has just been completed in EUCOM, the outcome of which was, briefly, that the Rhine line was held for 3 days following D-Day after which a necessary rapid withdrawal from France was effected.' This conclusion would have to be viewed as optimistic in light of our commitment of fighter assets to covering the airlift, if the Soviets were to attack."[39]

Royall responded: "President Truman made it clear, we are staying, period. But your instructions remain unchanged—not to initiate military action, but take defensive measures as necessary. If the Soviets want war, they have to start it."[40]

Sokolovsky, however, was under strict orders not to start a war. Stalin had other plans. He had already set up the Democratic People's Republic of Korea (North Korea) in September, under a Soviet-drafted constitution that named Seoul as its capital. In another six months, Stalin would begin laying plans for the Korean War in Moscow discussions with Kim II Sung.[41]

Frankfurt-Berlin Air Corridor: 1230, October 18,1948

On Monday, October 18, Sokolovsky's air regiments were to try again, for the last time, to intimidate Clay, LeMay, and Tunner into calling off the airlift and evacuating Berlin. However, as we have seen one of their pilots, whose name is lost to history, decided to shoot instead of intimidate, giving Lieutenant Russell Brown the first, but for more than 40 years unacknowledged, US Air Force kill of a Soviet fighter since World War II.[42]

While Brown and McCoy reported their Yak kills, Colonel Yevgeni Glinka was hung over and boiling mad. He had Lieutenants Rabotev and Khurchatov standing at attention in his office, and he had just finished berating them as cowards for running from the USAF F-80s—they had flown the other two Yaks in the flight that had shot down the C-54. His head throbbing, he ordered the two lieutenants out, and shouted for his operations officer, Major Ivan Kaberov: "Kaberov! Get in here!"

Kaberov, familiar with Glinka's vodka habits, came in on the run, expecting trouble. "Yes, Comrade Colonel?" Glinka said: "I want every pilot and aircraft in the regiment airborne as soon as possible. The Yankees have shot down two of our boys and those cowards ran from them!"

Kaberov, knowing not to argue with Glinka, replied: "I've got half the regiment in the air right now, but they're low on fuel. We need to recover, refuel, and issue orders..."

Cutting Kaberov short, Glinka shouted: "There's no time for that. Launch the ready fighters now, then recover!" "And what orders do I give the ready fighters?" asked Kaberov.

Glinka, full of scorn, snarled: "Find Americans and kill them!"

Glinka, in a rush, had made several serious errors. First, he was disobeying a direct order from his Air Army commander. Second, his regiment, the *158th Fighter Regiment,* was based at Staaken and two smaller fields in the immediate vicinity of Berlin. This meant that his fighters were under constant US radar coverage, right down to their takeoffs and landings. Third, he did not wait to mass his forces or brief them properly before sending them into the air. Fourth, he forgot that the *GRU* and the *NKVD* monitored his communications. Finally, he counted too much on the loyalty of his often-abused operations officer.

Kaberov, returning to the operations room, sounded the alarm and scrambled the ready fighters, a single squadron of Yak 9Us. By using the alarm, he triggered a link to *4th Fighter Division's* operations center, which was on the phone with the *158th* before the first aircraft left the ground.

"*158th,* this is *4th Division.* You've scrambled your alert force. What's going on there?" asked the voice over the direct line.

Kaberov had taken the call personally. "Comrade Colonel Glinka has ordered the launch to react to the shooting down of two of our aircraft by US F-80s," he reported neutrally.

4th Division: "What shoot down? Why wasn't this reported?"

Kaberov: "We learned of it when the flight returned to base and reported to the commander."

4th Division: "There was no radio report?"

Kaberov: "No. Standing orders are to report incidents only in person."

4th Division: "How did this happen?"

Kaberov: "Our pilots reported they were attacked without warning while flying across the Frankfurt-Berlin Corridor. They were jumped by F-80s, and one element went down in the fight, during which a C-54 was also hit and went down. The other element escaped the fight. That's what the pilots reported."

4th Division, incredulously: "And Comrade Colonel Glinka launched his ready fighters to attack the Americans? Is that what's going on?"

Kaberov: "Yes."

4th Division: "On my authority, launch no other fighters. General Orlov needs to report this to *Second Air Army,* and receive instructions."

With that, what became known to legend as the "Great Berlin Furball" kicked-off.

The leader of the ready fighter force, *3rd Squadron,* heard over his radio the excited voice of his commander, Colonel Glinka, as he gained altitude over the field.

"Bear, this is *Krasnya.* Fly to Tempelhof and knock down as many Americans as you can, over."

"Bear," Captain Sergei Anopov, listened in shock to his commander's voice. Like all the pilots in the regiment, he had been briefed on the rules of engagement the day before, and understood that these rules came from the highest levels of command—there was to be no shooting, no matter what—and here his commander was countermanding those rules.

"Krasnya, is this war? We've had no warning, over," *Bear* said.

"Bear, follow orders! They've killed two of our pilots today and we're fighting back!" responded *Krasnya.*

"Roger," said *Bear,* thinking he needed to be very careful in the next few minutes.

3rd Squadron formed into a combat formation by flights as it circled over Staaken, then headed for the spot six miles southwest of Tempelhof still over the Soviet Zone where Ground Controlled Approach (GCA) took control of incoming C-54s.

Berlin Air Safety Center, seeing the massed fighters in combat formation heading toward the critical point in the Tempelhof approach pattern, urgently called the C-54s closing on that point and ordered them not to begin their descents. The three C-54s next in line heard the call and began the standard go around procedure. (Aircraft that missed landings or had mechanical problems simply went home to Rhein-Main—Tunner had ordered an end to "stacking" aircraft over Berlin after one disastrous afternoon's experience.)[43]

Used to operating under strict Ground Controlled Intercept (GCI) procedures, *Bear* called his GCI controller: *"Stork,* this is *Bear.* Request heading and range to target."

Stork, the *158th's* GCI operation, was located in a room next to the *158th's* operation room, and had been visited by Colonel Glinka.

Stork responded: *"Bear,* this is *Stork,* your target is a large aircraft at heading 200, altitude 1,500 meters, range 9,000 meters. Climb to 6,000 meters, turn to heading 190. Possible enemy fighters at 6,000 meters, heading 210."

Stork had spotted a flight of P-47s, moving along above the transport stream, about 10 miles behind the C-54 the Yaks were vectored to intercept. *Stork* had, however, missed a flight of F-80s that was about 20 miles back of the target, and coming fast.

Tempelhof GCA had a radar range at altitude of 40 miles. The radar operator there could see the Yaks, the P-47s, and the F-80s. He called the P-47s: "Osprey flight, this is Berlin GCA. Bogies to your 10 o'clock and level. You have a heavy {the C-54] at 12 o'clock low."

The Osprey flight leader ordered his flight to climb and turn toward the bogies, taking the advantages of altitude and the sun. He knew the Yaks could outperform his "Jugs" in a dogfight, but he could out-dive and out-climb the Yaks—if there were going to be a fight, he wanted to fight vertically, not in the horizontal plane where the Yaks had the speed and turning radius advantages.

Gold flight, the F-80s, had also heard the call, and pushed their throttles while slightly nosing down to reach maximum air speed. (Compression would be a problem if they were going too fast—approaching the speed of sound would make the subsonic aircraft respond sluggishly, almost locking the controls.) They closed quickly on the much slower propeller-driven aircraft.

Suddenly, everything happened at once. *Bear* had ordered one of his flights to climb higher, to fly top cover against the US fighters he had been warned about but had not yet seen—that .flight almost ran into the oncoming P-47s, which refused to engage despite being fired upon.

Osprey flight rolled and dove toward the rest of *Bear's* force, now itself rolling in on the C-54. GCA called the C-54 and ordered it to dive, too. *Bear's* top cover called a warning, *Bear's* squadron scattered, with one element staying on the C-54 and the others turning toward the P-47s. The P-47s went streaking down toward the C-54, hoping to drive off the two Yaks still in pursuit, while still refusing to engage the balance of *Bear's* forces.

The Yaks chasing the C-54 heard their comrades call a warning, and broke to one side, away from Osprey flight's leader. His second element took a long range, high-deflection shot at them, but saw no results. Osprey flight was zooming back to altitude with the Yaks concentrating on getting some kind of shot at them when the F-80s arrived at speed.

Stork had seen the F-80s coming at last, and called a warning to *Bear,* but the P-47s were on them at that point and *Bear* could not react to the call.

The F-80s found both sides' fighters hanging on their props, struggling for altitude. Coming in hot, the F-80s couldn't turn and just picked targets for nearly head-on diving passes. Three of the four Gold flight F-80s scored hits on the distinctively painted Yaks as they shot through them.

Bear's squadron scattered again, while Osprey flight continued to gain altitude, and Gold flight pulled up into a straight zoom.

During this time, the startled C-54 had pulled out of its dive, and shot into the US sector low and fast, and coughing hard. (Its cargo was duffel bags full of coal, and coal dust, shaken loose by the abrupt maneuvers, had filled the cabin and cockpit.)

Bear, cursing *Stork* for letting the F-80s surprise him, ordered his wounded aircraft home while he fought for altitude and reassembled his formation—he knew he outnumbered the Americans two to one, and no matter how fast the jets were, they could not turn with him. And he wanted the P-47s.

The Osprey pilots wanted the Yaks just as badly, but were not about to fight on their terms. Gold flight, able to zoom to altitude much faster than the prop-driven fighters could climb, was already back on top, and called to Osprey to follow them down on the Yaks.

At that point, both sides heard their ground controllers call them off. *Bear* heard *Pelikan,* the call sign for *4th Fighter Divisions* GCI operator, order them to break off and head home. At just about the same time, Home Plate, the American's GCI, called Osprey and Gold, and ordered them to break off. Once again, both sides followed orders.

Berlin: 1300, October 18,1948

While all of this had been going on, much had been happening on the ground. Soviet air police, acting on General Orlov's orders, had arrested Colonel Glinka at Staaken. They arrested Kaberov, and, after he landed, Captain Anopov. They also arrested Major Petrinko, Glinka's executive officer, whom they found in his quarters in a drunken stupor (he had been Glinka's drinking buddy the night before, but did not have Glinka's capacity).[44]

LeMay and Tunner conferred, then LeMay called Clay. The airlift stayed on, despite the furball. They concluded that no other Soviet aircraft had been directed into combat, and no other preparations for combat were visible. They were going to proceed until the Soviets acted to stop them.

Gold flight had an interview with Colonel Baker in terms that Lieutenants Brown, McCoy, and Gibson would have recognized, while Osprey flight received similar orders from their commander. An airtight lid had been placed on the Great Berlin Furball, but rumors—probably started by radar operators and C-54 pilots—gave it life for years in Air Force ready rooms and clubs.

There was no further Soviet offensive action. Clay decided to report events to Washington, but to say nothing publicly or to the Soviets. He concluded that the ball was in Sokolovsky's court.[45]

Berlin: 1400, October 18,1948

The orders to the Yak fighter regiments had been explicit. Their pilots were not to open fire, not under any circumstances. They were only to buzz the transports. If American or British fighters approached, they were to fly to safe zones outside the corridor where Soviet anti-aircraft batteries were in position.

Sokolovsky had trouble rinding out the truth. He had radio intercepts of the American transmissions from the *GRU,* Soviet Military Intelligence, which monitored all American radio traffic during the airlift. After the first F-80 versus Yak dogfight, the *GRU* had translated and rushed the intercepts to him, beating a report that was making its way up the air chain of command from the fighter regiment to the air division to air army to the Soviet air commander in Germany. He also had the *Red Army* reports of the crashed aircraft before he received the report from the regiment whose aircraft had been involved. And he knew the *NKVD,* the secret police, was monitoring all of these events and would make a direct report to Beria, who might make a direct report to Stalin.

Sokolovsky received the report from General Yesov, his air commander. He read it with consternation, seeing that it claimed that the Yaks had been attacked without warning by the US jet fighters and the C-54 had gone down after getting caught in the middle of the dogfight. That report disagreed with the Berlin Air Safety Center radar plot, which the British and French also saw, with the army anti-aircraft force's radar and visual observations, and with what he knew the US pilots were reporting to their chain of command.

While he was studying this report, he received a phone call from a smoking mad Yesov who reported the second air battle of the day. This time the report was accurate. Yesov reported the battle was caused by a drunken colonel acting directly contrary to orders. He said no aircraft were lost—on either side, so far as he could tell—but five Yaks were damaged. He had placed all of the people responsible at the fighter regiment under arrest.

Sokolovsky was in a box. As head of the Soviet Military Administration for Germany, he reported directly to Stalin, and had received his orders from him. One of his pilots had grossly overstepped his orders. If the pilot were still alive, Sokolovsky would have had him shot. And now a fighter regiment commander, whose affection for vodka apparently outweighed his respect for orders, had started a second air battle. But Sokolovsky knew that even having everyone in the air force chain of command shot would not save him if Stalin held him personally responsible for the mistake.

He could try presenting the fighter regiment's report of the first air battle as accurate, but Stalin would know it was not, and a false report would kill him just as dead as a report of a (now deceased) subordinate's over zealousness. However, if he took strong disciplinary action against the drunkard, made an accurate report, and Stalin did not have him shot or sent to the *gulag*, he should be okay. A false report, if accepted, could lead to World War III, and if it did not, Beria would know he had lied, and so would the GRU. That was not a recipe for a long and healthy life.

Sokolovsky made the most difficult phone call he ever had to make in his life. He called Stalin.

Stalin came on the line: "Vassily Danilovich, you had trouble today?"

Sokolovsky, sweating, knowing Beria had made his report, replied: "Generalissimo, it is true. A fighter pilot shot down an American C-54 in the Frankfurt to Berlin corridor, right in front of American jet fighters. He and his wingman were shot down by the Americans. There were no survivors."

Stalin paused. Sokolovsky could hear him chewing on his pipe. "You took no other action?"

"Everyone was under strict orders not to shoot even if fired upon, but the downed pilots' regimental commander launched an attack on his own," replied Sokolovsky. "I ordered it halted."

Stalin said: "So they couldn't follow orders any better after first firing on the Americans?"

Sokolovsky, sure he was about to hear his own death sentence, said: "Generalissimo, I've arrested the regimental commander and the others involved."

Stalin, once again chewing on his pipe, paused again, and then said: "Vassily Danilovich, you will make certain that orders are strictly followed in the future, won't you?" He continued: "I see you are due to return to Moscow for another assignment soon. You must come and tell me about your progress with the Germans. And," and here Stalin paused again: "Don't talk to the Americans about this. I will handle it."

With that, Stalin hung up, and Sokolovsky thought he might live to see another sunrise. But he did not look forward at all to reporting to Stalin personally.[46]

Stalin's next call was to Molotov. Molotov was then in Paris for the meeting of the United Nations, as were his counterparts, Secretary Marshall, and Foreign Ministers Ernest Bevin (Britain) and Robert Schumann (France).[47]

"Vyacheslav Mikhailovich, this is Druzhkov," Stalin began.[48] "I need the Americans to stop sending fighters as escorts for their Berlin air transports. There has been an incident. Two of our fighters, contrary to orders, shot down one of their transports and were then shot down by American fighters. There was also a second fight with no losses. That's as far as it went. Sokolovsky is taking care of those who can't follow orders."

Stalin paused, then continued: "There can be no war in Germany. Approach Marshall and see if we can get their fighters to stand down. The risk is too high."

Molotov, who never addressed Stalin by his new title "Generalissimo," and got away with it, replied: "Comrade Druzhkov, it can be done. Marshall is here with his staff. We can have a corridor talk."

Molotov sent Valentin Zorin to make the contact. He encountered John Foster Dulles at one of the post-session cocktail hours and opened negotiations, suggesting that: "The US needed to reduce the chances of other unfortunate air incidents in the Berlin corridor, and that the Soviet Union was also sensitive to this issue."

Dulles recognized the initiative—he knew of the midair collision, but not the shoot-down or the subsequent air battle. He was appropriately noncommittal, but carried Zorin's approach to Marshall. Marshall had just finished a "telecon" with State, during which his Undersecretary, Robert Lovett, informed him of the shoot-down, the second fight, and the subsequent lack of additional military action.

Marshall was relieved to hear that nothing else had transpired, because on September 13, during a meeting at the White House: "Truman said that he prayed he would not have to make such a decision, but that if it became necessary they should have no doubt" that he would use the atomic bomb against the Soviet Union in an emergency. The following evening, this determination had been conveyed to a meeting of the publishers of 19 major US newspapers at the home of Philip Graham, publisher of the *Washington Post*. The publishers made clear to Marshall, Forrestal, Bradley, Lovett, and Chip Bohlen, who attended for the Truman administration, that there was a ground swell of public anger over the Soviet actions concerning Berlin.[49]

Marshall sent Dulles to seek out Zorin, to ask if the Soviets meant to honor the Berlin Flight Rules once again. Zorin indicated that if the Americans and British were willing to stop their fighter patrols in the corridors, the Soviets would resume following the Flight Rules.[50] Marshall then cabled Forrestal, and suggested that Clay should direct a temporary halt to the fighter patrols. Forrestal agreed, and Bradley cabled Clay to stand down the fighters.[51]

Clay called LeMay and told him to put the escort mission on hold temporarily. LeMay was glad for the respite, because the fighters were going through drop tanks at a great rate and stocks in Europe were dropping to a dangerous level. He needed replenishment if the effort were to continue.[52]

Clay also took the opportunity to send Colonel Frank Howley, commander of the US Berlin garrison, to talk to his Soviet counterpart at the

Berlin Kommandatura, General Alexander Kotikov. Howley and Kotikov discussed the repatriation of remains. There were now six American aircrew dead in the Soviet Zone. Kotikov repeated Sokolovsky's refusal to allow US teams into the "restricted military zone" to recover the remains, but said he would consider the request on a humanitarian basis.

The next day, at the Gleinicke Bridge, two Soviet military ambulances appeared. US military police inquired what they wanted, and a Soviet lieutenant stated that they were there to turn over the remains of aircrew who had crashed in the Soviet Zone. Colonel Howley was immediately notified, and the surprised US commander sent US ambulances and graves registration personnel to take custody of the bodies

Clay took the repatriation of remains as a positive sign, and LeMay reported no further incursions into the corridors. The peak of the crisis had been passed, but the blockade would continue for another seven months. The Soviets were hopeful that their old ally, General Winter, would win for them what diplomacy and intimidation had not. Thanks to good winter weather and steadily improving performance by the US Air Force, US Navy (two squadrons of Navy R-5Ds, the naval version of the C-54, were added to the airlift in late October), the British Royal Air Force, and civilian contractors, Soviet hopes were to be disappointed.[54]

Epilog

Stalin was a very unhappy man.

"The Truman administration refused again to recognize Stalin's quid pro quo in Germany. US propaganda turned the Berlin blockade into incriminating evidence of the ruthlessness and inhumanity of the Soviet regime. The US Air Force demonstrated its stunning superiority by supplying West Berlin for many months with everything it needed. Stalin never planned to start a war over Berlin, but he had to accept his defeat. In May 1949 he lifted the blockade. Khrushchev called the results of Stalin's policy 'a failure,' and said that 'an agreement was signed that made our position in West Berlin worse.' He was right. Until then the Soviets could refer to the documents of the Allied Control Commission in Germany which stated that Berlin, although the place of residence for this temporary body, still remained the capital of the Soviet zone of occupation.

In 1949, Stalin recognized the de facto permanent Western political rights in Berlin, and agreed, in a separate protocol, to the division of the city into West and East. Stalin's stubborn refusal to face the failure of his German diplomacy led to an even greater defeat for Soviet foreign policy in West Berlin. The outcome of the Berlin blockade, of course, was much more disastrous to Soviet security interests than Khrushchev wanted to concede. The majority of countries in Western

Europe, terrified by the 'red menace,' turned to the United States for protection, and thus NATO, an alliance of democratic countries that outlived the Soviet Union, came into existence—and constituted the Soviet military's biggest problem for four decades. Stalin's clumsy pressure put off those Germans who otherwise would have vacillated and perhaps even followed the pied piper of the Kremlin on the road toward German reunification under Soviet tutelage."[55]

Thus, first blood was drawn, but the ocean of blood a third world war would have spilled remained only a nightmare.

The Reality

The Soviets were more cautious. Stalin knew the Soviet atomic bomb was coming soon (first tested on August 29, 1949)[56] along with an aircraft to deliver it, the Tu-4, and already had his Korean plans in train. He could see that the harder he pushed, the harder the US and the Allies pushed back. The capitalist states were not crumbling or fighting among themselves. Instead, they were uniting in an alliance. He had some insight into US war plans and atomic capabilities, thanks to Donald Maclean, a British Foreign Service officer who was also a Soviet spy and who was in a critical position in the British Embassy in Washington during this period.[57] Also, it would take time for the grievous wounds World War II had inflicted on the Soviet Union to heal. 1948 was not the time, and Europe was not the place, to start World War III.

Accordingly, there was only one Soviet incursion into the flight corridors in October, not the rising number shown in the story above. No direct attack was ever made by the Soviets against an airlift aircraft. There was no second instance of fighter cover being ordered for the transport stream. In fact, in a memorandum for the Secretary of Defense on "Military Measures Appropriate in the Event of Soviet Interruption to the Berlin Airlift" dated October 20, 1948, a time exactly contemporaneous with the situation developed in this story, the Joint Chiefs wrote:

> "At present, General Clay's instructions restrict him from any overt action with respect to Soviet interference with the Berlin airlift operation. They also restrict him from any protective or defensive action of consequence in his effort to accomplish the operation in the safest manner possible in spite of interference. The Joint Chiefs of Staff do not believe that these instructions should yet be broadened. This belief is based on the presumption that it must, from a diplomatic viewpoint, be clear if and when serious incidents develop that American forces are in no way to blame and on the fact that the limit of what can be accomplished with our own forces in the Berlin area can so readily be reached that every effort should be made to postpone this contingency with its almost inevitable consequences."[58]

In short, the US did not want war.

The Soviets tightened the blockade, cutting off streets and restricting the movement of people and goods from their sector to the western sectors.[59] They then concentrated on political issues, building toward the advent of the German Democratic Republic, whose constitution was approved on March 20, 1948.[60]

The Berlin Airlift itself wrote history. The Allies did not have to abandon Berlin, a course of action that many thought would seriously undermine their position in western Germany, and thus on the continent as a whole.[61] Neither did they have to use armed force, a capability they possessed in enough quantity to start a war but not in enough quantity to win it, in order to supply their garrison and the city of Berlin. Instead, from June 26, 1948, through September 1, 1949, through 276,926 flights, sometimes in weather in which "even the birds walked," the US and Britain hauled 2,323,067 tons of supplies into Berlin. Of this effort, the US carried 76.7 percent, the RAF 17.0 percent, and civilian contractors 6.3 percent. This effort was not without a human cost: 31 American and 18 British military personnel, 11 civilian aviators, and 5 Germans were killed during airlift operations.[62] Thanks to the heroic sacrifices of the few, and the strenuous and often dangerous efforts of the many, the freedom of more than two million citizens of West Berlin was secured, time was bought during which the US rebuilt its military capabilities, and the West coalesced into the political, economic, and military alliance that eventually prevailed in the Cold War. In the opinion of General Omar Bradley, writing in 1983: "(the Berlin] airlift turned out to be our single greatest triumph in the Cold War."[63]

Bibliography

Bradley, Omar N., and Blair, Clay, *A General's Life: An Autobiography by General of the Army Omar N. Bradley and Clay Blair,* Simon and Schuster, New York, 1983.

Eisenhower, Dwight D., *Crusade in Europe,* Doubleday, Garden City, New York, 1948.

Leebaert, Derek, *The Fifty'-Year Wound: The True Price of America's Cold War Victory,* Little, Brown, Boston, 2002.

LeMay, Curtis E., and Kantor, MacKinlay, *Mission with LeMay: My Story,* Doubleday, Garden City, New York, 1965.

Newton, Verne W, *The Cambridge Spies: The Untold Story of Maclean, Philby, and Burgess in America,* Madison Books, Lanham, New York, 1991.

Parrish, Thomas, *Berlin in the Balance, 1945–1949: The Blockade, The Airlift, The First Major Battle of the Cold War,* Addison-Wesley, Reading, Massachusetts, 1998.

Pogue, Forrest C, *George C. Marshall: Statesman, 1945–1959,* Viking Penguin, New York, 1987.

Radzinsky, Edvard, tr. Willetts, H.T., *Stalin: The First In-Depth Biography Based on Explosive New Documents from Russia's Secret Archives,* Doubleday, New York, 1996.

Tusa, John, and Tusa, Ann, *The Berlin Airlift,* Sarpedon, New York, 1998.

United States, Department of State, *Foreign Relations of the United States, 1944,* vol. 1, Washington, D.C., 1966.

Zubok, Vladislav, and Pleshakov, Constantine, *Inside the Kremlin's Cold War: From Stalin to Khrushchev,* Harvard University Press, Cambridge, Massachusetts, 1996.

Notes

*1. The Air Force did remember. Brown retired as a major general in 1972.
*2. Russell Brown, *Flashpoint: Berlin, 1948* (New York, 1994), p. 28.
3. Pogue, *George C. Marshall: Statesman,* p. 49.
4. Parrish, *Berlin in the Balance,* p. 73.
5. *Ibid.,* p. 143.
6. *Ibid., pp.* 134–35.
7. Tusa and Tusa, *The Berlin Airlift,* pp. 107–08.
8. *Ibid, p.* 115.
9. *Ibid,* pp. 113–14.
10. Parrish, *Berlin in the Balance,* pp. 148–49.
11. Tusa, *The Berlin Airlift,* pp. 131–33, and 271.
12. *Ibid.,* p. 130.
13. Parrish, *Berlin in the Balance,* p. 168.
14. *Ibid, p.* 175.
15. Bradley and Blair, *A General's Life, p. 474.*
16. Memorandum for General Norstad, "Preliminary Appreciation of the Defense of the Rhine River," 26 Oct 48, signed S.E. Anderson, MG, USAF, Director Plans & Operations, RG 341, Entry 335, Box 807, National Archives.
17. Bradley and Blair, *A General's Life,* p. 488.
18. *Ibid,* pp. 488–89.
19. Pogue, *George C. Marshall: Statesman,* p. 304.
20. Parrish, *Berlin in the Balance, p.* 182.
21. *Ibid, p.* 198.
22. Tusa, *The Berlin Airlift, p.* 160.
23. *Ibid., p.* 176; see also Parrish, *Berlin in the Balance,* p. 216, and Pogue, *George C. Marshall: Statesman, p.* 302.
24. Allied Control Authority, Air Directorate, Flight Rules for Aircraft Flying in Air Corridors in Germany and Berlin Control Zone, 22 Oct 48, DAIR/P(45)71-Second Revision, RG: 341 Entry: 335 Box: 806, NA.
25. Pogue, *George C. Marshall: Statesman, p.* 307.
26. *Ibid, p.* 238.
*27. "Summary of Corridor Incidents," App VII-B: "USAF and the Berlin Airlift, 1949."
*28. *Ibid.*
29. Parrish, *Berlin in the Balance,* pp. 223–25.
30. For safety, the C-54s were separated vertically by 1,000 feet in altitude as well as horizontally by 3 minutes flying distance.
*31. Richmond, Lawrence, *The Airbridge* (New York, 1954), p. 354.
*32. Metzger, Gordon, *USAFE and the Airlift* (New York, 1977), p. 417.
33. Parrish, *Berlin in the Balance,* pp. 177, 208.
*34. Richmond, *The Airbridge, p.* 405.
*35. Metzger, *USAFE and the Airlift, p.* 482.
36. Secure conference via teletype, operated like an internet chat session.

37. Headquarters, European Command, APO 403, 30 Aug 48, "Orderly Evacuation of Berlin by Air," Appendix C, RG 341, Entry 335, Box 806, NA.
38. Bradley and Blair, *A General's Life*, p. 481, calling lack of direction from the NSC concerning war risk "outrageous," Bradley commented: "During the critical phase of the Berlin Blockade, when we were nose to nose with massive Soviet military power, the JCS was so poorly advised that we could not draw contingency war plans. Our exposure was enormous."
39. Memo for General Norstad, *op. cit.*, para. 6.
*40. Richmond, *The Airbridge*, p. 409.
41. Leebaert, *The Fifty-Year Wound*, p. 68.
42. LeMay and Kantor, *Mission with LeMay*, p. 414, reports a World War II Balkan incident in which US fighters shot down "three or four" Yaks.
43. Tusa, *The Berlin Airlift*, pp. 246–47.
*44. Kaberov and Anopov survived the arrests—likely because of their World War II records (both had been aces)—and stayed in the Air Force. Glinka and Petrinko were never heard of again.
*45. Richmond, *The Airbridge*, p. 412.
*46. Vassily Danilovich Sokolovsky, *My Service: Stalin's Red Army* (Moscow, 1993), pp. 223-35.
47. Pogue, *George C. Marshall: Statesman*, pp. 408–09.
48. Radzinsky and Willetts, *Stalin*, p. 509. "Druzhkov" suggests friendliness in Russian, and was an alias Stalin used with Molotov.
49. Pogue, *George C. Marshall: Statesman*, p. 315.
*50. Martin, Roger R, *Paris Corridors* (New York, 1977), p. 45.
*51. *Ibid., p.* 47.
*52. Metzger, *USAFE and the Airlift*, p. 495.
*53. Frank Howley, *In the Berlin Hot Seat* (New York, 1953), p. 335.
54. Tusa, *The Berlin Airlift*, pp. 305–09.
55. Zubok and Pleshakov, *Inside the Kremlin's Cold War*, p. 52.
56. Radzinsky and Willetts, *Stalin*, p. 515.
57. Newton, *The Cambridge Spies*, pp. 67 and 145–86.
58. RG 341, Entry 335, Box 806, NA.
59. Tusa, *The Berlin Airlift*, pp. 274–75.
60. *Ibid,* p. 341.
61. "The Secretary of State thought that the United States had the option of staying in Berlin or seeing the failure of their European policy." Pogue, *George C. Marshall: Statesman*, p. 305.
62. Parrish, *Berlin in the Balance*, p. 329.
63. Bradley and Blair, *A General's Life*, p. 481.

2

THE PUSAN DISASTER, 1950
North Korea's Triumph

James R. Arnold

Sadong, North Korea, May 1949

The massive tanks of the *15th Tank Training Regiment* halted in perfect wedge formation. Their turrets rotated in unison to point at a line of hastily dug earthworks. A thudding volley split the air. The 3 5-ton, Russian-made tanks rocked backward as their 85mm cannons fired. The gunners quickly found the range. Their second and third shots collapsed the trenches. Drivers engaged their transmissions and the tanks advanced again.

The riflemen defending the trenches did not run, the manacles around their ankles did not allow it. Some cowered. Others frantically worked their bolt-action Japanese Model 38 Arisaka rifles, but the 6.5mm bullets made no impression against the approaching tanks. A brave handful who were not secured with chains rose from the firing pits. The tanks responded with 7.62mm machine-gun fire from their bow and coaxial weapons. The infantry charged through the machine-gun fire to try to hurl their anti-tank grenades. The few who survived stood in hopeless disbelief when the detonations emitted thick, greasy smoke instead of the promised destructive armor-piercing explosion.

Major Vladimir Ivanovich Orlov smiled. Five years before, the then Lieutenant Orlov had commanded a platoon of T-34/85s during the drive against the Korsun Pocket. His own tank had eliminated 11 Fascist tanks and earned him the honor Hero of the Soviet Union. Few tankers possessed Orlov's wealth of combat experience. For the past year, Orlov's job had required him to pass on this knowledge to the *North Korean People's Army (NKPA)*. He firmly believed that nothing tested a soldier's resolve better than live hostile fire. Accordingly, for this last exercise he had asked his North Korean liaison officer for "volunteers" from the army's punishment battalions and the nation's prisons to serve as opponents against his well-drilled tankers. The response had been gratifying.

From a trench 200 yards away, a camouflaged anti-tank gun fired. Its feeble pop could not be heard above the roar of the tank engines. However, a voluminous cloud of dirty smoke gave away its position. The company commander's tank pivoted to face this new enemy and indicate the direction of advance. He barked an order to his platoon leaders: "Danger! Anti-tank gun. Bearing 0100. Advance and engage with machine-gun fire."

Orlov smiled again. His tankers were responding exactly according to their battle drill. The hidden anti-tank gun had been a surprise to test their mettle. Undoubtedly the keyed up crews believed themselves to be imperiled by this foe. In fact, the obsolete Japanese Model 01 47mm weapon could only penetrate the T-34/85's armor with a lucky shot. But the major did not want luck to interfere with this final training exercise. Accordingly, unbeknownst to either the gunners or their targets, his technicians had removed 80 percent of the propellant from each anti-tank round.

The gunners managed another two shots before the tanks methodically gunned them down. Meanwhile, the supporting company rolled over the shallow infantry trenches to crush the handful of still writhing survivors. Orlov fired his flare pistol. The exercise was over. The tanks dutifully formed a semi-circle and the tankers dismounted to stand at attention. Orlov entered the circle to provide his post-exercise critique. "You bastards are good, very good. You will now be assigned to new cadres and teach them the lessons you have learned here. Dismissed!"[1]

That evening most of the regiment received promotion to officer grade. It was a welcome reward for two years of hard service. Then they transferred to the newly activated *105th Tank Brigade*. This unit mirrored the organization of a World War II era Soviet tank division except that it lacked a heavy tank regiment, rocket launcher battalion, and anti-aircraft and mortar regiments. Still, the *105th* featured some 6,000 men distributed into three tank regiments with some 140 T-34/85 tanks and 16 SU-76 self-propelled guns supported by a mechanized infantry regiment, reconnaissance battalion, and engineer battalion.[2] Observing strict radio silence and using superb camouflage, in the early spring of 1950 the elite unit, redesignated the *105th Tank Division,* marched south to take up positions near the 38th Parallel. They were supremely confident because they knew that the enemy, the capitalist puppets belonging to the Republic of Korea Army, had neither tanks nor modern anti-tank weapons.

Washington, DC: January 1949 to June 1950

The formative military experience of the 33 rd President of the United States, Harry S. Truman, came in World War I during his service with a Missouri National Guard artillery unit. He rose from a humble private to be elected lieutenant on the eve of the unit's departure for France. He ably led his unit in combat and received promotion to captain. The experience of war taught him several things, including a deep contempt for professional military men and an awareness that the military seemed unable to manage itself without enormous waste. This bothered Truman greatly, because he prided himself on his thrifty nature. He wrote that West Pointers could not be trusted "with a pair of mules" because they would either lose the mules, or sell them and use the cash to buy whiskey.[3]

His keenness to root out waste received a forum during World War II. The then Senator Truman founded and ran a subcommittee that investigated waste and fraud in military procurement. The investigation confirmed his biases. His work attracted so much praise that President Roosevelt selected him to run as his vice-president in 1944. Roosevelt's death saw the one time Missouri National Guard private become commander in chief of the entire American military.

As soon as World War II ended, Truman set to work. He demanded a balanced federal budget and a reduction in the staggering national war debt. To achieve these goals he imposed strict budget ceilings on the American military. When the Pentagon recommended a minimum austerity budget of some $15 billion a year, Truman promptly cut it by a third. The result was a dramatic decline in the size of the standing military force and a reduction in the quality and quantity of its weapons. In 1945 the army had numbered six million well-trained, well-equipped men organized into almost 100 divisions. Three years later it numbered 677,000 men in ten under strength, poorly prepared divisions.

When Truman won his upset victory in the 1948 presidential election, he felt unbound from Roosevelt's towering legacy. To help implement his budget-slashing policies Truman selected Louis Johnson to serve as Secretary of Defense. Johnson brought two major attributes to this position: loyalty to his boss—he had been Truman's chief fund raiser during the 1948 election—and near total ignorance of military strategy or weapons systems. So, under Johnson's unenlightened supervision, the reduction in the military accelerated.

Simultaneously, Truman maintained a very tough policy toward communism. He saw international communism as a monolithic force controlled by Moscow and bent on world domination. He was determined to hold it in check. The discontinuity between his foreign policy and his evisceration of the US military never occurred to him.

In June 1950, Secretary of Defense Johnson and the Chairman of the Joint Chiefs of Staff, General Omar Bradley, undertook a two-week inspection of the Far East. They visited military installations and met with senior leaders including General Douglas MacArthur, the commander of US occupation forces in Japan. The head of the Korean Military Assistance Group, General Lynn Roberts, gave a briefing. Roberts enumerated the many daunting obstacles he had confronted, but asserted that training was progressing. Roberts assured his audience that the South Koreans were more than a match for the communists. Someone asked Roberts whether the *NKPA* possessed an armor capability. Roberts replied: "Korea is not good tank country."[4] Everyone accepted his judgment. After all, Roberts had commanded an armored combat command during the Battle of the Bulge and so presumably knew what he was talking about.

Johnson and Bradley concluded that everything seemed to be in order. There were no threats on the horizon. They returned to Washington on June 24. President Truman was on vacation at his home in Missouri. Late that evening Johnson learned about an Associated Press report that North Korea had launched a major attack. Johnson was skeptical. He replied that he had not heard any such thing, and that he had just returned from the region and no one had warned that such an attack was likely. Soon Johnson went to bed.

In contrast, the incomplete reports alarmed Secretary of State Dean Acheson. He telephoned Truman and the two men discussed the implications of the shocking news. Up to this point, the Kremlin had fought the Cold War without resorting to overt military action. Truman and Acheson agreed that clearly Joe Stalin had to have ordered the attack. But why now and why Korea? Was it a feint to draw American forces into a fight on the Asian mainland or to divert attention from a Chinese invasion of Formosa? Regardless of the answers, the event itself angered Truman. He had worked hard to build the United Nations into a forum to address international disputes. The UN, in turn, had sponsored and then supported South Korea. The communist attack was both a blow against the UN and a personal slap in the face to Harry Truman.

Truman Ups the Ante

Following a carefully detailed script written by their Soviet advisers, at 0400 on June 25, *NKPA* artillery and mortars had opened fire in a softening up bombardment.[5] Shortly thereafter, seven *NKPA* infantry divisions swarmed over the border. Tanks belonging to the *105th Division* spearheaded the advance. Surprise was complete. Only four of the eight Republic of Korea (ROK) divisions were deployed near the frontier. They lacked modern equipment. There were no pilots qualified to fly combat missions. Their heaviest weapons, 105mm howitzers, had been used in US infantry cannon companies during World War II. They were so worn that they could not fire full charges. The ROK armored force consisted of 27 obsolete armored cars. Most importantly, the army had no effective antitank weapon to fight the T-34/85s. Their 140 anti-tank guns were all 37mm weapons, a type proven already obsolete by 1941. ROK infantry had to rely upon their 2.36-inch bazookas to have any hope that they would stop the communist tanks. The first encounters obliterated that hope. Seoul fell on the third day of the North Korean offensive. The *NKPA* unit that contributed most dramatically to the capture of the city, the *105th Tank Division*, earned the honorific *"Seoul Division"* for this victory.

When North Korea ignored demands to withdraw, the US persuaded the United Nations Security Council to help South Korea. It marked the first time in UN history that it reacted to aggression with military force. Nonetheless, the American response to the unfolding disaster in Korea was one of gradual escalation. Misled by confident reports about the fighting capability of the ROK troops, at first only two ships, escorted by air and naval forces, were sent to deliver emergency ammunition supplies. The American role expanded to allow Air Force and Navy planes to fly ground support missions but to remain south of the 38th Parallel. Meanwhile, the head of an American survey team arrived in South Korea on June 27. A quick inspection tour revealed the truth. ROK soldiers were in full rout. Fleeing soldiers and thousands of refugees clogged the road south from Seoul. General MacArthur decided to visit the scene himself.

Looking exactly like he did in World War II—battered campaign hat, corncob pipe—MacArthur flew to Korea on June 29. He briefly toured the ROK defensive line at the Han River just south of Seoul. His judgment was harsh: "I haven't seen a single wounded man yet."[6] Then and there MacArthur concluded that South Korea could only be saved by the introduction of US ground forces. A generation of American fighting men had grown up believing that American soldiers should not become involved in fighting Asian hordes on the Asian mainland. MacArthur's snap decision reversed this long standing policy.

At 1700, Washington time, June 29, Truman and his senior advisers met secretly at the presidential guest quarters at the Blair House to ponder MacArthur's request. The outlook was grim. ROK forces were apparently running as hard as they could. It seemed that the best the United States could hope for was to establish some kind of defensive perimeter around the port of Pusan. Everyone worried about making too great a commitment to Korea and then being unable to react when the Soviets made their main push. The President wanted to take every step possible to push the communists back to the 38th Parallel. But he firmly kept in view the larger threat posed by the Soviet Union. Accordingly, the formal policy statement explained: "The decision to commit United States naval and air forces and limited army forces to provide cover and support for South Korean troops does not constitute a decision to engage in war with the Soviet Union."[7]

Among the conferees at the Blair House this seemed unambiguous enough. But in public Truman found he had some trouble articulating the US strategy. He emphatically stated that the nation was not at war. A reporter, searching for an appropriate headline-length description of the American involvement in Korea asked Truman if the situation could be described as a United Nations' "police action." The president agreed.

The Destruction of Task Force Smith

The first American soldiers sent to fight the police action belonged to the Eighth Army in occupied Japan. They had been enjoying a soft garrison life and were neither physically nor mentally prepared for battle. Yet on paper the Eighth Army seemed strong. It possessed four of the ten active divisions in the entire US Army. Because the 24th Infantry Division was based on the Japanese island of Kyushu, nearest to South Korea, MacArthur's chief of staff chose it to move first. Even the official readiness statement rated the division as only 65 percent combat ready. In fact, it was the least prepared division in the army. It was so under-strength that MacArthur's General Headquarters stripped 2,108 non-commissioned officers from the army's other three divisions and attached them to the 24th. A separate levy added some 2,600 more men. While these actions gave the division a strength of nearly 16,000 men, they ignored the fact that none of the new personnel had trained with the parent unit. Throughout history, corporals and sergeants have been the essential leaders who guide fighting men in combat. They provide the iron backbone that allows soldiers to face the horrors of war. As the men of the 24th walked up the gangplanks to board the transports for the quick trip to Pusan, they met these leaders for the first time.

The soldiers belonging to Task Force Smith had even less time to get squared away. General William F. Dean, the division commander, met Lieutenant Colonel Charles Smith at the airfield in Japan. Dean issued his orders: "When you get to Pusan, head for Taejon. We want to stop the North Koreans as far from Pusan as we can."[8] Dean had little doubt that when the North Koreans encountered American soldiers they would melt like snow. Unfortunately, the heavy C-54 transport planes carrying Smith's men tore up the flimsy runways at Pusan. Consequently, the Air Force halted transport operations. About half of Task Force Smith's heavy equipment remained in Japan. Nonetheless, the task force immediately headed to the front.

Early on the morning of July 5, Task Force Smith's 406th Infantry Regiment was dug in astride the Seoul-Pusan Highway. A mile behind it was a supporting 105mm field artillery battery commanded by Miller Perry. It numbered another 134 soldiers. At 0730 the morning fog lifted to reveal a *NKPA* tank column advancing along the highway. It was in route formation, apparently unaware of the Americans' presence. When the tanks closed to within a mile of the US infantry, the six 105mm howitzers opened fire. Truman's budget cuts had restricted the number of high explosive anti-tank (HEAT) rounds available to the Eighth Army. On all of Kyushu there were only 18 and Miller Perry's battery had one-third of this total. Perry decided to hoard these rounds and begin the fight with regular high explosive ammunition. The rain of shells seemed to have no effect on the enemy tanks.

A veteran of Guadalcanal, Smith had been in tight spots before. He calmly ordered his 75mm recoilless rifle teams to hold fire until the tanks were within 700 yards. Meanwhile, his ten bazooka teams remained concealed along the highway. The T-34/85s advanced. The recoilless rifles opened fire at unmissable close range. Each team scored numerous direct hits. But many of the rounds were duds. Worse, even the effective shells made no impression. The bazooka teams opened fire at point-blank range. One team fired 22 rounds at the tanks' weaker rear armor. Even at a range of 15 yards the bazookas had no effect. Just as they had done on the Sadong training grounds, the tanks rolled over the American infantry.

Battery commander Perry ordered his gunners to engage with their HEAT rounds. Finally the defenders' fire made an impression. The leading two tanks slewed off the road. One burst into flame. Three crewmen emerged. Two raised their arms in surrender. The third raised his submachine gun and killed a machine gunner, the first American loss of the war.

In total the defenders managed to knock out four tanks. After shooting up the American transport, the remaining 29 simply continued south down the highway. Next came the infantry. Their training and tenacity astonished. A survivor wrote:

> "Instead of a motley horde armed with old muskets, the enemy infantry were well-trained, determined soldiers and many of their weapons were at least as modern as ours. Instead of charging wildly into battle, they employed a base of fire, double envelopment, fire blocks on withdrawal routes, and skilled infiltration."[9]

Task Force Smith held on until 1430 before Smith ordered a retreat but the withdrawal degenerated into wild panic. It would take five more days for Task Force Smith to reorganize. A total of 185 men had been lost. Far worse was the impact on morale. News of the disaster swept the 24th Division and later spread throughout the Eighth Army. Above all was the ominous intelligence that the communists possessed a killer weapon that could not be stopped.

The NKPA Rolls South

It took almost two weeks for US intelligence officers to figure out what type of tank the enemy was using in Korea. It took far less time for the officers in the field to clamor for something to oppose these tanks effectively. World War II had clearly shown that the best anti-tank weapon was a better tank. But a search of the American arsenal found a cupboard literally stripped bare. In June 1950 not a single tank was in production. As a stopgap measure workers removed some M26 Pershing tanks from their display pedestals around Fort Knox and began to refurbish them. The Army's newest model, the M46 Patton, was merely a modified Pershing featuring a new turret atop a Pershing hull. Because Japanese bridges could not carry their weight, no Pattons were assigned to the Eighth Army. The only tanks immediately available were M24 Chaffees, light reconnaissance tanks armed with 75mm guns. Events soon revealed that the North Korean tanks completely outclassed them.

In the absence of effective tanks or anti-tank guns, there was one other alternative for the infantry. Recently a new 3-5-inch "super bazooka" had been developed. Ammunition production for this weapon had just begun. General MacArthur issued an emergency request for them on July 3. Until they arrived, the battle of men versus tanks was decisively tilted in the favor *of the NKPA.*

During the ensuing days, the *105th Tank Division* spearheaded the communist drive to overrun all of South Korea. The 24th Infantry Division rushed into position to establish a succession of blocking positions. The US Army post-mortem reported:

> "One by one, these positions... were outflanked or overrun, and the 24th Division reeled backward in retreat. After one week of fighting, the division had suffered heavy casualties, including 1,500 men missing in action."[10]

The next five weeks were little better as the *NKPA* rolled south at a very moderate cost. In sum, the six weeks following the initial North Korean invasion witnessed an unbroken string of ROK and American disasters.

Command Decision

On the evening of July 22, a captured American jeep carried the commander of the *NKPA 4th Division,* Major-General Lee Kwon Mu, north along the Taejon—Seoul highway. The jeep drove without headlights to evade detection by American planes. Mu was pleased with his unit's performance so far. It had helped capture Seoul and thereby earned the honorific *"Seoul Division."* Its great victory at Taejon brought it the title *"Seoul Guards Division."* Now it seemed that the senior leadership had a new mission in mind. The jeep passed several truck convoys carrying troops and ammunition south. Mu also saw a surprising number of battle-scarred and abandoned tanks. The comrades in the *105th Division* had paid a price, Mu reflected.[11]

Delayed by blown bridges and two bombing raids, Mu arrived late to the conference. To his surprise he found that almost the entire *NKPA* high command was present. Perhaps equally surprising, they had waited for him before beginning the formal meeting. A young staff officer, Lieutenant-Colonel Lee Hak Ku began the briefing:

> "Up to today, we have made satisfactory progress according to the timetable laid out in planning document 2-5. I want to remind everyone that while we did account for the possibility of American interven-

tion in contingency plan B-1.2, we rated the likelihood of imperialist ground involvement as less then 33 percent. We correctly anticipated naval blockade and correctly dismissed its short term impact. We underestimated the impact of enemy air power. Consequently, our logistical support for the front line troops is stretched very thin. We must recognize that each mile we advance lengthens our supply line and correspondingly reduces the logistical problems for the enemy. Furthermore, we have driven the imperialists and their puppets into a shrinking perimeter. It can be more easily defended than the linear position across the entire peninsula that they formerly held."[12]

The colonel paused to take a deep drag on his British cigarette. General Mu studied the colonel carefully. He had heard that Ku was a "comer," a brilliant, ambitious officer with good political connections. Ku's cogent summary and the fact that he had access to British cigarettes—something available to only the most favored of the party elite—confirmed the rumors. This man might be a very useful ally, Mu reflected.

Ku proceeded to describe the intelligence service's estimate of the enemy order of battle. For the next week the People's Army faced a badly depleted 24th Infantry Division, a bruised 1st Cavalry, and a fresh unit tentatively identified as the 25th Infantry Division. The South Korean forces had not yet recovered sufficiently to weigh heavily on the scales of battle. But the offensive had not been without cost. The *People's Air Force* was out of the equation. The crack *NKPA 3rd Division* had suffered heavy losses. The *4th* and *6th Divisions* had suffered moderately. Most significantly, the fearless tank thrusts by the *105th Tank Division* had been expensive. Enemy action and mechanical breakdown had subtracted nearly 60 percent of the unit's tanks.

After a dramatic pause, Ku came to his conclusion:

"In sum, the calculus of battle points in our favor, but time is not on our side. We have enough strength for one more big push. The question is where?"[13]

A furious debate ensued. Army commander General Chai Ung Jun observed that, to date, the tank-led frontal assaults had triumphed, but at ever-increasing cost. Meanwhile, the infantry had exhibited a surpassing ability to locate the American weaknesses and flow past or through lightly defended sectors. Everyone understood that the *NKPA's* infiltration tactics worked best in broken terrain. This fact argued in favor of a wide envelopment south to the coast and then east toward Pusan. But such an operation would take time.

Mu spoke for the first time. He argued for one more direct assault, a concentration of force to administer the *coup de grace* along the highway leading to Pusan. As Mu expected, Colonel Ku emphatically supported his notion. But the senior leadership had grown up in cut and thrust army politics where those who backed a plan that failed seldom received a second chance. They looked to General Jun for guidance before committing themselves, only to realize that Jun himself seemed unable to decide. It was apparent that Jun was positioning himself to land on his feet regardless of which plan was adopted.

The generals were evenly divided. Perhaps the older veterans of the long fight in China showed a preference for the tried and true indirect approach while most of the younger hawks favored a direct assault. At this decisive moment General Mu spoke again. Sound strategy, patriotism, ambition, all pointed in one direction: "Give me my division, the *6th Division*, and the tanks and I guarantee we will drive the Yankees into the sea." A collective gasp rose from the table. Several of the older generals shook their heads in disapproval. Another lengthy debate ensued but by the narrowest margin Mu's plan prevailed. The final offensive would being in the pre-dawn hours of July 25.

"Stand or Die!"

During the two days before the attack, General Mu was everywhere; inspecting the dug-in, well-camouflaged field artillery, rehearsing assault tactics with the company commanders, instilling a determination to conquer or die to the all-important infiltration teams. A quick visit to the *6th Division*, which was aligned shoulder to shoulder with his own division, convinced him that he did not have to spend much time there. Officers and men alike clearly knew their business. The unit traced its origins back to 1942 when the Chinese communists had formed a Korean Volunteer Army from Korean deserters from the Japanese Kwantung Army. The knowledge that there was literally no alternative but victory or death had forged the division into a veteran group of ruthless killers. He read with approval division commander Pang Ho San's rousing proclamation:

> "Comrades, the enemy is demoralized. The task given us is the liberation of Taegu and the annihilation of the remnants of the enemy. The liberation of Taegu means the final battle to cut the windpipe of the enemy."[14]

Mu was equally pleased with the *105th Tank Division*. The battlefield introduction of the 3- 5 -inch bazooka had forced the tankers to change their tactics. The enemy no longer ran simply when the tanks appeared. Unsupported tank thrusts had become too risky. Mu therefore ordered the tankers to assemble behind the lines for a refresher course in tank—infantry cooperation conducted by Major Orlov and his Russian advisers. The tankers closely attended to the Soviet lecture, particularly after the first class when a sergeant had tried to argue with Orlov. Mu had ordered the sergeant to stand at attention and nodded to his bodyguard. The

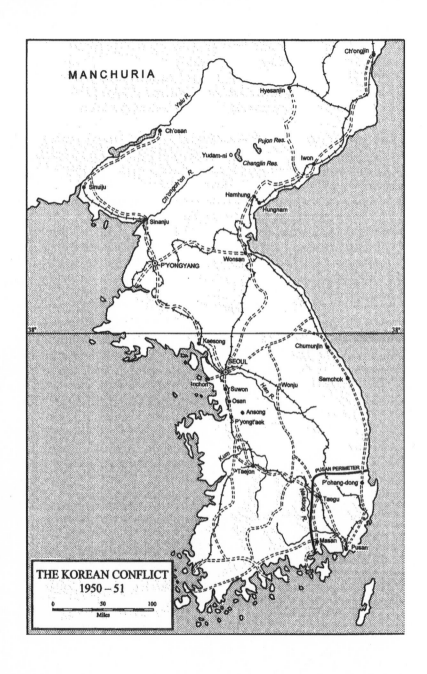

MANCHURIA

Ch'ongjin

Hyesanjin

Yalu R.

Ch'osan

Pujon Res.

Yudam-ni Changjin Res. Iwon

Ch'ongch'on R.

Sinuiju Hamhung

Hungnam

Sinanju

Wonsan

P'YONGYANG

38°   38°

Kaesong

Chumunjin

SEOUL

Inchon Suwon Wonju Samchok

Han R.

Osan

Ansong

P'yongt'aek

Kum R.

PUSAN PERIMETER

Taejon P'ohang-dong

Naktong R.

Taegu

Masan Pusan

THE KOREAN CONFLICT
1950 – 51

0   50   100
Miles

bodyguard drew his pistol and shot the sergeant dead. Mu then turned to Orlov and said: "Please continue."[15]

The night before the attack General Mu returned to his own head-quarters to summon his regimental and battalion commanders to a final briefing. He looked around and only with effort hid his surprise. Near reckless front line leadership had yielded victories but at high cost. Gone were many of the veterans of the China War. Still, Mu reflected, when only we few remain we are still enough. Confidence restored, Mu explained in detail what he wanted the *4th Division* to do.

Across the lines, Eighth Army Commander General Walker and his staff examined the map. His forces had retired into a defensive perimeter around Pusan. One front faced north and one west with the hinge in the middle at Taegu. South Korean forces manned the northern front from the Sea of Japan inland toward Taegu. They had rallied from the opening shocks and now seemed able to hold their own against the *NKPA* infantry. They would have to carry on alone because Walker had no US forces available to support them. The western front was altogether different. In fact it could hardly be called a front since there was no continuous defensive line running south from Taegu through Masan to the sea. ROK militarized police units had established strongpoints in the southern third of Korea. No one expected them to provide effective resistance when the North Koreans advanced. At least they could serve as an outpost line to warn if the communists were attempting a deep envelopment via Masan.

The key sector was clearly around Taegu. Besides being a critical rail and road center, the city was the hinge liking the northern and western fronts. Walker resolved to use everything he had to hold Taegu. He ordered the shattered remnants of the 24th Infantry Division back into line to defend the perimeter south of Taegu. The 1st Cavalry was barely in better shape. It also deployed south of Taegu with its strongest unit, the 7 th Cavalry Regiment, tied in to the 25th Infantry Division just south of Taegu. The 25 th Division, commanded by General William B. Kean, defended Taegu itself.

The division's only full-strength regiment was the all black 24th Infantry Regiment. Walker and Kean shared the widespread view that "Negroes won't fight."[16] Accordingly, they placed the 24th Regiment in the least threatened sector east of Taegu. The battered 27th Infantry Regiment occupied the high ground south of Taegu. Sandwiched between them was the 19th Infantry Regiment which took position astride the Seoul-Taegu highway.

To prepare his men for pending battle General Walker issued his orders:

"We are fighting a battle against time. There will be no more retreating, withdrawal, or readjustment of the lines or any other term you chose. There is no line behind us to which we can retreat. There will be no Dunkirk, there will be no Bataan, a retreat to Pusan would be one of the greatest butcheries in history. We must fight until the end. Capture by these people is worse than death itself. I want everyone to understand that we are going to hold this line. We are going to win."[17]

Five *NKPA* divisions deployed fanwise along a 40-mile arc west and north of Taegu. The offensive began just after midnight on July 25. Select infiltration teams made masterful use of the terrain to slip between American outposts and around the flanks of the main line of resistance. They had two objectives: to establish ambush sites deep in the rear along the roads and trails by which reinforcements and ammunition would move to the American front; and to attack and take out the American field artillery. The second objective was the more important. When given time to prepare, the American artillery showed a superb ability to shift fire rapidly and crush the *NKPA* assault infantry. General Mu planned for his infiltration teams to neutralize this US advantage.

A brief *NKPA* artillery bombardment heralded the beginning of the main offensive at 0400. Mu's Soviet advisers wanted the artillery to target the enemy guns in a classic counter-battery bombardment. Mu ignored them. Even when his divisional artillery was at full strength, the American field guns outranged his 76mm field guns and 122mm howitzers. Furthermore, the artillery had had trouble keeping pace with the rapid advance. American planes had taken a heavy toll. Accordingly, Mu ordered his guns to open fire with high explosive in hopes of cutting American communication wires and then to smother the front line positions with smoke shells.

In theory, the steep hills stretching around Taegu should have provided defensive advantages. If sufficient men had been available, the hills and ridges could have provided a succession of defensive positions to blunt the *NKPA* advance. Instead, the defenders were stretched thin. Lack of time had also hampered the defenders. Too many units occupied positions where nearby hilltops and undulations in the ground blocked lines of sight. Gullies and ravines penetrated almost every battalion-size defensive sector.

Still, the men of the 1st Cavalry, the "Wolfhounds" of the 27th Infantry, the all-black 24th Infantry, and even the remnants of the ROK Capital Division put up a good fight, slowing and even repelling numerous charges. But the *NKPA* infantry relentlessly maintained the attack. The trouble for the defenders came at critical moments when they called for their tactical trump card: the field artillery. In some sectors the artillery responded with a gratifying barrage that pinned the communist infantry to the ground. Too often requests for support brought a puzzling crackle of static. In some cases, the initial *NKPA* bombardment had cut communication wire. More often, infiltration teams cut the wires themselves. At battery headquarters signal men also discovered that their antiquated switchboards failed under the pressure of high demand. However, the major reason that the artillery support slowly petered out was that too many gun crews were involved in desperate hand-to-hand fighting against NKPA infiltrators who seemed to rise from the very ground to attack the flanks and rear of the battery positions. The NKPA pinning attacks directed at the units defending Taegu's flanks continued through the morning. They accomplished their purpose by both tying down front line defenders and forcing local reserves to counter-attack to maintain the position. Meanwhile, the decisive breakthrough came along the poplar-lined Taegu—Sangju road seven miles north of Taegu. This road ran along a narrow valley dominated on the west by the Yuhak-san mountain mass that rose to a height of 2,700 feet. On the eastern side the Ka-san towered 2,900 feet above the valley. From the heights the road seemed to stretch on a nearly straight north-south axis. The men of the 19th Infantry who defended this sector called it the "Bowling Alley." Their position blocked the road and extended up both sides into the mountains. About one mile in front of the American line was the village of Sinjumak. Here the road curved behind a series of hills that blocked direct fire from the American line. This was the staging area for the 105th Tank Division.

The defenders belonged to an outfit rich in unit pride. As one of the handful of regular US Army units in the Civil War, the 19th had conducted a famous fight that earned it the sobriquet "The Rock of Chickamauga." The soldiers in Korea proudly called themselves "Chicks." The Chicks had had two days to prepare their positions in and around the Bowling Alley. Accustomed to Japan's soft garrison life, they found that the effort to scramble around rugged terrain while exposed to blazing heat and jungle-like humidity was enervating. Wild rumors about North Korean power and brutality also took a toll.

The initial NKPA bombardment unnerved the Chicks. They were new to combat and more than a few men were simply terrified. Even before the bombardment ended, the defenders saw a triple wave of enemy infantry advancing toward their trenches. The advance appeared hesitant and disjointed. American automatic weapons mowed down the NKPA soldiers in the first wave. A pair of M-16 half-tracks, each mounting four .50-caliber machine guns, added their terrific fire to riddle the second wave. The third wave refused to advance and went to ground. A near silence fell on the field. The Chicks looked at one another with amazement. It had been much easier than they expected.

In fact, this initial assault had been a sacrificial forlorn hope. Unlike the traditional forlorn hope composed of brave volunteers, this forlorn hope comprised 1,000 new replacements—South Koreans conscripted at gunpoint in the streets of Seoul. Their task was to locate American strongpoints. In this they had succeeded.

A salvo of green and red flares rose above the NKPA position. Next came bugle calls and the dreaded sound of revving tank engines. Then came a series of shattering explosions as the *NKPA* regimental 120mm mortars began pounding the US strongpoints.

The T-34/85s rolled steadily toward the American line. Sheltered behind each tank came a combat squad armed with burp guns. In an astonishing display of accuracy, the 90th Field Artillery Battery used its 155mm weapons to knock out five tanks with HEAT shells. Then the battery itself fell to a frenzied assault conducted by a late-arriving infiltration team.

The Chicks' recoilless rifles had little effect against the enemy armor. When the tanks came to within 30 yards of the Chicks' trenches, brave men rose to fire their 3.5-inch bazookas. Their first shots knocked out numerous tanks. Now the training in tank—infantry teamwork paid off for the attackers. The *NKPA* infantry spread out in a protective cordon around the tanks. The tanks then worked in pairs, one providing covering fire while the other made a short advance to neutralize the enemy firing positions.

It quickly became apparent to the GIs that the bazooka was a suicide weapon. A bazooka team might take out a T-34/85 but it always brought on a hail of burp gun fire that forced the team to take shelter or to die. Fewer and fewer teams showed a willingness to expose themselves to this deadly fire. One battalion commander showed that he fully understood the meaning of Walker's "Stand or Die" order. Shouting to nearby soldiers that: "as long as I'm in command, this outfit will not withdraw another inch," he seized a bazooka to stalk a T-34/85. He got the lead tank but an 85mm round from the tank's twin cut him in two. Ignoring the pleas of their officers, riflemen began moving to the rear. Some paused to turn and fire at the nearby *NKPA* infantry but many threw down their weapons and simply fled. The second wave of tanks penetrated the trench line and continued south along the road. Behind them, the *NKPA* infantry used grenades to begin methodically rooting out the remaining defenders. How Walker's "Stand or Die" order had affected the Chicks cannot be determined because most of those who did stand did indeed die.

Throughout the morning, ground fog and overcast conditions had limited US air support. Around 1000, planes belonging to the Far Eastern Air Force intervened briefly on the battlefield. The cloud ceiling was under 500 feet. Nonetheless, two flights of F-80s volunteered to make an attack. They dropped through the clouds to appear over the battlefield like ghostly, shrieking birds of prey. They found an *NKPA* mechanized column clogging the highway leading to Taegu. The powerful General Electric J-33 jet engine delivered very fast airspeeds. Consequently, the *NKPA* infantry did not have time to scatter to safety before the Shooting Stars were on them. Their six .50-caliber nose guns poured out a concentrated stream of accurate fire. The results were lethal. Trucks exploded. The heavy bullets scythed down running infantry.

But the flyers knew that the battle hinged upon the tanks. The F-80 pils had learned that the only effective weapon against enemy tanks was the 5-inch high-velocity aircraft rocket (HVAR). They had discovered that an approach toward the tank from a 4 o'clock position worked best. The optimal firing position was from a 30-degree angle at a range of about 1,500 feet. However, on this day the low cloud cover forced them to attack at a flat approach angle, which made aiming difficult.

It required enormous concentration to operate effectively in this environment and it cost one pilot his life. While lining up a target he flew too low and plowed into a hillside. The remaining three pilots carefully fired rocket salvos and took out five T-34/85s. However, fuel constraints limited the jets' time over the battlefield to 20 minutes before they had to return to their Japanese bases.

Even as they departed the clouds seemed to sink lower and the field became obscured by blowing rain, fog, and smoke.

The air strike momentarily stalled the communist tank thrust. Their Soviet instructors had drummed into them the lesson that rapid exploitation against a disorganized defender produced startling results. Accordingly, dedicated junior officers quickly reorganized their units and the T-34/85s resumed their advance along the highway. Their haste almost proved their undoing.

Unbeknownst to the attackers, the US forces possessed some armor assets of their own. Two reduced platoons of M24 Chaffee light tanks occupied a reserve position in a gully adjacent to the highway. The Chaffees waited until the enemy were only 400 yards away before firing. Unfortunately, the American tankers had also been victims of deep budget cutbacks. For two years they had been requesting recoil oil so they could fire their main guns on the practice range. Instead, the first time the guns spoke came on July 25. Since their firing buttons did not work, the gunners relied on old-fashion lanyards. Two guns misfired so badly that they blew the turrets off. Several other tanks achieved hits that failed to penetrate. Realizing that they had no hope of penetrating the T-34/85s' frontal armor, the remaining US tankers skillfully maneuvered to achieve enfilade shots. They managed to disable one North Korean tank at the cost of all their remaining Chaffees.

Backstopping the Chaffees were three medium Pershings that had just arrived in Korea. The lieutenant commanding the Pershings ordered the tanks forward to just below the crest line. Drivers engaged the transmissions. The wet ground made for heavy going and a new problem emerged. The tanks lacked adequate fan belts. After one tank's belt shredded, the motor quickly overheated and the tank skidded helplessly to a stop on the steep slope. The remaining pair reached the designated location. They now enjoyed a textbook defilade firing position with the NKPA tanks moving from right to left across their front. Twin reports from the Pershings' 90mm guns rent the air. Two T-34/85s slewed to a stop and caught fire.

The Pershings knocked out three more tanks before the enemy located them.

Typically, when confronting the unexpected, *NKPA* units lacked the command flexibility to adjust quickly. Even the well-trained crews of the *105th Tank Division* revealed this flaw. They were primed to fight American bazooka teams but their recently rehearsed tank-infantry battle drills had not prepared them for fighting enemy armor. So the confused communist tankers reacted haltingly. They provided easy targets to the Pershings. Even the immobilized Pershing managed to take out two enemy tanks. Indeed, had more Pershings been present, the *NKPA* armored spearhead might have been blunted. Instead, sheer weight of numbers swamped the American tankers. After an exchange that left 15 T-34/85s burning, the communist gunners managed to knock out the last Pershing and thereby eliminate the last barrier before Taegu.

Adequate reserves also might have stopped the North Koreans in Taegu itself. But the pressure all along the front had consumed General Walker's resources. When the 25th Division's last reserve, a combat engineer battalion, tried to move north along the highway to man a delaying position, it was ambushed by *NKPA* infiltration teams. Then the T-34/85s caught the engineers while they were still trying to fight their way clear and easily rolled over them. By now the GIs were badly infected with "tank fright." They failed to heed their officers' pleas to rally. On the road between Taegu and Pusan one fleeing soldier spoke for them all when he told a reporter: "Just give me a jeep and I know what direction to go in. This mama's boy ain't cut out to be no hero."[18]

Truman Folds his Hand

The Chairman of the Joint Chiefs of Staff gave the President the situation report:

> "Mr President, I have an emergency message from General MacArthur. Our troops are fleeing back toward Pusan. Fortunately the weather has cleared so our planes are pounding the Commies again. But the forecast is not good. Besides the ground fog in the morning a weather front is moving in and we are not too sure if we will be able to put in another maximum air effort. Consequently, General MacArthur is again requesting major reinforcements. He believes that it will ultimately take two field armies with eight divisions."

Truman interrupted. "What do we have in the pipeline?" "We've already combed out all available manpower in Japan and flown them over as individual replacements. A Marine regimental combat team and the 2nd Infantry Division are en route and are the closest major formations." "When can they get there?" "We estimate August 7 or 8, if the port at Pusan is still open." "Hell," Truman growled. "Anything else?"

"As you recall sir, we had ten divisions when the communists attacked. The four in Japan went to Korea and the 2nd Infantry is en route. The 1st Infantry Division is of course committed to Germany. We didn't think Korea was good tank country so we kept the 2nd Armored here in our General Reserve. Candidly sir, neither the 3rd Infantry nor the 11th Airborne Divisions are anywhere close to ready for action. They are terribly under strength. That leaves the 82nd Airborne. But if we send it then we have nothing left to respond quickly if something else happens. Besides, the paratroopers aren't really equipped for sustained ground combat."

"So what do we do?" Truman asked. A glum silence followed. The Secretary of the Air Force cleared his throat loudly. The Chairman hesitated and then nodded. "Well sir, given the situation, General MacArthur is requesting freedom of action up to and including using atomic weapons."
The predictable explosion came immediately.

"I'll be damned if I'll risk atomic war with the Russians to save a bunch of Koreans who couldn't be bothered to fight to defend themselves. Is MacArthur nuts? Does anyone here think that that's a good idea. Does anyone here have any other idea?"

Truman fixed his advisors, one by one, with a steely glare. Some shook their heads from side to side. Others simply looked down at their briefing papers. Only brash Matt Ridgway, the Deputy Army Chief of Staff spoke:

"Sir I agree. We have already dangerously depleted our reserves. We shouldn't yield now to the temptation to give General MacArthur a book of blank checks, just because he is presently front stage in what may after all prove to be a mere affair of outposts."[19]

Emboldened by this speech, Ridgway's boss, Chief of Staff J. Lawton Collins added: "And sir, just like in 1941, we still put Europe first, the Pacific second."
A long pause ensued. It was now clear that the hasty decision to intervene on the Korean peninsula was a mistake. What to do now was far less clear. No one saw an easy solution. President Harry Truman fully recognized that the decision was his alone to make. The painful silence continued. Finally Truman spoke. He had always enjoyed poker so the analogy came naturally to him:

"Gentlemen, I have learned from long experience that it's how you play your poor hands rather than your good ones which counts in the long run. We took a gamble and it has failed. To continue is to throw good money after bad and I won't do it. Tell MacArthur to order Walker to evacuate the troops. This, at least, is something MacArthur ought to be good at."

The Reality

With the exception of the story's beginning and end, almost everything described did indeed happen. The initial training exercise is my invention. However, as explained, the *15 th Tank Training Regiment* did provide the nucleus for the *105th Tank Division*. Regarding the sacrifice of the prisoners, recall that the *NKPA* killed both American and South Korean prisoners of war (as shown by numerous, gruesome US army photos of dead American soldiers with their hands tied behind their backs) and conducted "People's courts" in the streets immediately upon capturing Seoul. A regime that did these things was certainly capable of acting as described in the introduction.

To "liberate" South Korea, the Soviets apparently planned a *Blitzkrieg* to capture the whole peninsula and present the West with a *fait accompli*. At first it appeared that the tank-led spearheads would accomplish this mission. However, the tanks suffered from a crippling lack of mobile maintenance units. Numerous tanks broke down alongside the roads and were then destroyed by air strikes. The *105th*—with an initial tank strength of between 120 and 140 T-34/85s—received only some 30 replacement tanks during the campaign. Yet the total almost proved sufficient because Truman's crippling budget had failed to deliver needed weapons and ammunition. At a minimum the GIs urgently required the new 3.5-inch bazookas, HEAT shells for the artillery, modern tanks, and 90mm anti-tank guns. Even if they had been fully equipped, it is impossible to know how they would have fared. A regimental commander wrote: "There was no incentive for our men to fight well... They saw no reason for the war... [and] had no interest in a fight which was not even dignified by calling it a war."[20]

My *NKPA* staff officer is also an invention, except for the name. The real Colonel Lee Hak Ku was chief of staff of the *13th Division*. He surrendered on September 21, 1950, the highest ranking North Korean prisoner of the war. He later became notorious as the leader of communist prisoners in the riots on Koje Island in 1952.

The Chicks' first fight in Korea came on July 16 when about 900 men faced an attack at the Kum River line. The battle was a debacle. Only about half the Chicks could be found the next day. The l/19th lost 43 percent casualties including 17 officers killed. In contrast, at Chickamauga the l/19th entered battle with 194 officers and men and lost only one officer and six men killed. However, the unit reported many missing, for an overall loss rate of 70 percent.

Taegu was probably the most embattled city of the entire war. It was the anchor for the whole Pusan Perimeter. The North Koreans launched two major offensives to capture Taegu. By the narrowest margin both failed. Without a doubt, the *NKPA* made a huge strategic blunder around July 23, the time of my conference. Instead of massing to administer what could very well have been the *coup de grace,* the communist high command sent the *4th* and *6th Divisions* on a wide envelopment south to the coast; the option discussed but not chosen in my story.

Bibliography

Appleman, Roy E., *South to the Naktong, North to the Yalu, June-November 1950,* Department of the Army, Washington, DC, 1961.

Blair, Clay, *The Forgotten War,* Times Books, New York, 1987.

Futrell, Robert F, *The United States Air Force in Korea, 1950–1953,* US Air Force, Washington, DC, 1983.

Matloff, Maurice, ed., *American Military History,* US Army, Washington, DC, 1969.

Robertson, William Glenn, *Counterattack on the Naktong, 1950,* US Army Command and General Staff College, Fort Leavenworth, KS, 1985.

Sandler, Stanley, ed., *The Korean War: An Encyclopedia,* New York: Garland Publishing, 1995.

Truman, Harry S., *Years of Trial and Hope,* Doubleday, Garden City, NY, 1956.

Notes

*1. Colonel-General Vladimir Ivanovich Orlov, *Tank Commander! My Experiences in Three Wars* (Red Hero Press, Moscow, Kim II Sung City, Ho Chi Minh City, 1976), p. 230.

2. Joseph S. Bermudez, Jr., "Korean People's Army," in Sandler, *The Korean War,* pp. 182-88.

3. Blair, *The Forgotten War,* p. 5.

4. *Ibid.,* p. 61.

*5. Sergei V Ushakov and Vasili G. Golitsyn (Kutuzov Artillery Academy), *An Analysis of the Preliminary Bombardment Preceding the War for Korean Unification* (Red Artillery Press, Sevastopol, 1962), p. 18.

6. Blair, *The Forgotten War,* p. 77.

7. Truman, *Years of Trial and Hope,* p. 341.

8. Appleman, *South to the Naktong,* p. 60.

9. Blair, *The Forgotten War,* p. 102.

10. Robertson, *Counterattack on the Naktong,* p. 6.

*11. General Pak Ho San, *Memories of Comrade Mu* (Veterans' Collective Press, Kim II Sung City, 1972), p. 283.

*12. General Lee Hak Ku, *Planning for the Final Victory* (Unified People's Army Press, Kim II Sung City, 1958), p. 15.

*13. *Ibid,* p. 17.

*14. General Pang Ho San, *War and Reunification* (Unified People's Army Press, Kim II Sung City, 1963), p. 780.

*15. Orlov, *Tank Commander!,* p. 383.

16. Sandler, *The Korean War,* p. 160.

17. Appleman, *South to the Naktong,* pp. 207–08.

18. Blair, *The Forgotten War,* p. 107.

19. Ridgway actually used the phrase "affair of outposts," in a memo cited in Blair, *The Forgotten War,* p. 123.

20. Blair, *The Forgotten War,* p. 113.

3
VIETNAM
The War That Nobody Noticed

Paddy Griffith

The Pentagon: December 1,1963

Sir Robert Thompson[1] entered the office of Secretary of Defense Robert S. McNamara, in a pugnacious frame of mind. He knew that the campaign in South Vietnam had been going very badly and that he, as a counter-insurgency (COIN) advisor to the late President Ngo Dinh Diem, could credibly be blamed for some of the failures. Nevertheless he was more than ready with his counter-attack, because he sensed that now, at the start of December 1963, there was a unique opportunity to shake up both Vietnamese and American attitudes, and to make policies stick that in the past had not been properly pursued.

It was only a month since Diem had been killed in a *coup d'etat*, to be replaced by a new and more promising military government. Then only ten days ago President John F. Kennedy, had also been assassinated.[2] New administrations had thus unexpectedly been installed in both Saigon and Washington within a few days of each other, and so the stage was suddenly clear for bold new initiatives, if only the moment could be seized. Thompson believed he knew exactly what those initiatives should be, and he was now about to sell them to the US government.

Thompson himself was a British colonial civil servant who had risen to prominence in the 1950s during the successful British campaign against communist insurgency in Malaya, where from 1959 to 1961 he had served as the Secretary of Defence. He had then moved on to Saigon, where he had tried to explain British counter-insurgency methods and the ways they might be adapted to South Vietnam—which he recognized as being a significantly different and less promising theater of war than Malaya. Unfortunately under Diem he had experienced many frustrations, as his advice had been comprehensively diluted, distorted or simply misunderstood. He had found a corrupt government machine in which simple things were very difficult to achieve, and anything more complicated was quite impossible.

Of particular importance was the chaotic lack of unity in the chain of command, since the government, the senior army generals, the younger army officers and the police had each established their own private fiefdoms which constantly plotted against each other, not always without exchanges of gunfire.[3] On top of this there were conflicting pressures from a number of competing American agencies, and between their representatives in-country and those in Washington. It all made for a very fragmented governmental machine in which the implementation of any policy was infinitely complex and intractable. In Malaya, by contrast, the British had found it relatively easy to integrate all military and civil power within a single and unitary administration, and had quickly been able to centralize all aspects of the COIN campaign under a single hand.

Nor was it as easy to win the hearts and minds of the South Vietnamese people as it had been to placate the majority of Malays. In Malaya the insurgents had emerged from an unpopular segment of the Chinese ethnic minority which could be identified and isolated, whereas in Vietnam the insurgents came from the ethnically Vietnamese majority numbering at least 13 million out of a total population of around 16 million. They enjoyed natural access to almost the whole country, especially outside the towns. Apart from anything else, this implied that the whole scale of the insurgency was far greater in Vietnam than it had been in Malaya, with the *Viet Cong (VC)* being able to mobilize a battalion or even a regiment of guerrillas for every squad that had been available to the Communist Party of Malaya. Equally the long land frontier with Laos and Cambodia offered many entry points into South Vietnam to supporters of the insurgency coming from outside, whereas in Malaya almost all of the access had been by sea, and therefore easy to close off by a naval blockade.

In terms of political incentives, it was unfortunately not possible for the South Vietnamese government to offer any greater measure of independence to its population than they already enjoyed. An independent non-communist administration was already in power, so a promise of self-government could no longer be used as an inducement in the way that it had been by the British in Malaya. On the contrary, the *VCs* popular appeal rested partly upon its call to reunify South with North Vietnam; but this was specifically unacceptable to both the Saigon and US governments.

South Vietnam owed its very existence to the fact that it was the alternative to North Vietnamese communism; whereas, as far as the Americans were concerned, their main interest was defined as preventing all communists, including those in North Vietnam, from extending their rule or influence in any way at all. If the South should fall, it would represent the toppling of the first domino in a line that might stretch all the way to India, Indonesia, the Philippines, or even beyond. Reunification was therefore not a concession that the Americans could grant without admitting defeat, and so by extension they were not in a position to offer the nationalist majority the political solution that it desired.

However, Thompson was only too well aware that the Vietnamese masses really wanted far more than reunification, which was surely little more than an abstract idea to most peasants. What was much more important to them was attentive, good and fair local government, combined with fewer arbitrary taxes and a reduction in absentee landlordism in favor of land ownership by the farmers themselves. These were all things that the VC promised to its followers, and actually delivered in several parts of the territory it controlled. They were also the things that the South Vietnamese government should have been able to deliver far more effectively than the VC, especially with the benefit of generous US assistance, even though it was unable to grant political concessions by reversing the split between North and South. Thompson clearly understood that reforms in local government and land ownership were precisely the things that the US should insist were central to winning hearts and minds, and therefore central to winning the war as a whole.

In Malaya the British had forced the peasants to live in "strategic hamlets" which ensured good local government at the same time as they protected the population and separated it from the guerrillas. Such strategic hamlets had naturally been a major theme of Thompson's teaching when he arrived in Saigon to advise Diem, and an ambitious building program had indeed been implemented. Unfortunately, however, the program proved to be far too ambitious for the resources allocated to it, even when those resources actually found their way down the chain of command to the hamlets themselves, which was rarely the case. Corruption and backhanders at every level sucked off the necessary financial and logistic means, while politics and propaganda conspired to conceal this fact from the resource-giving authorities. Many of the hamlets were built only on paper, while most of the rest involved the enforced creation of masses of homeless people who were thereby thrown directly into the arms of VC recruiting sergeants. Nor did proposals for land reform fare any better, since many of the rich absentee landlords were influential friends and supporters of the Saigon political elite. If the government had deprived them of their land, it would at the same time have been depriving itself of its key backers.

Thompson had pondered these failures long and hard by the time he arrived in Secretary McNamara's office, and he was more than ready to explain his proposed solutions in detail. He especially demanded a unified chain of command for the COIN effort, clearly ring-fenced as a distinct entity, and completely separate from all the confusing overlaps, inefficiencies and vaguenesses that normally applied to both the South Vietnamese and US command hierarchies. Then he wanted far more resources allocated to the building of strategic hamlets, but this time guaranteed by trusted local authorities, each subject to strong US supervision, so that everything would be done properly and carefully, with the minimum of corruption. The scheme could not be applied to the whole country all at once, as Diem had tried to do it, but should begin with relatively small areas and then expand systematically outwards as and when solid bases had been fully established. In Thompson's view each village should contain a small group of US civilian and military personnel led by a junior officer or NCO who would possess sufficient personal qualities and initiative to help the local people to organize themselves, and hence keep the program as a whole well on track.

In the event Thompson was relieved to find that McNamara was a very receptive host, not only willing to hear him out, but even actively egging him on. The Secretary of Defense was a man who perpetually asked questions of everyone he met, and now he revealed that during the final months of the Diem regime he had come to distrust the uncritically optimistic answers that he had been getting back from the higher echelons of the CIA and the Pentagon, particularly on the progress of counter-insurgency in the Mekong Delta. He now needed to hear more independent voices who could point him in the direction of new policy guidelines. He remembered that President Kennedy had made great play with the idea of teaching counter-insurgency doctrine to the US military, but that the impetus had fallen on stony ground, and the lessons had never been properly absorbed.[4]

The military had insisted on clinging to their time-honored answers to conventional warfare problems, such as "firepower" and "mobility," and were too little prepared to understand that in an insurgency war it was far more important to win hearts and minds. In McNamara's opinion that situation had to be reversed as a very high priority and, provided he explained it all properly to the new President, he was sure that it could be. The main reason was that Lyndon B. Johnston was currently taking his advice pretty straight about matters of this type, since he did not see Vietnam as his number one priority in December 1963. From the perspective of the White House, Pentagon politics and Indochinese insurgencies seemed to be little more than irritating distractions from the main project, which was to build a "Great Society" within the United States. Yet McNamara was convinced that if Vietnam were not given serious and urgent attention, the security situation there would only degenerate until it came to dominate the whole political horizon in Washington.

Between them, McNamara and Thompson agreed that for the time being they effectively held the con on Vietnam, and so they sat down to sketch out their five key objectives, together with some of the key obstacles that would have to be overcome. The objectives were these:-

1. Ring-fencing the COIN chain of command, to free it from interference from the many agencies, both South Vietnamese and

American, which were currently making coherent policy-making impossible. In particular this implied a much stronger coordinating role for the US ambassador in Saigon, who at that moment was the newly-arrived but very shrewd Republican patrician, Henry Cabot Lodge.[5] It was essential to give him day-to-day control over all military and intelligence agencies, since the Pentagon in particular had already shown that it instinctively distrusted COIN thinking—or indeed any solution that included the words "political" or "civilian." Equally the ambassador would have to adopt a newly tough posture towards the South Vietnamese government itself, since in the past it had all too often failed to follow through on US-sponsored initiatives. In the new Thompson–McNamara view the situation had now become too important to the essential interests of the USA for the theoretical independence of its Southeast Asian ally to continue to be allowed the full respect normally expected by diplomatic protocol. The tail, in short, could no longer be allowed to wag the dog.

2. **The careful building of a revitalized strategic hamlet program,** including increased participation by US professional soldiers and civilians, plus a major effort to identify, support and protect effective South Vietnamese local administrators, teachers, medical and agricultural staff. Thompson had learned by bitter experience how badly these things could go wrong unless they were carefully and closely monitored, so he was determined not to make the same mistakes again. He was particularly anxious to involve the US Army and Marines in low level civic action, in units of no more than four, eight or twelve men, rather than the companies of 120 or more that still seemed to be their favoured tactical grouping. Despite the anguish that he knew it would cause among the straight-laced champions of the conventional line army, he demanded an immediate doubling of the Green Berets, to be followed by a gradual subsequent expansion until their numbers approached those of Armor Branch. Yet in order to avoid overstraining the active army worldwide, there would be a major call-up of reservists and National Guard personnel.

Of vital importance to this decision was the dramatic moment when Army Chief of Staff, General Harold K. Johnson, confronted the President. The general had made it plain the Army could not make a commitment to Vietnam without calling out the Reserves and National Guard. LBJ had agreed and then reneged out of fear of the political backlash. General Johnson put his stars on President Johnson's desk, and for once LBJ backed down.

Of paramount importance in calling up the Reserve Components was the leading role given to the Army Reserve's Civil Affairs units. These units were filled with experts from civilian life in just about every form of civil government from sewage treatment to the protection of arts and monuments and in a wide range of commercial and industrial skills. In World War II such units had restored shattered governments and economies, while at the same time demonstrating the value of the democratic model. Thompson felt the constructive orientation of these citizen soldiers was just the right fit for COIN. By the same token there would be an insistence on "the minimum use of force" and the maximum respect for ordinary Vietnamese civilians. Equally a target was set for 90 percent of all US aid to South Vietnam to be dedicated to programs which supported civilian rather than purely military operations.[6]

3. A major program to buy out the absentee landowners, in order to return land to the farmers who actually lived on it and worked it. Thompson saw this as the real key to winning the hearts and minds of the local peasant hierarchies, and an essential accompaniment to the strategic hamlet program. By giving land to the peasants he would win their loyalty and create strong democratic local government structures to replace the existing fragile and undemocratic ones imposed from Saigon. In many ways Thompson saw the small but ultra-rich group of absentee landowners as a worse destabilizing factor in Vietnamese society than the VC—but a great deal less difficult to neutralize.

4. The rule of law and eradication of corruption were aspirations of the Vietnamese people every bit as powerful as their desire to own their own land. The military and local government authorities should therefore in future be held strictly accountable for all their actions, and governed by due legal process by an independent judiciary. Assassination and torture were to be outlawed as instruments of state policy, and much greater funds dedicated to the welfare—and it was hoped conversion—of prisoners. The South Vietnamese police should be built up and supervized by sophisticated anti-corruption measures. All this was truly revolutionary in the security environment created by the Diem regime.

5. A reduced role in local-level counter-insurgency for the Army of the Republic of Vietnam (ARVN), but an increased role in protecting the borders from infiltration from North Vietnam. According to the new Thompson-McNamara thinking, the ARVN was ineffective in the village war, but could be more effective as a conventional force, thereby obviating the need for a major deployment of US troops to fulfil this role.

If the 20,000 US military advisers currently in-country could be quietly increased to, say, 80,000, it would not seriously disrupt the American military posture worldwide, but it could offer a solid backbone for a battle-ready and effective Vietnamese Army. Considerable "Vietnamized" forces of tanks, armored personnel carriers (APCs) and some helicopters would be needed in border areas, supported by as big a tactical air force as the Vietnamese could operate. However, there was no need for more than a small US Air Force in support except in times of great crisis, and an assessment was made that any strategic bombing campaign into North Vietnam, Laos or Cambodia was doomed to be counter-productive. Since there were no strategic targets worthy of the name, it would be a complete waste of Air Force assets (let alone involving the Strategic Air Command!) to undertake such a campaign. On the contrary, all the experience of earlier wars showed that strategic bombing only strengthened the target population's will to resist, as well as winning it precious international sympathy. The large scale use of American air power in this campaign would therefore surely undo all the "hearts and minds" progress that was being made on the ground, and so it was not contemplated.

At the same time as they set out their objectives, Thompson and McNamara naturally considered the obstacles they were likely to encounter. The big two were both deeply political, inside Washington and Saigon respectively. What was being proposed was a radical shake-up of the whole chain of command within the Pentagon—where McNamara was already deeply unpopular for his independent business-based solutions in many other areas—and within the South Vietnamese military dictatorship, which was excessively centralized, undemocratic and corrupt. In effect the Thompson-McNamara agenda represented a radical "anti-militarist" program, in the interests of democracy and civilian primacy. In order to succeed it would require the sustained support of the President over a long period of time, together with some favorable spin in the media. The American people would have to be persuaded not only to get behind a COIN effort that would last for decades rather than months or years, but also that it had to be won by civilian rather than military means.

There was of course also a distinct military dimension to the problem, since the *VC* guerrillas were roaming free in the South Vietnamese countryside, assassinating government agents, organizing logistic and political bases, and from time to time engaging the ARVN in some large scale firefights. Behind them lay a growing potential for *North Vietnamese Army (NVA)* intervention, as increasingly large parties of regular troops were identified making their way down the Ho Chi Minh Trail through Laos and Cambodia into the South. The border they had to cross was notoriously long, permeable, mountainous and jungle-clad. It did not make a defensive line that was easy to hold, although on the other side of the coin it certainly demanded a debilitatingly long and difficult march from the heavily-burdened infantry who were being ordered to invade the South. They had to operate at the far end of a perilously over-extended line of communication.

After Thompson and McNamara had thought through their plan and consulted other advisors for about a month, the Secretary of Defense finally felt ready to present it all to the President as a firm recommendation. Distracted as he was by the many other cares of his new office, LBJ was more than ready to wave it through without argument. As a civilian himself he was quite happy to buy into the idea that pacification should be led by civilians, and in any case he accepted that, despite all military criticisms, Robert McNamara was still very much the head of the Pentagon. If the man in that particularly key position was saying that the military should be subordinated to civilians, there was ostensibly little alternative to accepting his opinion. As a first mark of his commitment to this policy the President immediately applied his charms to persuading the civilian Cabot Lodge to remain in station as ambassador in Saigon. At the same time General Maxwell D. Taylor, who had originally been earmarked as Lodge's successor, was tactfully diverted to a prestigious ambassadorial role with NATO in Brussels—not so many miles away from his triumphant 1944 battlefield at Bastogne.

Saigon, South Vietnam: January 1964

When Thompson returned to his office in Saigon in early January there was already a fierce bureaucratic battle in full swing between the newly-empowered US ambassador and the entrenched interests at the head of Military Assistance Command Vietnam (MACV), the CIA and the other US agencies. It soon became clear that Ambassador Lodge was winning. He was not personally easy to work with, and he was certainly making a lengthy list of enemies by his new tough policies, but he was industrious, effective and respected by his staff. With the backing of the President he was now able to bang heads together and move towards a coherent chain of command. Many old Vietnam hands reported how refreshing it was to see someone "cutting through the BS" and forcing the cozy mandarins to see some reality at last.

When it came to relations with the new Vietnamese government, led by Generals Duong Van Minh ("Big Minh") and Nguyen Ngoc Tho, Lodge found a mood of unprecedented willingness to cooperate with the Americans at all levels. There was still a widespread sense of relief that the oppressive Diem regime had been removed, and a rare willingness to pull together. As soldiers, moreover, the Vietnamese leaders were excited by the prospect that the Americans would relieve them of much of the burden of fighting the "village war" against the VC, thereby releasing the ARVN to operate in formed units in the frontier areas. Conversely they were made aware that if they did not accept a greater US primacy than had hitherto been the case, the new US administration would be ruthless in cutting its aid. Lodge spelled it out credibly that Lyndon Johnson was mainly interested in domestic politics, and did not think it was too late to pull out of Southeast Asia if full cooperation were not forthcoming. This was a threat that would not have carried as much weight while the internationalist Jack Kennedy had still been in office.

There were naturally some sections of the ARVN which resented and resisted this new state of inter-allied relations, just as there was an influential section of the South Vietnamese political class which refused to accept the compulsory purchase of their estates, regardless of the generosity

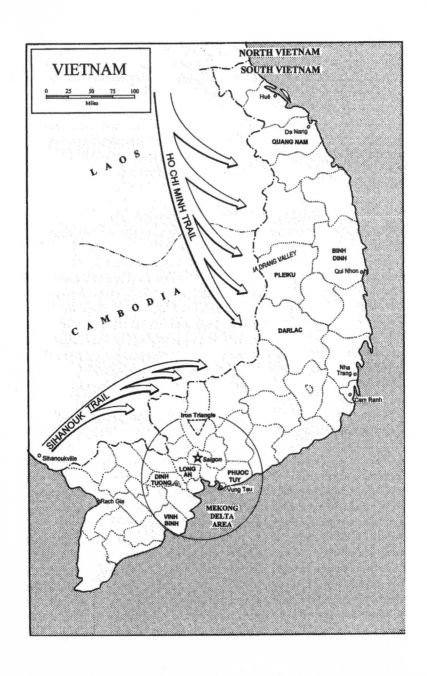

of the compensation to be paid. They felt the policy of eradicating absentee landowners was a direct assault on their traditional way of life, rather than on their finances. Of course many were compliant and willing to be bribed, especially those who had received no rent in recent years because their lands were controlled by the *VC*. Nevertheless there remained a hard core of opponents at the top of Saigon society.

In these circumstances it soon came to Lodge's ears that a second military coup was being plotted. The plan was that Major-General Nguyen Khanh would topple Big Minh on January 30, to restore what he called "national pride" in the face of "outrageous American demands." If this coup had succeeded, the country would have been plunged back into chaos and any hope of building a systematic COIN policy could be forgotten. However, by a mixture of good luck, good intelligence work and an unprecedented US willingness to become directly involved, the coup was defeated, Nguyen Khanh was retired and persuaded to emigrate to Paris, and the Big Minh regime was saved. It was given a chance to consolidate its power throughout the army, the absentee landowners and the provincial governments, and despite some failures and even a few spectacular disasters, it generally succeeded very well. Stability was at last assured, at least for the medium term.[7]

On the wider diplomatic plane the State Department announced to the world that the USA was going to commit greatly increased manpower and funds to its campaign to create a newly democratic style of government in Vietnam, and it appealed to all its allies to send aid and specialized assistance, especially in the form of specialist civilian workers, trained police and high quality infantry. Naturally the nations that were most beholden to America, and geographically closest to Indochina, were the most enthusiastic in their response: South Korea, Thailand, the Philippines, Australia and New Zealand. Perhaps unexpectedly, however, a wider circle of US allies also felt enough confidence in the new policies to overcome their natural suspicions of a situation which under Diem had seemed to be going from bad to worse. For widely different but equally understandable reasons Japan, Malaysia, India, France, West Germany and Israel felt they could send only civilian teams; but Britain and Canada caused a minor diplomatic stir when they also committed detachments of elite troops, and even Italy sent a combined battalion of construction engineers and a Bersaglieri security guard. In no cases were the contingents numerically large, but the key point of note was that they were fully dedicated for what everyone understood would be at least a ten-year mission.

Lodge's revised political settlement within South Vietnam, reinforced by worldwide diplomatic support, served to establish the essential preconditions for pacification. This was the main interest of Sir Robert Thompson, who now got down to picking key provincial leaders, ARVN military staff and US advisers to begin setting up "expanding oil stains"[8] of government control in the countryside. He rejected Diem's concept of setting up thousands of new strategic hamlets all over the country all at once, just as he also rejected the idea of starting off with the worst trouble-spots, such as Long An and Dinh Tuong provinces in the Mekong Delta. Instead, he decided to set up his first safe areas in provinces where the government already exercised a greater, albeit still disputed, control. He selected five initial target provinces—two in the Delta, two on the coast of central South Vietnam, and one in the north around Da Nang. His long term plan was to expand from there in a gradual and measured way until he could eventually nibble effectively into the truly intransigent hard core *VC* centers.

With new professional American manpower and massive funds for civilian aid now assured for the immediate future, it was possible to give a great boost to the South Vietnamese police and civilian aid agencies. The plight of the many refugees and political prisoners created by Diem was noticeably ameliorated, and it was observed that the lightened national mood of optimism that had followed the fall of Diem seemed to be holding up well into the new year. The early political gains were not rapidly dashed, as many had feared, and so the road was opened for the Thompson— McNamara plan to be put into effect in the full spirit that it had demanded. It was not shelved or side-lined into one of the many bureaucratic backwaters that had previously plagued this particular theater of operations.

Da Nang, South Vietnam: March 1965

The coastal town of Da Nang was regarded with special affection by the 9th US Marine Expeditionary Brigade, which had made an exceptionally fine job of pacifying all the neighboring hamlets in the course of the previous 12 months. There had been no noisy beach landing as at Iwo Jima; no vast invasion of armored vehicles and heavy guns; but simply the quiet infiltration of a battalion-sized base from which almost microscopically small units were sent out into each hamlet, supported by a major effort of police, intelligence and civic reconstruction teams, not to mention a great deal of logistic resources to ensure health, prosperity and education. Because expertise rather than merely manpower was being concentrated upon a relatively small number of target communities, a high rate of success was assured. The false accounting by which a hamlet was routinely reported as "fully under government control," quite regardless of its true status, became a shameful thing of the past—as did the wanton creation of refugees. Whenever isolated outlying settlements were closed down and their inhabitants brought into the larger hamlet, there would always be excellent housing and other facilities ready for them. Among those facilities the best of all, from the peasants' point of view, were large free grants of land. The proportion of land on which rent had to be paid fell from 86 percent to 22 percent, and of that only 4 percent was owned by landowners who lived outside a ten-mile radius of the land itself.

As far as security was concerned, each village was fortified, and the villagers were organized and armed to provide their own night garrisons, under Marine direction. If the worst came to the worst an emergency reaction and counter-attack platoon might be sent out from the central Marine base, but essentially the posture was defensive and local. The real offensive against the VC lay in the creation of contented and loyal communities in which intelligent police work could accurately pinpoint the worst enemy activists, but in which the ordinary peasant's natural ambivalence was well understood and accommodated. There was no provocative talk along the lines that "those who are not with us are against us." There was no vainglorious rhetoric about "search and destroy" missions; no futile sweeps through the countryside on the off chance of encountering an occasional guerrilla; no wasteful speculative barrages against unidentified targets, and no air strikes against small groups of personnel who might possibly be hostile.

It was recognized that the more powerful the ordnance used, the greater was the risk of mistakes and "collateral damage." The tired old PR line that collateral damage was "unfortunate but sometimes unavoidable" was now perceived as the shocking affront to humanity that it had always been. Instead, any unintentional damage to civilians or their property was seen as a major setback to the central task of winning the hearts and minds of the peasantry. It was taken very seriously and generous compensation, reconstruction or other appropriate after care was guaranteed. Those responsible for mistakes were arraigned and punished while—perhaps most important of all—a full and honest report of the incident was issued to the press. The culture of security forces lying in the interests of short term cover-ups was rejected in favor of a long term determination to tell the unvarnished truth. If any other policy had been followed, it was predicted that the support and belief of the American public would not have survived beyond, say, the presidential elections of 1968.

Up to the spring of 1965 Lyndon Johnson had experienced little public criticism over his Vietnam policy. It was recognized that he had acted decisively in January 1964, after which there had been no great moments of crisis, few memorable headlines, and no dissent outside a number of universities on the left of the debate, and presidential candidate Senator Barry Goldwater on the right. Goldwater was easily discredited as too hawkish, so that LBJ was duly confirmed in the presidency in November 1964, and empowered to devote himself to his program of domestic reforms.

Vietnam had been relegated to the status of a relatively minor and containable sideshow, little more perceptible to the general public than the many other small covert wars currently being fought and won by US advisers in Latin America. Nor was the public troubled by any sudden or massive increases in troop deployments, or expansions of the draft. Almost all the personnel sent to Vietnam were volunteers and professionals, supported by an expanded obligation on reservists, National Guardsmen and civilian specialists. As a result, no particular fear of death in a paddyfield was felt by non-volunteering civilians of draftable age, regardless of whether they were college students who could obtain deferment or ghetto blacks who could not. If a young man was drafted, he would join the active army in exotic but peaceful foreign places such as Korea or West Germany, or more likely in less exotic home garrisons somewhere to the south of the Mason—Dixon Line. In sum, the social pressures within USA were not particularly exacerbated by any mass requirement for manpower in Indochina, and the popular music industry had to seek its inspirations elsewhere.[9]

The government nevertheless had to wrestle with the major difficulty that the war would be a very long one. It had to be repeated to the public, over and over again, that victory was not yet in sight and that a long hard struggle, with an ever-mounting toll of casualties, was unavoidable before it would be. For example the pacification of the Da Nang area was completed to an acceptable standard only 12 months after it had begun, and only after that was it possible to expand the "oil stain" into neighboring sectors of Quang Nam province. At that rate it was estimated that the whole process, country-wide, might take something like 12 years, or three presidential terms—presumably two of LBJ following through his chosen policy of January 1964, and then a third of someone unknown, and of an unknown party. It was the uncertainty of that third presidential term that most bothered the planners, but there was nothing much they could do about it in 1965. They simply had to keep faith that the only key to success in Vietnam lay in consistently applying the correct principles of counter-insurgency, and not in any brash short term fix.

The other major difficulty that had to be confronted was the possibility of escalating North Vietnamese intervention. In 1964 this was not running at a high level, and a welcome breathing space was granted during the "campaigning season" of the northeast monsoon from November 1964 to March 1965. This was a great help not only for the start of the pacification program, but also for the ARVN build-up of conventional forces on the frontiers. Then during the southwest monsoon from May to October 1965 the climate made troop movements difficult, although there were reports of NVA activity along the Ho Chi Minh Trail in Laos and Cambodia, and in the central highlands. At this juncture the question for the North Vietnamese government was whether or not it should significantly reinforce that area for the next campaigning season.

On one side of the argument was a group of impatient commanders who argued for an immediate assault with regular troops against the ARVN, which was still perceived as inefficient and vulnerable. They believed they could cut South Vietnam in half by a bold thrust from the la Drang valley in Pleiku province to the coast in Binh Dinh province. Against this view General Vo Nguyen Giap, the triumphant victor at Dien Bien Phu in 1954, pointed out the uncertain hazards of a premature escalation into a more conventional phase of warfare. He argued that in the absence of a massive US deployment, the village war in the South was still being won very handsomely by guerrilla methods alone. Indeed, the commitment of NVA regulars on a large scale might well provoke a US response in kind, which would make the whole task very much more difficult. For him it was better to exploit what he saw as America's weak response in a quiet rather than a noisy manner.

At the end of much debate the veteran Giap had his way, and there was only a two-battalion attack in the la Drang that October, against the Montagnard special forces camp at Plei Me. It defended itself very well and the ARVN was able to relieve it with an armored column from Pleiku. The robustness of the ARVN response was itself something of a surprise to the northern troops, although it was immediately negated by a very successful VC ambush on November 11 against an ARVN infantry regiment at Ap Bau Bang on Highway 13 north of Saigon. The Hanoi planners could still draw the conclusion that the ARVN was weak and the VC strong, but they had not yet noticed the long term shift in the balance that was slowly taking place on the ground.

The Iron Triangle, January 1967

By the time the Thompson-McNamara plan had been running for three full years the situation had already changed quite significantly. The village war was progressing more or less according to plan, despite some notable setbacks. Equally the "Vietnamization" of the mainforce war was going forward very well, with an emphasis on armor, artillery and basic fighter ground-attack aircraft. Everyone was delighted with the new Ml6 rifle, which gave the soldier an equivalent weapon to the communist AK-47, and removed the South Vietnamese suspicion that they were being offered only a second rate inventory. By contrast the helicopter was confined to only an auxiliary role, since it was recognized as too vulnerable, and its armament too light, for serious combat. If it were used to deposit infantry in the jungle, moreover, that infantry would be deprived of its heavy weapons and would be all but immobile on foot. It would have no tactical advantage over the enemy, and would in all probability have to retreat out of any firefight to find a secure landing zone for resupply and casualty evacuation. Instead of becoming the main instrument of warfare, therefore, the helicopter was used selectively for armed reconnaissance, resupply and a variety of liaison and medical tasks. Despite the futuristic claims of its highly-funded lobbying groups, it could not truly replace the tank and the APC as the best means of providing battlefield firepower and mobility.[10]

The first real test of the new ARVN mainforce capability came during the campaigning season of 1966-67, when the North Vietnamese finally decided to release a major regular army attack across the frontier. Obviously they had at last come to realize just how far the underlying balance of power in the South was shifting against them, and so they decided to build up a major force in the "Iron Triangle" area just south of Ben Sue and Ben Cat villages, some 25 miles north of central Saigon, to launch what they hoped would be a mortal blow to the capital. Good intelligence alerted the ARVN forces to the threat, and a series of fierce battles began on January 8, 1967, which would come to be known as the Sin Loi campaign. It continued through March, and at the end of it all neither side could credibly claim to have won the victory.[11] Admittedly the ARVN troops were not fighting as effectively as the Americans might have done in their place, but on the other hand they did not take the risks of all-out offensive combat against deeply-entrenched fortified zones. They had some dismal failures, but then again they also had some solid successes. This campaign represented the real start of the mainforce war, and by and large the South Vietnamese troops did not disgrace themselves in the way some cynics had been predicting.

One major intelligence coup was the unexpected discovery by the British SAS that the communists in the Iron Triangle traced their line of communication not northwards up the long overland Ho Chi Minh Trail to Hanoi, but westwards to the Cambodian coast at Sihanoukville, where Soviet bloc and Chinese shipping was able to send supplies up a much shorter route into the heart of South Vietnam.[12] A major operation, code-named Toan Thang, was planned against this "Sihanouk Trail" in May. It involved a clear infringement of Cambodia's neutrality, but President Johnson prepared the way by showing the world detailed photographs of just how the North Vietnamese had already abused Cambodian hospitality by their own military presence. Because there had been no clandestine bombing or other operations in Cambodia, and no widespread protest movement against the Vietnam war itself, this frank diplomatic initiative was internationally accepted in the same spirit as Kennedy's had been when he displayed photographs of Soviet missile bases in Cuba. The ARVN Toan Thang operation itself was certainly very successful, and large stocks of food and ammunition were uncovered in the jungle not far from the border north of Saigon. The port of Sihanoukville was mined to prevent the importation of more, but without harming the Cambodian population.

Meanwhile, in the village war, the felicitous mix of military and civilian professionals, both South Vietnamese and allied, was bearing sturdy fruit. In Phuoc Tuy province, for example, the Australians had brought in teachers and nurses to supplement the section-level military teams in every hamlet which, together with the vital land reform programs, seemed to have the effect of negating the attraction of the *VC* to many of its potential recruits.

To be sure there was still a continuing toll of friendly casualties caused by sniping, mining and the occasional full-blown company assault. On one occasion in August 1966 the whole hamlet of Xa Long Tan was overrun, with 22 dead among the security forces and civilian aid workers. That defeat caused some powerful negative headlines worldwide, but at the end of it all the general opinion was that if serious counter-insurgency at hamlet level had not been undertaken, the scale of the battles and casualties might well have been at least ten times greater. The grim total of non-Vietnamese freeworld personnel killed between January 1964 and January 1968 added up to the horrific figure of 2,896, including six journalists and 148 medical personnel. However that added up to an average of only 724 per year or 2 per day, which was well below the level experienced in any other major war the world had known, and considerably lower than the 18,000 dead in four years (making 4,500 per year, or 12 per day) that some experts estimated as the minimum toll to be expected if the Americans had escalated the mainforce war, and if less well-controlled circumstances had obtained in the village war.

As the number of pacified villages grew, so the demands on Western manpower also grew. New tasks were constantly being found for them, ranging from an accelerated program of training for the ARVN, to the creation of a new deep water port at Cam Ranh Bay, as well as a number of jet-capable airstrips. Logistics personnel were needed to handle the massive quantities of supplies that came rolling in, especially building materials, agricultural machinery, motor vehicles, medicines and consumer goods of all sorts for the new hamlets. The overall contingent of non-Vietnamese personnel in-country gradually increased from 80,000 to more than 120,000, although the high rate of volunteering for second and third tours meant that by the end of 1968 the grand total of those who had served in Vietnam was still as low as 250,000. As one tenth of one percent of the overall US population, this was such a small proportion of the whole that their experiences scarcely scarred a generation.

The US Embassy, Saigon: January 31,1968

When Ambassador Lodge looked out of his office window, he was troubled by reports of a new *NVA* offensive at Khe Sanh and the A Shau valley, north of Hue, as well as in Pleiku and Darlac provinces in the central highlands. The ARVN was suffering heavy losses, and the enemy had even sprung a tactical surprise at Lang Vei by using a few light tanks.[13] The whole country was on edge with a fear of the unknown. Nevertheless the ambassador had been reassured that there were adequate ARVN reinforcements at hand, behind which as many as 400 USAF combat aircraft were already on their way across the Pacific from California to meet the crisis. The battle line would hold and the village war would continue to be won. "Land to the tiller" had turned out to be a wonderful trump card which had massively eroded support for the VC, even if there were still mutterings of bitterness among the fat cat landlords who had been dispossessed—and richly compensated. He sighed and turned away from his window—but as he did so he noticed movement out of the corner of his eye, so he turned back quickly to look again.

Two men dressed in black were scrambling over the garden wall of the embassy, and a police siren could be heard from the street outside. There was a crackle of gunfire. The ambassador rushed to alert the Marine guard, fearing that a VC commando unit was mounting an attack. There was a moment of confusion, but it rapidly passed. Apparently two street urchins on a motorbike had snatched a watch from a tourist, but had quickly been pursued by a police patrol car. They had selected the embassy wall as their line of flight by pure chance, and had been lucky to escape unscathed as a policeman emptied his revolver at their disappearing profiles. The embassy Marines immediately arrested them and handed them straight back to the frustrated patrolman on the sidewalk outside, and in future a much enhanced security watch was put in place in the building.

This incident was widely reported in the international press, but it was seen as an amusing curiosity rather than a matter of deep moment. The wider NVA assault, which would be known to history as the Tet Offensive, generally caused little more of a stir in the USA, although of course it was a very different matter for the ARVN troops who had to oppose it on the ground. Some serious battles were fought and heavy sacrifices were accepted, but the ultimate result was a great boost to South Vietnamese confidence. It seemed that the ARVN had successfully resisted the very worst that the North could throw against it, even though the fighting did not finally die down for some six months. But throughout this crisis the US pacification of the Vietnamese villages continued to progress more or less as planned, and despite some noted setbacks, most of the news seemed to be pretty good. For example the press, especially the European press, gave great play to the positive Italian construction effort in Vinh Binh province, where the Bersaglieri celebrated the completion of each of their building programs by a march past at the gymnastic pace, all complete with feathers in their hats and promiscuous bugle-blowing. The American press found the perfect "mom and apple pie" stories in the Army's Civil Affairs community where down-to-earth reservists, still half-civilians, were more interested in building schools and sewage systems than in closing with the enemy. The Peace Corps' selfless, almost monastic style appealed to the American audience as well. Where the Civil Affairs troops did see combat it was in more than a few heroic attempts to defend "their villagers" from VC assaults.

President Johnson was re-elected in November with an increased majority. His Great Society programs for domestic reform had been a success at home, at least in the short term, and had helped to dampen down racial tensions. His first term had certainly not been blown off course by entangling foreign adventures.

The Saigon Embassy: April 30, 1975

In the aftermath of Tet there were annual *NVA* Christmas season assaults into the largely uninhabited frontier regions, although they encountered an increasingly self-confident and resilient ARVN defence, backed by US expertise and logistics. In the densely populated coastal strip the village pacification program was gradually picking up pace and depth, until in 1974 the 432 insurgent hamlets of Long An and Dinh Tuong provinces could finally be tackled—the ultimate bastions of *VC* control. South Vietnam was gradually becoming the proud and self-reliant independent state that it had so obviously failed to be under the Diem regime of a decade earlier.

Meanwhile in the USA President Johnson came to the end of his second term in 1972, and his chosen successor was the bubbly and positive Hubert H. Humphrey, formerly LBJ's vice president. The Republican candidate was Richard M. Nixon, already a failed runner for the White House, who now committed political suicide by burglarizing the Democratic offices in the Watergate hotel, which caused a considerable national scandal. Humphrey sailed through with a massive majority. The impact of all this was wholly positive for South Vietnam, in that it consolidated the essential continuity of US policy over a 13-year period, and guaranteed the long term future of the programs and aid that had already been working so well. Sir Robert Thompson felt he could at last retire to enjoy his favourite chilled highballs in a peaceful environment.[14]

On April 30, 1975, a helicopter landed on the roof of the US Embassy in Saigon, in order to escape the enthusiastic crowds blocking the streets below. Out of it stepped President Humphrey with a message of congratulation to his new ambassador and to President Ky of South Vietnam. It had just been announced that the hamlet pacification program had now successfully been completed to cover the whole country, and that the *VC* had all but totally withered away. The *NVA* had been defeated in the field and had effectively abandoned its campaign of aggression. Ho Chi Minh was dead and his successors in the Hanoi government were talking seriously about a lasting peace. There was much to celebrate in Saigon. When the presidential helicopter finally took off to visit an aircraft carrier waiting for it in the bay, it was immediately seized by Navy deck hands to be put into mothballs as a museum exhibit, symbolic of the final victory. One of them joked "We should throw this over the side to save us the trouble"—but that advice was not followed.

During the remainder of the 1970s and 1980s the heightened military posture of South Vietnam could gradually be stood down, and most of the allied contingents returned home, well satisfied with a job well done. Booming prosperity replaced warfare, although a residual US garrison was left in place, very similar to that in South Korea. Meanwhile the collapse of international communism was brewing in the background, until in 1990 the Berlin Wall was torn down and the Soviet Union dissolved. At that point a welcome message was received from North Vietnam that Hanoi was prepared to negotiate reunification with the South on fraternal terms that the South might care to suggest. The offer was accepted with alacrity, and so it was that in 1992 the unified nation state of Vietnam joined the tiger economies of Southeast Asia as a leading player.

The Reality

There was indeed a "window of opportunity" for South Vietnam in the weeks following the deaths of Diem and Kennedy in November 1963. However the moment was lost, and Nguyen Khanh's second military coup on January 30, 1964, plunged the country into escalating instability which was ably exploited by the VC. By the following year the Americans had recognized that their COIN preparations had been too disorganized and too fragile, and the only remaining alternative to retreat was a major deployment of mainforce conventional troops, which rapidly grew to over half a million men, many of them draftees, which in turn caused notorious social strains within the USA. On the North Vietnamese side there was an immediate attempt to match the American escalation with their own regular forces, and General Giap failed to persuade his comrades that the war should be left to the VC. As a result an entire NVA division was sent into the Ia Drang battle, to be defeated by the 1st Airmobile Cavalry Division. Meanwhile the action at Ap Bau Bang was a triumph for US armored forces. After that, many further mainforce battles were fought, among which a good proportion were arguably avoidable, since they were initiated by optimistic US helicopter-borne offensives into unpopulated areas where the NVA was certainly lurking, but from whence it could probably have done no more than beat its head fruitlessly against secure freeworld fortresses.

Although US tactics and weaponry could generally overwhelm the enemy in the mainforce war, the strategy was badly flawed because it concentrated maximum efforts and firepower on the border areas, while leaving the village war to a corrupt ARVN establishment, which it did not try to reform. The present chapter is predicated on the assumption that these priorities had been diametrically reversed, and that the vital chain of command had indeed been unified, as apparently Ambassador Maxwell Taylor had signally failed to do among the heady crises of 1966.

Lieutenant General Curtis LeMay, commander of US Air Forces in Europe during the Berlin Blockade. *(National Archives)*

Above: After a USAF attack, a disabled T-34/85 perches atop a wrecked bridge south of Suwon, South Korea. Despite such successes US air power could not halt the victorious North Korean advance.

Both left: C-54 and C-4 7 transport aircraft at Rhein-Main Air Force Base in July 1 948 as the Berlin airlift got under way. Two C-54s from the base's 61 st Troop Carrier Wing were destroyed in the worst incidents of the crisis in October. *(National Archives)*

Above: Black soldiers of the 24th Infantry move toward the front line, Korea July 1950.

Above right: An Australian Centurion tank and a group of infantrymen at Xa Long Tan, scene in 1966 of a rare setback for the freeworld forces in their successful pacification of South Vietnam. *(Paul Handel)*

Right: A common memory of Vietnam-a Civil Affairs soldier standing guard in one of the countless strategic hamlets that so successfully deprived the communists of access to the population. *(US Army)*

Above: Soviet MiG-23 Flogger-B fighters escorted the Tu-16 bomber squadron that struck the America carrier battle group on June 21 , 1967.

Above & right: Damage aboard the USS America after the Soviet missile strike.

Above: An A-4 Skyhawk ready to take off from the USS Saratoga for the attack on the Soviet anchorage at Kithira, June 21 , 1967.

Right: A signal station aboard the Soviet all-gun cruiser Kirov, sunk at the Kithira anchorage in the Sixth Fleet counterattack following the strike on the *America* battle group.

Above: Kiowa helicopters from the hastily-formed 444 Squadron prepare to support coalition operations near Montreal in the wake of the disastrous urban operation in the downtown core.

Left: A Lynx patrol, from 2 Troop, B Squadron, 8th Canadian Hussars, participates in an anti-FLO clear and secure operation north of Ottawa.

Above: FROG tactical nuclear surface-to-surface missiles. These weapons delivered the first nuclear strikes since the end of World War II as the Soviets lashed out to break the growing stalemate of the war in China.

Above right: Motorized infantry dismounting for the assault deep in Manchuria during the crushing attacks of the initial stages of the Soviet invasion of China.

Right: At 0636, October 25, USS Aubrey launched two SM-1 SAMs at a circling Soviet Tu-95 Bear, inadvertently initiating the Confrontation of 1973. *(US Navy)*

Above: Dzerzhinski, sister ship of the ill-fated Admiral Ushakov, reinforces the Fifth Eskadra on October 26, 1973. Note that an aft turret has been replaced by an M-2 Volkhov SAM launcher, testimony to the Soviet respect for American naval air power. *(US Navy)*

Above: Soviet airborne troops patrol a road on the outskirts of Kabul
shortly after the Soviet invasion of Afghanistan began.

Left: A formation of Soviet Mi-24 Hind-D helicopters covers a mechanized
column in action in Afghanistan. Such operations would not have been so
straightforward had the US administration decided to allow Stinger SAMs to be
sent to the Afghan resistance. *(Jamiat-e-/slami Afghanistan)*

Above: A US Army rocket launcher firing the secret KICAS-AM munition.

Above: Men of the Rogachev Motorized Rifle Division surprised by the mass of strange little orange parachutes floating down upon them, May 20, 1989.

As for specific events, Operation Sin Loi was actually a US offensive known as Cedar Falls, and it did indeed begin on January 8, 1967, as a considerably more ambitious—but scarcely more triumphant—US enterprise than the ARVN battle outlined here. Operation Toan Thang was not mounted in 1967 but in May 1970, and under a far greater diplomatic cloud than assumed here. Then again the Australian battle of Xa Long Tan in 1966 was a freeworld victory, whereas the Tet invasion of the Saigon embassy in 1968 was a serious media defeat. Overall the total of American dead by the end of 1968 numbered something not far from the 18,000 dismissed in this text as a perfectly avoidable and excessive total.

Bibliography

Blaufarb, Douglas S., *The Counter-insurgency Era*, The Free Press, New York, 1977.

Donovan, D., *Once a Warrior King*, New York, 1985.

Frizzell, D.D., and Thompson, W.S., *The Lessons of Vietnam*, New York, 1977.

Galloway, Joseph L., and Moore, Harold G., *We were Soldiers Once... and Young*, Harper Collins, New York, 1992.

Griffith, Paddy, *Forward Into Battle*, Crowood Press, Swindon, Wilts., 1990.

Halberstam, David, *The Making of a Quagmire*, Bodley Head, London, 1965.

Race, Jeffrey, *War comes to Long An*, University of California Press, Berkeley, 1972.

Starry, Donn A., *Mounted Combat in Vietnam*, Department of the Army, Washington DC, 1978.

Valentine, Douglas, *The Phoenix Program*, Avon, New York, 1990.

Notes

1. Thompson was head of the British advisory mission in Saigon 1961–65, after which he continued to give advice and write shrewd commentaries on the evolving situation.
2. Diem died in the coup of November 1, 1963, which was engineered by Generals Duong Van Minh ("Big Minh"), Tran Van Don and Le Van Kim. Kennedy died in Dallas on November 22, to be succeeded by Vice-President Lyndon B. Johnson.
3. For the amazing double-dealing that led up to the coup of November 1, see Halberstam, *The Making of a Quagmire*.
4. Blaufarb, *The Counter-insurgency Era*.
5. "Today in Washington he is considered to have been the best ambassador we ever had there," Halberstam, *The Making of a Quagmire*, p. 248.
*6. If this target had not been specified at an early date, it is only too likely that the actual expenditure would have been a shockingly inefficient 90 percent spent in military aid and only 10 percent in civilian—as was amusingly speculated in Thompson and Frizzell's 1977 alternative history *The Lessons of Vietnam*, pp. 200–17.
*7. In late 1967 Minh was succeeded by the smart, charismatic and aggressive Nguyen Cao Ky, the chief of the Air Force.

8. 8. A concept originally outlined by French colonial officers around 1900, such as Gallieni and Lyautey, and subsequently embraced as a central tenet of counter-insurgency theory.

*9. For example Joan Baez made a speciality of updated folk versions of Civil War songs, while Bob Dylan concentrated on rapid-fire lyrics about race issues. The two never met. Country Joe Macdonald and the Fish attended the President's reception to celebrate his re-election in 1968, where they performed their very popular football songs.

10. For the tactical superiority of tanks over helicopters in Vietnamese terrain, see Starry, *Mounted Combat in Vietnam*. For an analysis of the weaknesses of heliborne assault tactics, see the present author's *Forward Into Battle*, pp. 136–62.

*11. ARVN casualties in the Sin Loi operation mounted to some 12,500 killed and wounded, although they claimed *NVA* casualties were twice as high. The disparity is explained by the ARVN tactic of holding small but heavily armed defensive posts, upon which the cream of the northern army sacrificed itself in attacks that were usually—but not always—futile. Conversely there could be little ARVN progress against the *NVA* fortified 2.ones and tunnels.

*12. For details of the epic "Papa Six Five" SAS patrol behind enemy lines, see the book of that name by Jockey O'Hara (London, 1971).

*13. The Khe Sanh firebase was overrun and not subsequently re-occupied, since it was too far from support. Equally the Lang Vei special forces base was overrun but all nine of the attacking PT-76 tanks were knocked out in the battle. The A Shau became an *NVA* enclave, but the key coastal area around Hue and Quang Tri remained firm—as did Pleiku and Darlac. Some 30,000 ARVN killed and wounded were reported.

14. The author was once castigated by Thompson for failing to chill the glass that he offered to him.

4
TO THE BRINK
The Middle East, June 1967

John D. Burtt

"Danger, and it is grave danger, lies in misadventure and miscalculation. There is risk that those in authority in area may misapprehend or misinterpret intentions and actions of others.
Secretary of State Dean Rusk, May 22, 1967

The Eastern Mediterranen
The Task Force escorts, five destroyers and the guided missile cruiser *Little Rock,* spread themselves out around the giant carrier while the USS *America* itself buzzed with the usual activity of preparing and launching aircraft. The activity took on an intensity that all members of the Task Force felt. Ashore, about a hundred miles away, Israeli and Arab armies clashed from Jerusalem to the Sinai. Of more immediate concern was the Soviet force of destroyers and a cruiser lurking just over the horizon. Their intentions were unknown, but the current level of Soviet rhetoric against Israel and the West made the reinforced naval presence ominous. That uncertainty had the battle group at a Condition Three state of readiness, with most weapons ready for immediate use. The focus of much of the uncertainty, the Soviet *Kashin* Class guided missile destroyer, *381,* covered their every move and was even now steaming directly into *America's* path.

Captain Donald Engen, the carrier's captain, swore under his breath and ordered his helmsman to alter course slightly away from the Soviet vessel. Behind him, Rear Admiral Lawrence Geis, Commander TF 60, picked up a phone. "Signal the *Lawe* to move that Red ship out of the way," he barked.

Engen looked at him with raised and questioning eyebrows. The situation was tense enough with Israeli and Arab forces locked in battle and their sponsors arguing it out in the United Nations and court of world opinion. Additional risk of a US-Soviet confrontation was not needed. Geis nodded to his senior captain. "Sixth Fleet orders," he explained.

The order went out to the USS *William C. Lawe,* a *Gearing* Class destroyer, which nimbly moved to place itself between the carrier and *381.*

Almost immediately the airwaves filled with Soviet protests and American counter-protests. The two ships approached and swerved, nearly colliding on several occasions. The USS *Thomas* began moving in to help its sister ship, when the two destroyer captains miscalculated. *Lawe* and *381* ground their sides together, throwing sailors on both ships off their feet.

The exact sequence of events following the collision will always be in doubt as neither captain survived, and US and Soviet sources reported conflicting stories. The Soviets stated that the American ship deliberately caused the collision and opened fire, to which *381* responded. The US insisted that the Soviet ship opened fire without true provocation.

Regardless of the actual cause of the event, what occurred is not in doubt. Two Goa missiles roared off the bow of the Soviet ship and hit the *America,* steaming 1,500 yards away. One missile hit an A-4 Skyhawk on the deck, detonating it and its armament. The other plowed into *America's* hangar deck, setting off a series of explosions and a huge fire.

The Cold War had turned suddenly hot.

Background

By 1967, the Cold War had been going on for more than 20 years. For the Union of Soviet Socialist Republics, it had been a difficult time. They were just now emerging from the Stalin and Khrushchev eras that had put them militarily and economically behind the West.

Adding to their discouragement was a series of setbacks for the international communist movement. The United States had intervened in Vietnam, forestalling a promising takeover of the South. Communist forces in the Congo had been defeated. Several leftist leaders had been removed: Sukarno of Indonesia, Ben Bella of Algeria, and Nkrumah of Ghana. More recently, in April 1967, the left wing government of Greece had been overthrown. Worse, however, was the continuing dispute with the Communist Chinese over the philosophical and international leadership of the movement.

The only place in the world that seemed to be going the Soviet way was in the Middle East. Problems and mistakes made by the West had opened the door for the Soviets in 1955 when they concluded an arms deal with the Egyptians. Their status improved dramatically when the United Kingdom, France and Israel had combined to attack Egypt in 1956 over the Suez Canal. The Soviets had become the major supporters of several key Arab states since that time, most notably Egypt and Syria.

Egypt interested the Soviets on a global level. Through that country, they had a friendly association with an Arab leader of international stature, President Gamal Abdel Nasser, giving them political access to Africa and the Arab world. This access gave them the potential to affect a region crucial to the West, due to the region's oil reserves. Although their chief nemesis, the United States, was not dependent on Arab oil, the Americans'

European allies obtained 80 percent of their oil from the Middle East.[1] Their interest in Syria was primarily national, adding to the security of their southern flank.

With their influence in the region on the upswing, the Soviets naturally looked to this area for a chance to embarrass, defeat, or at least degrade the West, and especially the United States.

For the United States, international stability was the chief goal in 1967. Americans, too, felt that they were losing the Cold War. Economic woes and political squabbling were adversely impacting the North Atlantic Treaty Organization (NATO). West Germany found itself unable to purchase new weapons or pay for the upkeep of its allied defenders. Great Britain was having to shift forces from east of Suez to meet its NATO commitments. And the year before, France had pulled out of full military participation in the alliance.

In addition to these problems, communist insurgencies were springing up virtually worldwide, especially in Latin America. Communist-inspired riots disrupted Hong Kong. And the morass of Vietnam, despite 460,000 American troops, seemed no closer to a resolution, much to the growing displeasure of the American people.

The Middle East, as noted above, was important to the West, and United States' policy in the region was quite complex. It had brokered the deal that "settled" the Suez War, and established what came to be known as the Eisenhower Doctrine, committing the United States to "preserve the independence and integrity of the nations of the Middle East" against aggression by anyone. Ties with conservative Arab regimes such as those of Jordan, Saudi Arabia, and Kuwait were pursued, along with substantial support for Israel. The chief problem in the region for the USA, other than the Soviet presence, was the declining relationship with the Egyptians. That relationship had been improving under President John F. Kennedy, but suffered under President Lyndon Johnson.

There were many irritants between the two countries. America was unhappy with Nasser's rhetoric and subversive actions against the conservative Arab regimes, including his backing of the revolution in Yemen.[2] Nasser was unhappy with the American use of foreign aid, such as wheat and debt rescheduling, as a political lever. And there was clearly a personality conflict between the two presidents. The Egyptian leader distrusted Johnson for his pro-Israeli advocacy and his stand against Nasser's brand of revolutionary Arab nationalism. Nasser felt certain Johnson was out to humiliate and destroy him personally.

Unfortunately, the region, where the Soviets looked to turn their international fortunes around and the United States looked to maintain the *status quo,* was one of the most unstable in the world, fraught with internal and external strife among its nations, especially Egypt, Syria, Jordan and Israel.

Egypt was in bad shape. Despite governmental stability—Nasser had been in power since 1952, although officially president only since 1956—the country stagnated under an enormous debt. Egypt owed more than $4.0 billion in foreign and domestic debt; international banks were no longer lending the country money, causing social programs to grind to a halt. Nasser's overextended political and strategic commitments did not help. The war in Yemen, for example, tied down a large portion of Egypt's military and cost nearly $60 million annually with no end in clear sight. Many of the problems in the region stemmed from Nasser's personal quest for leadership in the nationalist Arab revolution. It put him at odds with most other Arab countries, as noted earlier.

Syria had most of the same problems Egypt had and added extreme political instability to the mix. In its 21 years of independence, it had had 23 separate governments with eight military coups to make things more volatile. The last coup, in February 1966, saw the current leftist Ba'ath leadership take control, but they had already suffered two abortive coup attempts against them since taking power. Syria's leaders tried to mask their instability with internal repression and an unrelenting focus on external enemies, especially Israel and the United States. The Syrians backed the Palestinian organization Fatah,[3] including support for its raids across the border into Israel. Harsh rhetoric attacked Jordan and Egypt for cowardice in not supporting armed attacks against the Jewish state.

The Hashemite Kingdom of Jordan was relatively stable, but it was the weakest of the three Arab states neighboring Israel. Under the rule of King Hussein bin Talal since 1953, the small country differed from the other two because of its considerable dependence on Western economic and military support. Its territories west of the Jordan River, commonly called the West Bank, virtually surrounded the split city of Jerusalem and made Jordan vulnerable to conflicts with Israel, which coveted the area. Its moderate stance toward the Jewish state and its western ties put Hussein and his country at odds with Syria and Egypt.

And then there was Israel. The state was formed after the Palestine Partition plan, adopted by the United Nations on November 29, 1947, divided the old British mandate for Palestine into a Jewish state, Arab state, and the open city of Jerusalem. The United Nations plan started an armed conflict between Jewish settlers in the Mandate and their Arab neighbors. Israel declared independence on May 14, 1948, which resulted in an immediate invasion by Arab forces from Egypt, Syria, Jordan, Iraq and Lebanon. United Nations intervention forced one cease-fire, but renewed fighting broke out. Against the fractured and uncoordinated Arabs, Israel actually gained territory before the fighting was stopped again. Significantly, no Arab Palestinian state was ever formed.

In the intervening years, sporadic fighting continued, including the Suez War, which saw Israel take most of the Sinai Peninsula from Egypt.

Peace negotiations after that war gave back most of Israel's territorial gains in exchange for guarantees from the United States. In 1965, Arab terrorist (or freedom fighter, depending on the outlook) raids across the border began and increased in intensity and ferocity. Israeli requests for UN action against the raiders and those that supported them were ineffective. Reprisal raids also failed to stop the attacks.[4]

By mid-1967, Israel was caught in an economic recession and an internal debate on how to handle the Arab raids. The current dominant party in Israel's Parliament, Mapai *(Mifleget Poalei Eretz Israel* or Israel Workers' Party), led by Prime Minister Levi Eshkol, favored a defensive strategy relying on deterrence with very specific events that would trigger military action. Mapam *(Mifleget Poalim Hameuhedet* or United Workers' Party) supported military action only if the concrete support of a major power was obtained. Military activism, Mapam felt, would inevitably lead to placing Israel in the middle of the Cold War. Other parties, like Herut *(Tenuat Haherut* or Freedom Movement) demanded the government occupy territory to halt the raids and liberate all the lands of ancient biblical Israel.[5]

In the increased tensions of the region, all sides looked to their armed forces to provide security and deterrence. Egypt had the largest armed forces in the Middle East, equipped exclusively by the Soviet Union. The Egyptian military had some 210,000 troops backed by 1,300 tanks (including some 450 of the Soviet T-54/55 main battle tanks with 100mm cannon), and over 400 combat aircraft. Of particular concern to the Israelis were the 30 Tu-16 medium bombers in Egypt's arsenal. This twin-engined subsonic bomber was capable of carrying a 9,000kg payload or two standoff Kennel missiles, each with a 1,000kg warhead. To Israel's north, Syria could muster 63,000 troops with 750 tanks and 127 aircraft, including 15 Tu-l6s. In November 1966, Egypt and Syria momentarily put their animosity aside and signed a Soviet-sponsored defense pact, agreeing to work together in the event of an Israeli attack. However, the two countries disagreed on exactly what would constitute an "attack." Thus the pact was more show than reality. To the east, Jordan fielded ten brigades with 50,000 infantry and 280 US M48 Patton and British Centurion tanks.

To deter this multi-directional threat, a fully mobilized Israel could field 250,000 troops, 1,000 tanks, mostly M48s, Centurions and retooled Shermans, and about 300 combat aircraft, primarily French built Mirages and Super Mysteres.

On April 7, 1967, a small border clash near the Sea of Galilee escalated into an engagement between Israeli and Syrian tanks, artillery and aircraft, leading to the destruction of six Syrian MiGs and a flyover of Damascus by the victorious Israeli jets. The incident sparked a renewed attack by Syria on Egypt for not becoming involved to help its defense pact partner. The charge was echoed by Jordan, further embarrassing Nasser. The incident played a key role in the ensuing crisis.

The April clash also triggered an internal crisis within Syria, threatening once again the Ba'ath government. Subsequent Soviet actions started a chain of events that threatened a world war.

The Crisis

The aftermath of the air clash over Syria provided the Soviets with an opportunity to help their Middle East clients and create another trouble spot for the West. Syria was again facing an internal crisis, and Israel was threatening major retaliatory action against them for continued Fatah raids. On May 13, 1967, through three different diplomatic channels, the Soviets warned Egypt's government that Israel had massed significant forces on the Syrian border and was about to invade to overthrow its government.[6]

Soviet leaders calculated they could heighten tensions enough to get the United States actively involved economically, politically and possibly even militarily, on the side of Israel, thus suffering a major loss of influence among the Arab nations. The fictitious threat would also allow Syria's leaders to regain complete control of their country through an outside threat, deter Israel from any real plans against that country, and involve Egypt in a way that would enhance its Soviet ties. They calculated that the tensions should not result in a shooting war between Israel and the Arab nations, as had happened when the threat had been used before.[7] But they were also confident that if fighting did break out, Arab military forces, with their Soviet equipment, could handle the armed conflict. Indeed, a hard-fought Arab loss could make Nasser even more dependent on Soviet aid and less hostile to communism.[8] Finally, they were certain that the tensions would not bring US and Soviet forces into direct conflict.

Nasser reacted strongly to the information. Without waiting for proof that the threat actually existed, he ordered troops into the Sinai to threaten Israel's southern border. Some of his immediate reaction was based on the charges of cowardice that his Arab neighbors had been leveling at him after the April clash over the Sea of Galilee. Advance troops were on their way the following day, with an armored division right behind.

The Israelis reacted moderately. They denied the accusation—a denial backed up publicly by UN observers—and offered to take their Soviet Ambassador on a tour of the suspected concentration sites. The Soviets turned down the offer, stating baldly that they knew what they knew and did not need proof.

By May 16, Egypt had 30,000 troops and 200 tanks in the Sinai. Israel limited its own military movement as it felt the Egyptian force was purely defensive and was no immediate threat. Arabs outside Egypt, however, reacted jubilantly—accolades from other governments poured in, and the Arab media blared approbation of Nasser's move.

Fueled by the accolades and exhilarated by his sudden rise to heroic stature, Nasser made an impulsive decision on May 16 to demand that the

United Nations Emergency Force withdraw from its positions. The UNEF had been patrolling the Sinai since the Suez War as a deterrent to renewed fighting. In making this decision, Nasser did not discuss it with any of his high level advisors nor did he discuss it beforehand with his Soviet sponsors. UN Secretary-General U Thant, in a very controversial decision,[9] sent the order to pull out to his commander in the field, Major-General Indar Jit Rikhye, who began the UNEF withdrawal on May 19- By that time the Egyptian force in the Sinai had grown to 70,000 troops and 700 tanks. The UNEF withdrawal and the size of the Arab force created the potential for offensive action against Israel, which responded to the threat by mobilizing its military.

The Soviets were surprised by Nasser's order to the UNEF and somewhat discomfited by the growth in the military forces facing each other. But the crisis was still within the limitations they had planned and their primary target, the United States, was starting to take serious notice of the situation. President Johnson and his administration had limited themselves to simple messages of restraint to both sides early in the crisis. But with the withdrawal of the UNEF, they began to watch the region more carefully.

Egypt continued to put troops into the Sinai and by May 22 had four full divisions at the border. With no overt Israeli reaction, other than mobilization, and continued adulation from Arab countries, Nasser moved impulsively again. Assuming the United States was too involved in Vietnam to take any role in the Middle East and assuming Israel would not act for fear of the Soviet Union, on May 23, he announced that the Strait of Tiran was closed to Israeli shipping and strategic goods.

The Strait of Tiran was an 800-1,000 yard channel lying between Egypt and two rocky islands, Tiran and Sarafir, at the mouth of the Gulf of Aqaba. The gulf itself was 100 miles long and ended at the Israeli port of Eilat. Although it had been 18 months since an Israeli flagged ship had passed the Strait, Eilat did contribute some $3 million in monthly imports and exports to the Israeli economy, representing about 5 percent. However, nearly 90 percent of Israel's oil imports, an obvious strategic commodity, came through the Strait.

But closure of the Strait was more of a political challenge than an economic one to the Israelis. The blockade of the Strait had been a significant cause of Israel joining with Britain and France in the Suez War and its opening had been the only real result that had remained of Israel's victory over Egypt in that conflict. Golda Meir, in a 1957 speech to the United Nations, had stated baldly that:

"Interference by armed forces with ships of the Israeli flag exercising free and innocent passage in the Gulf of Aqaba and through the Strait of Tiran will be regarded by Israel as an attack entitling it to exercise its inherent right of self defense... and take all measures as are necessary."

Nasser's action caught everyone by surprise, especially the Soviets. But he had not simply triggered a potential *casus belli* for the Israelis; he had changed the complexion of the crisis for the United States. The US had virtually guaranteed free passage of the Strait in the settlement of the Suez War. Johnson assumed that the Egyptians were acting under direct orders from the Soviets and sent a strongly worded message to President Kosygin on May 23, stating that the "blockade is an extremely grave matter, challenging the commitment of the United States and would be met with its fullest opposition."

In fact the commitment of the United States was anything but clear. The Eisenhower Doctrine, established in 1958, had committed the United States to maintaining the territorial integrity of all Middle East nations against aggression. An *aide-memoire* in February 1957 promised force if US ships were denied free passage of the Strait, but only to join with others to defend the rights of other nations' ships. Complicating the matter even more was the fact that, although America had written defense agreements with 42 other nations, it did not have such an agreement with Israel. All that was recognized was a strong moral commitment to the Jewish state.

The closure of the Strait forced Israel into a major internal crisis. With a well-advertised *casus belli* in place, most Israelis demanded military action, if only to make their military deterrence credible. Eshkol, and especially Foreign Minister Abba Eban, disagreed, feeling Israel needed to secure Western support first. Grudgingly, the rest of the cabinet went along. Eban left for the Western capitals that day.

Eban's trip was just one of the major diplomatic moves being made by all sides. U Thant met with Nasser and Foreign Minister Mahmoud Riad. Both Egyptians stressed that closure of the Strait removed the last vestige of Israel's 1956 aggression and was an action well within their rights since they considered themselves at war with Israel. Nasser, however, agreed in principle to a two-week moratorium on enforcing the blockade to allow negotiations to proceed. US Treasury Secretary Robert Anderson and retired Ambassador Charles Yost, sent by President Johnson, heard much the same thing.

Initially, Eban's trip was far from helpful. France's President Charles de Gaulle only advised the Israelis to let the major powers work things out and not to attack. In Britain, Prime Minister Harold Wilson offered his moral support for an international flotilla of ships to break the blockade and enforce free passage, but little else.

In Washington, Eban requested a statement that action against Israel would be an action against the United States. Both President Johnson and Secretary of State Dean Rusk opposed such a blanket statement. They wanted Israel to wait for the international community to act and remove the blockade. Johnson stated flatly that: "If Israel attacked, she'd do it alone." The President suggested that Israel abide by the UN moratorium that U Thant had negotiated with Nasser, and allow them to put together the international regatta, as it came to be called, that Britain supported.

Eban replied that Israel needed more concrete assurances in exchange for waiting the two weeks. He gave pointed notice that more delay would mean the loss of their military credibility to deter future attacks, opening up the specter of continual war. Johnson did not want to commit the US further without Congressional support, but Rusk, in a private meeting with the President, noted that the US could easily lose major prestige among its allies if it failed to act.

When Eban left Washington on May 27, he took with him a promise that America would act unilaterally to open the Strait on June 14, if the international regatta failed to form. As an added show of faith, Johnson authorized the covert transfer of a photo-reconnaissance squadron of RF-4Cs from Ramstein Air Force Base in Germany to help Israel monitor Arab movements on their border. The RF-4Cs gave the Israelis night-time reconnaissance capability, something all other parties in the area lacked. In addition, orders went out to the US Sixth Fleet to move into the Eastern Mediterranean. Two separate carrier groups, one with the USS *Saratoga* and one with the USS *America,* started moving immediately toward Crete.

While the diplomacy was taking place at high levels, media rhetoric was altering the crisis hourly. The Soviets, despite assurances to Washington that they were counseling restraint to their clients, bombarded the airwaves with warnings about Israeli and US intentions. Arabs were told that thousands of US Marines and seven aircraft carriers were on their way to fight for Israel.[10] The USSR also announced its intention to strengthen its small naval force in the Mediterranean as a counter to the Sixth Fleet.

Arab rhetoric was even more strident. The stated goal of Egypt's move into the Sinai was no longer just to deter Israel from attacking Syria. The goal had become war with the Jewish state and its complete annihilation. Nasser stated flatly that in the coming inevitable war, the objective was to destroy Israel.

In Jordan, Hussein found himself in a quandary. His people were completely enthralled by the "holy war" rhetoric of vengeance and victory being shouted from every Arab radio station—staying neutral could create a backlash against him. He had no illusions about Arab military capability. No common plan, nor even coordination existed among the Arabs, a situation that could only lead to disaster. However, he also knew that any Arab attack against Israel would result in an Israeli invasion of the West Bank, something he alone could not withstand. Thus, on May 30, Hussein flew to Cairo and signed a defense pact with the Egyptian leader. The pact allowed foreign troops into Jordan—Iraq and Saudi Arabia promised troops immediately—and put Jordan's military under an Egyptian commander in the event of war.

With the signing of the Egypt-Jordan pact, Israel found itself fully surrounded by what appeared to be an Arab unified front, bent on its destruction. General Yitzak Rabin, the Israeli Chief of Staff, demanded immediate authorization to attack before Syria, Jordan and Egypt were fully organized. His reasoning could not be faulted. First, mobilization of the full Israeli Defense Force (IDF) was devastating to the Israeli economy, due to the expense of military actions and the lost productivity of workers called to duty. Second, sitting in defensive works, waiting for an Arab attack, was debilitating to army morale. Finally, lack of credible military action in the face of such a clear *casus belli* as the closing of the Strait, sent the wrong signal to their enemies and invited further aggressive action.

But, Eshkol, backed by his cabinet, refused the military's demand, citing the US promises as reason to wait. On June 1, the Prime Minister made a radio address to his nation that heightened tensions more than helped. Flat, unemotional, devoid of inspiration, the halting address started building pressure toward a change in the Israeli government.

While Israel faced its internal problems, Washington struggled to develop a working international program to open the Strait. By June 7, however, it was becoming apparent that the idea was not going to be viable. Of the countries approached, only the Netherlands and Australia promised support. Even Great Britain declined, stating that renewed British involvement in the region after the 1956 Suez debacle would only inflame the situation. Johnson and his advisors came face to face with the fact that they would have to back up their promises to Israel with unilateral action.

US assets were skimpy for such action. North of the Suez Canal, two carrier battle groups were on station, each with one carrier and six escorts. In the Red Sea, the US had the USS *Valcour,* a tactical fleet command ship and three destroyers, plus the USS *Intrepid,* a smaller carrier that had transited the Canal on June 1, ostensibly on its way to Vietnam. New orders kept the *Intrepid* with the *Valcour* in case its aircraft were needed.

A week before the moratorium ran out events in Israel brought political matters to a head. News that four Iraqi brigades had entered Jordan drove the military to renew its demands. The resulting debate kept the military in check, but Eshkol accepted the need for changes in the government. He invited Gahal into what he termed a National Unity Government with two ministers without portfolio positions and relinquished his own duties as Minister of Defense. In his place stepped Moshe Dayan, the hero of Suez.[11] Morale in Israel soared.

On June 14, 1967, the moratorium set by the United Nations ran out. There was no new accord, no new diplomatic initiatives, no compromises from Nasser, and no international effort to break the deadlock. At dawn the following day, the United States moved.

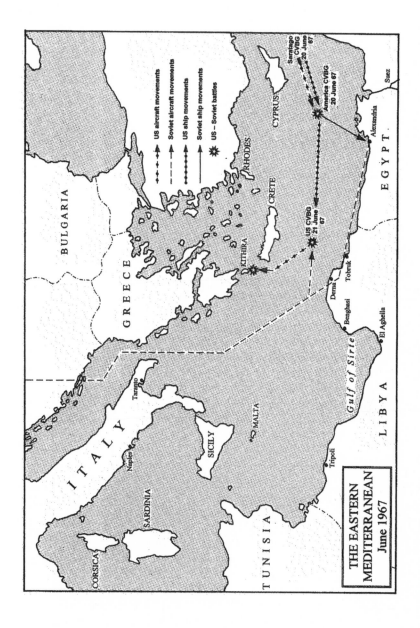

THE EASTERN
MEDITERRANEAN
June 1967

Explosion

The ship was called the *Coral Sea,* a 68,000-ton tanker. Normally it flew the Liberian flag, but as *it* approached the Strait of Tiran that Thursday morning, the Israeli flag waved from the fantail, an unmistakable challenge to Nasser's blockade. Leading the way for the cargo ship sailed the USS *Dyess,* a *Gearing* Class destroyer, its crew closed up and ready for action. Overhead F-4 Phantoms and A-4 Skyhawks from the *Intrepid's* airgroup, circled and waited for any Egyptian response.

Warned of the ship's approach, Nasser found himself in a terrible quandary. He had not really expected his blockade to be directly challenged, certainly not by the United States. His Soviet sponsors had assured him that the US was far too involved in Vietnam to risk another conflict. Worse than this miscalculation was the fact that Nasser had been bluffing with his blockade. Other than two recently emplaced coastal guns, there was nothing at the Strait to enforce the blockade. Exposing his bluff would embarrass the Egyptian President and virtually destroy his resurgent leadership among the Arabs. However, not responding would do much the same. He could only fall back on the Soviet promise to provide him direct support in the event of war.[12]

Radio communication with the *Dyess* from Egyptian authorities in Sharm el Sheikh, simply resulted in pro forma statements about free passage. Backed into a corner by his own words, Nasser felt compelled to respond. He ordered the guns to open fire.

The action, once it started, was anti-climatic—one shell hit the *Coral Sea* causing little damage. The *Dyess* returned fire with its single forward 5-inch mount, but American airpower terminated the action. Diving in, the US Navy Skyhawks obliterated the battery with bombs. Two Egyptian motor torpedo boats in Sharm el Sheikh did not budge; neither did the Egyptian Air Force. The *Coral Sea* and its escort sailed on.

The brief action heralded another intense round of loud diplomatic debate. The Arabs complained bitterly about the US intervention. The Soviets, somewhat stunned by the turn of events, backed Arab complaints at the United Nations, put their armed forces on heightened alert worldwide, and ordered their reinforced Mediterranean squadron to close on the American Sixth Fleet carriers. The Soviet *Fifth Eskadra* flagship, the *Sverdlov* Class cruiser *Dzerzhinski,* led a mixed group of destroyers and escorts to a position just over the horizon from the USS *America's* battlegroup, sailing 100 miles off the entrance to the Suez Canal.

While the superpowers raged and postured, Nasser was making decisions that would compound his problems. Deeply embarrassed by his dismal showing at the Strait, he contemplated several options. First, he could accept a *fait accompli*—he had gambled and lost—and endeavor to hold on to whatever prestige he could through diplomacy. Second, he could attack the *Coral Sea* again, this time with air power—his Tu-16 bombers could attack with standoff Kennel missiles and sink the ship before it got to Eilat. That option, however, would place his air force in more direct conflict with the Americans, with immediate Soviet aid questionable. His final option was to unleash his army against the real enemy—Israel. Such an attack would remove the embarrassment and allow him to lead the Arab world to a victory. His decision was preordained by his makeup.

The Egyptian high command, particularly Field Marshal Abdel Hakim Amer, and his Sinai Front commander, General Abdel Mohsen Mortagui, were taken aback by Nasser's new orders. All of their plans had been predicated on Israel attacking as it did in 1956. Their existing plan drew the Israelis into well-planned Sinai kill zones near Bir Gifgafa and Jebel Libni. Once the bulk of the IDF had been destroyed, Egyptian forces would then advance. The current Egyptian deployment in the desert was based on this plan. Significant redeployment would be required to change from a defensive posture to an offensive one.

The plan was quickly formed. The *7th Division* would hold its position near the coast and support the *20th Palestinian Division* in Gaza. To the deep south, the *6th Mechanized Division*, supported by the *1st Armored Brigade's* three T-54 battalions and an armored task force under Major-General Saad el Shazli, would advance into the Negev, cut off and take Eilat. *The 2nd Infantry Division*, supported by an armored brigade from the *4th Armored Division*, and its own tank brigade, would make the main attack toward Nitzana. A third armored brigade, the *Presidential Brigade*, a force of 100 tanks, nominally attached to the *3rd Infantry Division*, was also added to the main attack. These three latter brigades, along with the artillery support, had to redeploy. This movement started on June 16 under cover of darkness, which should have concealed the movement from the Israelis.

One part of Nasser's orders became controversial in his own camp immediately—Nasser decided not to inform his allies of the planned attack. He reasoned that bringing Syria and Jordan into the plans now would simply delay the attack and potentially compromise security. On a more personal level, he was feeling the time pressure to attack because of his own embarrassment. He informed his generals that they would announce that Israel had attacked them, initiating a massive Egyptian counter-attack. Time would be saved and secrecy maintained.

Israeli intelligence, however, aided by the night seeing capabilities of the American RF-4C reconnaissance aircraft, spotted the movement almost as soon as it started. News of the redeployment of armor and artillery forward in the Sinai galvanized the new Israeli government, with the military calling again for an immediate attack. The US sent a note of caution and restraint, suggesting that Israel allow the Egyptians to make the first overt aggressive move. The Israelis would then hold the moral high ground regardless of the outcome. Johnson, through embassy cables, again reiterated his guarantees that Israel would be protected.

Dayan was at first unwilling to withhold an Israeli attack. His primary concern was the initial air battle that the Israelis felt would precede any Arab attack. Such an attack would be costly to the Arabs, given the qualitative advantage the Israeli Air Force held, but could conceivably cause serious damage to cities and civilians. Air Force commander General Mordechai Hod stated, however, that with enough early warning, his pilots could meet the enemy in the skies, disrupting and destroying their cohesion.

There was another factor that led to Dayan's accepting the US position. Although there was definite movement in the Sinai that presaged an attack, there was no corresponding movement in Jordan or Syria. Without an immediate worry of a three-front war, Israeli commanders could see opportunity in the coming Egyptian attack. There were three *ugdot,* or divisional equivalents, in place in the Sinai. Brigadier-General Yisrael Tal commanded two armored brigades and the reinforced 202nd Parachute Brigade, facing the Egyptian *7th Division.* The brunt of the initial Egyptian assault would land on Brigadier-General Avraham Yoffe's two armored brigades and Brigadier-General Ariel Sharon's division of one armored and two mechanized infantry brigades. Both Yoffe and Sharon liked the idea of meeting the enemy armor in the open, followed by an immediate counterattack. Further south, Colonel Avraham Mendler's independent armored brigade would have to fend off the reinforced *6th Mechanized Division's* attack on the Negev and Eilat.

Before dawn on Monday June 19, American radar aircraft *off the America* picked up massive air activity developing above the Sinai— Egyptian aircraft taking off and forming up. The formations turned toward the Israeli border as Nasser's massed artillery opened fire on Israeli positions; 122mm shells and 240mm Katyusha rockets slammed down onto the Israeli defenses, while tanks and armored personnel carriers moved forward to their lines of departure.

To the north, the Egyptian attack aircraft were thrown into confusion by the sudden presence of American F-4 fighters circling conspicuously off the Suez entrance. As pilots and controllers argued the problem, Israeli Mirages swept in from the desert side and blasted through the Egyptian planes. Formations disintegrated as the MiGs struggled to ward off the unexpected attack. The Tu-16 bombers, loaded with ordnance, could not maneuver well and could not dive to low level for safety because of their own artillery barrage. They had to press on. Very few made it to their targets and those were distracted by anti-aircraft fire and did little damage. Over 30 MiGs fell from the sky, along with seven Israeli jets. The Americans fighters did not engage.

Below them, ignorant of the air battle, the Egyptian armored assault formations moved forward. Each of the three main attacking columns followed the classic Soviet style of attack: two tank battalions up front followed by a second echelon of armor and mechanized infantry. The primary assault column of the *4th Armored Division* reinforced its drive with an extra tank battalion of 40 T-54s. Fully a third of Egypt's tanks in the Sinai were involved in this attack. Further south *6th Mechanized* and *Task Force Shazli* moved forward as well.

Initial movement went well as the T-54 battalions plowed into and through the Israeli positions blasted by their hour-long hurricane barrage. Exuberant commanders signaled their superiors in the rear with claims of an overwhelming breakthrough. Then the Israelis opened fire.

Sharon and Yoffe had moved their troops back from their border positions some five miles—the Egyptians' opening barrage had fallen on empty desert. Now the massed tanks of the two Israeli divisions tore into the advancing Egyptian armor.

Two hours into the battle, the situation had changed completely. Egyptian aircraft had returned to their bases following the initial dogfights. While there, they fell victim to General Hod's secret weapon—turn-around time. Whereas most air forces measured the time to refuel and rearm aircraft for further sorties in hours, the Israelis measured the time in minutes. Israeli aircraft swept in again, blasting the Egyptian combat air patrols from the sky, then shooting up runways, planes, control towers and fuel storage facilities. After several waves, the Egyptians had no air force left. On the ground, the attacking columns from the *2nd Infantry* and *4th Armored Divisions* streamed back toward their own lines, having lost 230 of 270 attacking tanks. Right on their heels came the Israelis.

Ignorant of the actual state of affairs, Nasser went public, announcing that Egypt had repulsed an Israeli ground and air attack in the Sinai. Egypt had gained air superiority, he claimed, and "victorious" Egyptian tanks were advancing into Israel. He called upon his Arab brethren to join the fight.

His announcement shocked his allies. Both the Syrians and Jordanians had tentative plans for an attack into Israel, but neither was fully prepared to implement them. The Syrians had Operation *Nazzer* (Victory) where a divisional force would sweep around the southern end of Lake Tiberias through the town of Deganya, while a brigade attacked toward Tel Dan at the northern end of the lake. The Jordanians had Operation *Tariq,* which called for cutting the Jerusalem corridor from the north and taking West Jerusalem. These plans were dusted off, but it was early afternoon before Jordanian guns opened fire.

The Soviets were equally stunned by the outbreak of full-scale warfare, especially since Nasser had not informed them beforehand. They were extremely pleased at the Egyptian progress, however, and responded to the news with the obligatory vilification of Israeli and American aggression against peaceful Arabs and praising Arab military prowess in repulsing the "infamous" attack. Hours later they received their second shock when their military advisors got through to explain the real situation.

As other Arab military leaders were meeting to plan their attacks, the Egyptian position in the Sinai went from bad to worse. The *12th Infantry Brigade,* defending the fortifications at Um Katef, was celebrating the announced victory as their officers were trying to make sense out of garbled and frantic radio signals from their outposts, when the first remnants of the Egyptian attack rolled into their position. The position was ostensibly a strong one, with three lines of infantry trenches and positions for artillery and armor support. But the demoralizing sight of their fleeing tankers became panic when Israeli armor blasted its way in right behind the Egyptian tanks. Isolated strongpoints fought bravely, but shock and surprise overwhelmed the Arabs. Resistance disintegrated. The Israelis paused briefly to refuel, then surged forward toward Abu Aghiela. By Tuesday morning, that fortification was in Israeli hands and the *2nd Infantry Division* had virtually ceased to exist. Sharon's division refueled, then continued west while Yoffe pivoted north toward Bir Lahfan and El Arish.

Things were not much better further south. Mendler's armored brigade caught *Task Force Shazli* by surprise. The *128th Armored Brigade's* older T-34s were no match for the Israeli Centurions and the Egyptians were routed. A relieving force from the *6th Mechanized's 125th Armored Brigade* ran into an ambush by Israeli Super Shermans[13] and was sent reeling. Egypt's southern thrust was stymied.

By the morning of June 20, serious fighting was continuing in the Sinai and the Israelis had counter-attacked the Jordanians in Jerusalem and the West Bank. That was when *381's* missiles hit the *America* and changed the regional conflict into a global one.

Cold War Hot

A moment of disbelief froze most of the US sailors who witnessed the missile explosions on the *America*. The big carrier began to turn away as its deck swarmed with damage control efforts. The *Lawe* responded first from 100 yards away from the Soviet ship. As the Goa missile launchers recycled with new missiles, the US destroyer opened fire with its forward 5-inch mount, the only one closed up and ready at Condition Three. The point blank shots shattered the *381's* bridge. Two other destroyers veered to engage the Soviet ship as it began to trade shots with the *Lawe*. The other two ships were hampered by the *Lawe's* close proximity to their intended target, but by ten minutes after firing its missiles, a deluge of US 5-inch shells had left the *381* holed, drifting and on fire.

Two miles away, billowing black smoke marked the location of the *America* as fires continued to rage. Condition Three had placed a full squadron of armed A-4 Skyhawks on its deck. Explosions as these planes were engulfed spread the fire and cut down the personnel who tried to fight the blaze. Vice Admiral William Martin, Commander of the Sixth Fleet,[14] from his vantage point on the bridge of the USS *Little Rock,* ordered the carrier and one destroyer to turn west and move toward his other carrier group, some 150 miles away.

Martin then turned his attention to the threat on the horizon. Twelve miles away, the Soviet cruiser *Dzerzhinski* and its eight escorts were closing in on the battle scene at nearly 30 knots. With *America* limping away at half that speed and most of its aircraft out of operation, Martin had just his cruiser and three effective destroyers—*Lawe* was heavily damaged—to face the Soviet squadron. Air cover was limited to six F-4s of *America's* combat air patrol and whatever the USS *Saratoga* could provide. He ordered the *Sara* to get planes in the air and close on his position as soon as possible. He also authorized them to get rid of their Soviet tattle tail.[15]

Overall the odds against the remaining US ships were not particularly good. In 1967 US carrier battle groups depended on air power to provide most of their offense and defense. The escorts were expected to deal with submarines and aircraft. As ship-to-ship gun duels were thought to be a thing of the past, escort shipboard weaponry was being converted to missiles and anti-submarine torpedoes. The remaining naval guns were solely for shore bombardment.

Little Rock and the US destroyers were prime examples of that thinking. The best long-range anti-surface weapon was the twin Talos missile launcher on the *Little Rock*. The Talos missile carried a 100kg warhead and rode a beam to its target. It was expected to be an anti-aircraft weapon, but could be used against ships as well. Other than the Talos, the *Little Rock* had a single turret with three 6-inch guns with a range of 12,000 yards, plus a twin 5-inch turret. The remaining escorts altogether sported 15 5-inch guns with a much shorter range. All of their torpedoes were anti-submarine weapons.

The Soviet Navy was in the midst of a major transformation to missiles as well, so the squadron bearing down on Martin was not all that much better prepared for surface action. The *Dzerzhinski* sported three triple turrets of 152mm guns that outranged the *Little Rock's* by a good mile. The two *Kotlin* Class destroyers had four 130mm naval guns and the three *Riga* Class frigates each had a single 100mm mount. The two *Kashin* destroyers, and the *Kynda* Class cruiser *Varyag* only had short range 76.2mm antiaircraft mounts but, as the *Lawe* had discovered, these could be used against ships.

The biggest advantage in a surface engagement lay with the *Varyag's* primary weapon system. Designed solely as an anti-carrier ship, it carried two quadruple missile launchers fore and aft, holding massive SS-N-3 Shaddock anti-ship missiles. The radar-guided Shaddock had a range of over 250 kilometers and held a 1,000kg high explosive warhead—ten times the size of a Talos.

The escort ships trailed after the *America,* limited by its speed and the need to stay between the Soviets and their charge. To the west the *Saratoga* began launching its ready squadron of 14 Skyhawks, armed with bombs, plus two F-4 fighters for cover. The Soviet intelligence trawler *Alidada,* tailing the *Saratoga,* had monitored the verbal warfare going on to the south and its sudden escalation. The *Alidada* was reporting the aircraft launches, when the USS *Galveston* fired on it from 8,000 yards away. The two Talos missiles, fired from the rear launchers of the cruiser, impacted eight seconds later, leaving the trawler sinking.

The US came on the receiving end minutes later when the *Varyag* fired its missiles at the *America* and its escorts. One of the big ten-meter long missiles failed as it launched, splashing down near the Soviet flagship, but the other three quickly crossed the 16,000 yards between the two squadrons. Circling F-4 fighters screamed the warning as did an E-1B Tracer Early Warning aircraft, but it took only 15 seconds for the missiles to reach their target area.

Radar-guided in their terminal phase, the missiles locked on to the escorts. The US ships got off only a few anti-aircraft rounds at the incoming missiles—an incredibly lucky hit exploded one missile. But another slammed into and through the aft Talos missile launcher and exploded deep in the *Little Rock's* engineering spaces, its 1,000kg warhead nearly cutting the ship in half. Some 1,500 yards away, the other Shaddock impacted the *Lawe,* virtually destroying the ship.

The *Varyag* was maneuvering to bring its aft launchers to bear, when an F-4 dove on it through a curtain of anti-aircraft fire. Without guns aboard, the fighter could only fire two Sidewinder air-to-air missiles point blank into the rear of the Soviet vessel. The launcher exploded, detonating the missile's fuel and warheads and turning the rear of the cruiser into an inferno.[16] The Phantom was hit moments later, but the two crewmen were able to eject.

Despite the sudden loss of the *Varyag,* the Soviet commander, Rear-Admiral N.I. Khovrin, continued his rush forward. With the *America* still visible on the horizon and only three small destroyers in his way, the advantage in the battle seemed to be his.

But the Soviets suddenly paid a heavy price for their high-speed pursuit. Their anti-submarine frigates, whose sonar performance was severely degraded by the squadron's speed, picked up incoming torpedoes. The warning came too late. Two of the weapons hit the *Dzerzhinski* and another ripped off the bow of the *Kashin* destroyer 383- The cruiser drifted to a halt as its engine rooms flooded. The torpedoes had been launched from the *America's* unseen escort, a nuclear attack submarine.[17]

As the Soviet squadron dealt with the sudden loss of their flagship, A-4 Skyhawks from the *Saratoga's* VA-44 Hornets squadron arrived overhead. The Soviets sent up a swarm of Goa missiles, destroying one Skyhawk and sending another limping north trailing smoke. But the others bore in, hitting the floundering *Dzerzhinski* with three 250kg bombs and *Kashin*

296 with two others, leaving the destroyer on fire. With attacks mounting and submarines in the area, Khovrin called off his pursuit, ordering his ships to aid in rescue and salvage from their damaged consorts.[18] His opponent, Martin, called off further American attacks as well and had his remaining ships stand by to help his derelicts.

The 45 minutes of battle had left the sea littered with burning and sinking ships. The US ultimately lost the *Little Rock* and *Lawe,* plus extensive damage to the *America.* The carrier finally got its fires under control but at a cost of nearly 135 lives and the loss of 40 aircraft.[19] The Soviets lost their only two guided missile cruisers, the *Dzerzhinski* and the *Varyag,* and two destroyers, the *381* and *383,* plus damage to a third.

The Jordanians Are Left Holding the Bag

In the Sinai, oblivious to the events off shore, the Israelis continued their attack, with Tal's division breaking into the Egyptian *1th Division'%* lines toward Khan Yunis. Egyptian resistance was faltering as rumors of a disaster in the south circulated. In mid-morning, on learning that the Abu Agheila defensive position had been overrun, leaving Israeli armor a clear path to cut off the *7th Division,* Field Marshal Amer sent messages to all his commanders, ordering them to fall back immediately across the Suez Canal. He then left his headquarters to break the news to his president and try to find a way to explain the disaster. Egyptian resistance fell apart quickly after the orders, leading to a destructive rout to the Canal.

Elsewhere the Jordanians struggled to hold Jerusalem and the West Bank against the converging Israelis. Most of their infantry brigades were poorly positioned and ill equipped to react to the fast moving Israeli columns. The bulk of the fighting fell to the tanks of the *40th* and *60th Armored Brigades,* but these units had to fall back as Israeli air superiority made itself felt.

Two other factors made the situation worse for the Jordanians. First was the total inactivity of the supporting Iraqi division. The four brigades had been invited in to Jordan under the Egypt—Jordan defense pact, expressly to help the Jordanians defend their territory. Now, they refused to move from their bivouacs despite continuous requests for help by Hussein. Second, to the north, the Syrians also did little, apart from some desultory artillery fire and minor probes. Fighting alone, Hussein had little choice— he ordered his troops to pull back to the East Bank of the Jordan River.

The events of June 20 led to intense posturing by diplomats and serious internal discussions within each government. For the first time the Washington—Moscow hot line was used, but there was little resolution as President Johnson and Premier Kosygin simply reiterated their own side's sketchy story and blamed the other. Stunned by the Arab military collapse and the sudden conflict with the USA, the Soviet leaders found themselves in a quandary. They could not afford to ignore the provocative attacks on their ships in the Mediterranean, but retaliation would almost certainly lead to escalation to a global war, something the Soviets were not prepared for. Some form of middle ground had to be found. The Egyptians gave them the opening.

Nasser and Amer had been at a loss on how to deal with the disaster unfolding in the Sinai. However, on learning of the US-Soviet clash at sea, Nasser chose to go public with the "explanation" that US aircraft had aided Israel in destroying the Egyptian Air Force and that their Soviet allies had come to their aid. Given the unilateral US actions at the Strait of Tiran, the lie was believable to most Arab governments. Algeria, Syria, Iraq, Sudan and Yemen all joined Egypt in breaking diplomatic relations with the United States. In addition, Nasser asked for more Soviet aircraft to replace his losses.

The Soviets decided to grant his request—with a side task for the aircraft in question.

The United States was as stunned by the turn of events as the Soviets, but pictures of the burning *America* and the sinking of the *Little Rock* brought Congressional demands for President Johnson to reinforce the area. Orders went out to the *Franklin D. Roosevelt* (CVA.42) and the *Wasp* (CVS. 18) to sail immediately into the Mediterranean from the Atlantic. The British offered two carriers, *Victorious* and *Hermes*, as well. In the Mediterranean, the *Saratoga* battle group had merged with the *America's* and Admiral Martin transferred his flag to the *Galveston* from the *Massey*, the destroyer that had rescued him from the water. The combined group set course east for Malta.

Claws of the Bear

The Soviet plan was a calculated risk. Normal Soviet doctrine for strikes against a carrier group called for a coordinated effort by air, sea, and submarine forces all hitting at the same time. However, the Kremlin leaders felt strongly that such an attack would trigger the feared all-out global exchange. So their plan was fairly simple. A regiment of 36 Tu-16 bombers, each with two AS-1 Kennel anti-ship missiles, would take off for Egypt from bases in Yugoslavia. MiG-23s would accompany the bombers, carrying Atoll air-to-air missiles and drop tanks. Flying in squadron groups of 12, some 100 miles apart, they would ostensibly be heading for Alexandria as replacements for the Egyptians. They expected the US would intercept the bombers, but they gambled that the US would not engage if the bombers stayed out of range of their combined carrier force. A single squadron would turn and run toward the US ships and launch missiles at the escorts at maximum range. By using only a third of the bombers in the attack, they expected the US would get the point without a risk of global war.

At 0230, June 21, 1967, the bombers began to take off. Bombers and escorts formed up over Albania and headed south. About 45 minutes later NATO radar picked up the flights and passed the word to the US Sixth Fleet.

The activity worried Admiral Martin. The *America* was out of action, its planes unavailable except for five F-4s from the VF-102 Diamondbacks which had been in the air prior to the attack. The *Saratoga* could put up 22 F-4s from its two fighter squadrons; armed with Sparrow and Sidewinder missiles, they should be able to handle the Russians. He had more concerns about the possibility of some bombers and their missiles getting through. Much of the vaunted US electronic hardware touted by current naval literature was a bluff. Half their three-dimensional height-finding radars were inoperative, and their electronic jamming system, the ULQ-6, would be effective only if a small number of missiles attacked the battlegroup.

The *Saratoga* launched its F-4s, dividing the two squadrons into three groups to cover each of the three Russian formations. Flying to within two miles of the Russians, the F-4s sent the Russian commander an explicit ultimatum that no Russian plane should come within 200 miles of the US carriers or it would be shot down. The Soviets did not respond, but their flight course kept them outside the restricted zone.

Two hours later, however, at 0515, the Russians made their move. Twelve MiGs, escorting the third bomber squadron, turned toward the F-4s and launched Atolls. Two F-4s went down to the sudden barrage and the remaining fighters found themselves locked in a dogfight. Twelve Tu-l6s dove and accelerated toward the US ships.

Martin waited momentarily to see what the other Russian groups would do; when they continued on their way, he ordered half the Phantoms escorting the nearest group to intercept and sent his combat air patrol to do the same. Eight Phantoms went to full power to converge on the Russian bombers as far from the ships as possible.

The US fighters caught up with the bombers 20 miles outside their Kennel launching distance. Nine bombers were shot down, but three made it through to launch. Six Kennel missiles roared off to continue the attack. All three bombers fell to the Phantoms moments later.

Martin had his battle group reverse course, unmasking the three missile launchers he had. The *Galveston* began firing Talos missiles as soon as the turn was complete, taking advantage of the longer range of these missiles. The system, however, malfunctioned after six missiles were launched. His two guided missile destroyers, the USS *Sellars* and *Sampson,* began firing their Tartar missiles when the range closed to around 17 miles, but *Sampson's* missile control radar failed to guide. The remaining ships opened fire with 5-inch guns at five miles range.

Two Kennels fell to the missiles and guns. One barely missed the *Sampson,* detonating 50 yards off its port side. Its sister ship, the *Sellars,* was not as lucky. The missile slammed home, detonating the missile magazine and blowing the *Sellars* stern off. The third missile hit the *Galveston* amidships, tearing into the superstructure and exploding below the bridge. The warhead's explosion killed most of the Sixth Fleet staff, including Admiral Martin, and caused a massive fire. The final missile failed to lock on the wounded cruiser and targeted the *America* instead. However, the Kennel ran out of fuel and splashed into the ocean just short of the carrier. The fact that only a third of the bombers participated in the attack was not lost on Admiral Geis, who assumed command after Martin's death. Both he and his superiors in Washington recognized the demonstration for what it was. The demonstration had cost the US six F-4 fighters, the USS *Sellars* and heavy casualties on the *Galveston*. The Soviets had spent nine MiG-23s and 12 Tu-l6s to make their point. In no mood to compromise and with Congress supporting action, the US chose to respond.

Counter-Punch off Kithira

The Soviet Navy had negotiated an anchorage for their Mediterranean squadron at the southern end of the Greek island of Kithira with the previous left-wing Greek government. The island lay 50 miles northeast of Crete and 20 miles off the Greek mainland. Shortly after 0800, June 21, 1967, radar on a patrolling Soviet destroyer picked up low flying aircraft approaching the anchorage. There were 11 ships at anchor that morning, the largest being the *Kirov,* an all-guns cruiser. More importantly, all the service and support vessels for the squadron were there. In the three minutes between the first warning and the onslaught, these ships had little time to do anything other than man their guns.

Twenty A-4 Skyhawks of the *Saratoga's* VA-216 Black Diamond squadron swept in. A barrage of Shrike anti-radar missiles that preceded the A-4s nullified what missile defenses the Soviets had left, limiting the defense to 37mm and 45mm guns. One A-4 was shot down and four others damaged, but the attack devastated the anchorage. When the planes departed, *Kirov* was burning from eight 250kg bomb hits. The Soviets' only tanker was on fire and settling. One cargo ship had already capsized; another burned, throwing rockets of flaming debris from exploding ammunition all over the water. The stored torpedoes in the submarine tender *Victor Kotelnikov* blew up, ripped the big ship apart and sank the *Foxtrot* submarine moored next to it.

The loss of all their support vessels at Kithira put the Soviets in a difficult position, as the US had intended with its response; with the naval battles heightening global tensions, NATO member Turkey refused permission for other Soviet ships to transit the Bosphorus Straits from the Black Sea. Mediterranean options closed, the Soviets turned to the only card they had to play. Their troops in East Germany went to full alert and overtly began to prepare for battle.

The Soviets had three tank and two combined arms armies immediately available in East Germany. They massed some 370,000 men and 7,000 tanks in 20 divisions and were backed up by *16th Air Army's* 900 planes. Another 30 divisions were in various states of readiness in Poland and Czechoslovakia. The forward movement of men and materials transmitted the threat clearly to the United States and its NATO allies and they had no choice but to respond. Five American, four British, and 11 West German divisions went to full alert and began their move toward their forward defensive positions.

While world attention was fixed on the two superpowers, Israel completed over-running Sinai and the West Bank. Egypt lost over 90 percent of the tanks it had committed to the Sinai; Israel also captured 400 artillery pieces and nearly 10,000 military vehicles. Over 5,000 Egyptians had died with twice that many captured or missing. The Jordanians had lost 200 of their 270 tanks and 75 percent of their artillery along with 6,000 troops killed or missing. Israel had lost 600 dead and 2,500 wounded.

The battle left just one outstanding vulnerability to the country—the Golan Heights occupied by Syrian forces. On June 23, while diplomats traded accusations and NATO troops dug in to the German countryside, Israel attacked the Heights with an *ugdah* of nine infantry and four armored battalions. Twenty-four hours later, Syria began its own withdrawal.[20] By the end of the day, Israel held the Heights and had begun to dig in.

With Soviet tanks moving forward and NATO defenders digging in, the hot line between Moscow and Washington was used again. Neither Johnson nor Kosygin wanted the war that was brewing, so the two finally got past the finger-pointing stage, agreeing to let the United Nations investigate the events of 20-21 June. Word of the agreement spread and both sides began disengaging.

Conclusion

Very few changes in the world followed the close encounters of June 1967. The United Nations could not determine a clear cause or culprit for the naval clash off Suez, and both the US and USSR declared themselves the victims of aggression. Internally, both sides assessed the results and made improvements in their forces. Cruise missiles like the Shaddock had proved their power and both navies worked to gain offensive and defensive advantages from the new technology.

Elsewhere, the Soviets quietly removed certain key officials who had started the crisis moving. They covered this housecleaning with massive overt aid to the shattered Arab militaries. The US continued to support Israel. Arab and Israeli clashes continued as did the heated rhetoric. Fighting in Vietnam grew heavier; revolutionary wars, both pro-communist and pro-Western, cropped up sporadically. In short, the Cold War grew cold again.

Reality

Everything up to the results of Abba Eban's May 26 meeting with President Johnson is historically accurate. However, at that meeting, Johnson did not give Israel the assurances they wanted in lieu of a preemptive strike nor did he commit to any unilateral action. Other commitments and the current public fervor over Vietnam were too great. In addition, the Navy could not promise that the USS *Intrepid's* air group could take out all of the Egyptian batteries believed to be protecting the Strait, so the carrier was allowed to continue its journey to the Far East. This decision was a tribute to the excellent bluff by Nasser, as there were in fact no batteries in place at that time. Johnson simply told Eban that he could do little without Congressional support and told Israel not to attack. However, there was no real leverage applied to the Israelis to stop them from doing so.

With no overt US assistance and no US impediments to an attack, Israel formed its National Unity Government on June 1, 1967, the day after Jordan signed its defense pact with Egypt, making Moshe Dayan Defense Minister. On June 5, the Israeli Air Force attacked and destroyed the Egyptian Air Force in the space of a few hours, followed by a ground assault by Tal's, Yoffe's and Sharon's *ugdot*. The rest, as they say, is history. Six days later, Israel held the Sinai, West Bank, Jerusalem, and the Golan Heights.

During the crisis that it had itself created, the Soviet Union did reinforce its Mediterranean naval presence five fold, but that was the extent of its support to the Arabs. Already shocked at the uncontrolled nature of the events they had initiated, the Soviets were further stunned by the military reverses suffered by their clients. Although they succeeded in putting a major strain on US—Arab relations, they had also suffered a severe decline in their military reputation.

US and Soviet ships played tag, but held their tempers in check, even following the attack (by the Israelis, but unknown at the time) on the intelligence gathering ship USS *Liberty*. The Cold War had grown intense, but not hot.

Some final notes:

The problems the USS *America* had in fighting its deck and hangar fires were taken from actual events. On July 29, 1967, off Vietnam, an inadvertent missile launch on deck of the USS *Forrestal* (CVA.59) caused a massive fire and the destruction of some 64 aircraft and 134 lives. The problems cited in the fictitious *America* inquiry were those found in the *Forrestal* investigation.

The tanker *Coral Sea* was actually involved in a high seas incident when attacked by members of the Popular Front for the Liberation of Palestine.

On June 11, 1971, the PFLP fired bazookas from small boats at the ship, striking it seven times, but causing no serious damage.

The Soviet *Kynda* Class cruiser *Varyag* was available for deployment to the Mediterranean in June 1967, but the Soviets had become very nervous about Nasser's actions and held the anti-carrier cruiser in the Black Sea in order not to make the US Sixth Fleet too nervous.

On June 7, 1967, the USS *Lawe* had a "near collision" with a Soviet patrol craft, *PC-160*, which was maneuvering near the USS *America*. Admiral Martin had ordered the destroyer to clear the Soviet vessel out of the carrier's way.

The limitations cited for the US Navy's electronic suites for air searches and jamming were all too real during this period.

Bibliography

Bar-Siman-Tov, Yaacov, *Israel, the Superpowers, and the War in the Middle East,* Praeger, New York, 1987.

Bond, Larry, and Carlson, Chris, *HARPOON-4: Rules for Modern Tactical Naval Combat,* Clash of Arms Games, Phoenixville, PA, 1996.

Burdett, Winston, *Encounter with the Middle East: An Intimate Report o ' what lies behind the Arab-Israeli Conflict,* Atheneum, New York, 1969.

Dupuy, Trevor N., *Elusive Victory: The Arab-Israeli Wars, 1947–1974* Harper & Row, New York, 1978.

Gerges, Fawaz A., *The Superpowers and the Middle East: Regional tnd International Politics, 1955–1967,* Westview Press, Boulder, CO, 1994.

Glassman, Jon D., *Arms for the Arabs: The Soviet Union and War in thj Middle East,* John Hopkins University Press, Baltimore, MD, 1975.

Howe, Jonathan T, *Multicrises: Sea Power and Global Politics in tl Missile Age,* MIT Press, Cambridge, MA, 1971.

Laquer, Walter, *The Road to Jerusalem: Origins of the Arab-Isi eli Conflict, 1967,* MacMillan, New York, 1968.

Parker, Richard B., *The Politics of Miscalculation in the Middle Eas* Indiana University Press, Bloomington, IN, 1993.

Notes

1. In 1967 the United States only imported 20 percent of it il requirements, and most of that came from Venezuela. However, almost all s oil used by the US in Vietnam came from the Middle East.
2. Nasser's subversive activities among the Arab states   were widespread: his military attaches had been kicked out of Morocco,»   nisia, Libya, Sudan, Jordan, Syria, Iraq and Saudi Arabia at various times djig his presidency.
3. *Harakat al Tahrir al Falistine* (Movement for the Lib .tion of Palestine, or Fatah) was a Palestinian organization formed in 1959. II   ould   later merge with the Palestine Liberation Organization in 1968 and assij   2 a leadership role the following year. Fatah's military wing, Al-Asifa, carried) it its first cross-border raid into Israel on January 1, 1965.

4. In fact, the UN reacted more harshly to Israeli repii   ils than the raids that provoked them. The November 1966 reprisal raid on   lie Jordanian village of Samu by Israeli paratroopers and tanks, for example, turned into a four-hour pitched battle with Jordan's Arab Legion. The raid was censured by the United Nations, and Israel was warned that military reprisals "cannot be tolerated."

5. Herut joined forces with the Liberal Party of Israel, forming a party called Gahal. The merger gave the more radical Herut members a stronger political base to work from.

6. Soviet Ambassador Dmitri Pojidaev passed the information to Egyptian Foreign Under-Secretary Ahmad Hassan al Feki in Cairo. Soviet Deputy Foreign Minister Vladimir Semyenov informed National Assembly President Anwar Sadat as he was leaving Moscow for home. Finally a Soviet KGB officer passed the warning to Salah Nasr, Director-General of Intelligence in Egypt.

7. In February 1960, the Soviets had also warned Nasser of an Israeli threat to Syria that had resulted in an Egyptian build-up in Sinai on Israel's southern border. The Egyptians had stayed in the desert for several months before pulling out with no further confrontation.

8. Nasser had run a domestic anti-communist campaign in 1959 that resulted in the Egyptian Communist Party dissolving, much to the Soviets' embarrassment.

9. U Thant argued that since the UNEF positions were solely on the Egyptian side of the border, he was obliged to withdraw them if the host country requested it. Three of the UNEF contingents—India, Pakistan and Yugoslavia—agreed with him. Five contingents—Canada, Brazil, Denmark, Norway and Sweden—felt the UN General Assembly should have discussed the matter first.

10. This was in the public Soviet announcements. One of those publicly identified "carriers" was the USS *Valcour,* a former seaplane tender now acting as a fleet tactical command ship in the Red Sea. Privately, they assured Nasser that no US Marines were accompanying the Sixth Fleet and that their own *Fifth Eskadra* in the area would neutralize any Sixth Fleet naval threat.

11. Moshe Day an was the Israeli Chief of Staff and the prime architect behind the stunning Israeli victory in the 1956 Suez War.

12. In late May, Soviet Defense Minister, Marshal Gretchko, had told his Egyptian counterpart, Shamseddin Badran: "Stand firm. Whatever you face, you will find us with you. Don't let yourself be blackmailed by the Americans or anyone else." *Later, after his arrest and interrogation for crimes against the state, Gretchko insisted he was only trying to buttress Egyptian resolve.

13. The Super Sherman was a heavily modified version of the venerable US M4 Sherman medium tank of World War II fame. The French originally added a 75mm high velocity gun, calling it the M51HV The Israelis further modified the design to include a larger 105mm medium velocity gun, designating it the Super Sherman.

14. William I. Martin was a 1934 graduate of the US Naval Academy and an aircraft squadron commander from World War II, in which he won the Silver Star. After a stint as Assistant Chief of Staff of Naval Operations for Air, he was promoted and assigned as Commander Sixth Fleet in April 1967.

15. "Tattle tail" was the derisive term the US Navy coined for the small Soviet vessels that tagged along with their carrier battle groups. The name was appropriate since, in the event of hostilities, the Soviets would know where

to find the carriers. It was particularly worrisome to the US forces since they assumed the Soviets would strike without warning.

*16. The F-4 pilot Lt. Cdr. Mike "Paper Boy" Myron (he always delivers) was awarded the Navy Cross for his actions.

*17. While it is "common knowledge" that attack submarines accompany all US carrier battle groups, the US Navy has never publicly released this information. The identity of the submarine that took part in this battle is still classified.

*18. For his part in the battle, Khovrin was reassigned to the Pacific Fleet. However, in 1974, he returned to the region as the commander of the Black Sea Fleet.

*19. The formal *America* inquiry after the crisis cited the lack of damage control training, lack of good weapons handling procedures, poor fire protection on deck and unsafe aircraft fuel systems as contributors to the magnitude of the fire damage.

20. Syrian officials began their withdrawal after announcing the fall of Kuneitra following a "valiant defensive effort" by Syrian troops—hours before the Israelis even approached the city.

5
ANOTHER SAVAGE WAR OF PEACE
Quebec, 1968

Sean M. Maloney

Montreal: July 25,1967

"In a speech in Montreal today, French leader Charles de Gaulle publicly supported the creation of an independent Quebec nation. To a cheering crowd, President de Gaulle uttered the phrase 'Vive Quebec! Vive Quebec Libre!' Fifteen spectators were injured in the melee that ensued." *Associated Press, Toronto.*

Ottawa: July 26,1967

"Nobel Peace Prize winner Prime Minister Lester B. Pearson declared this evening on a Canadian Broadcasting Corporation broadcast that the French leader's remarks were improper and that no part of Canada needed liberation. President de Gaulle has been declared *persona non grata* in the Dominion of Canada..." *Canada Press, Montreal.*

Origins of the War

It was almost five years since the first bombs had gone off in Montreal during the spring of 1963- The shadowy operatives of several disparate separatist terrorist groups, the most prominent of which was called the Front de Liberation du Quebec, or FLQ, had blown up mail boxes in the predominantly English-speaking Westmount district and had hit several Militia armouries and a Royal Canadian Air Force establishment in the south end. The capture of one FLQ cell by the police in 1965 curtailed most of these activities, but the de Gaulle speech emboldened many into emulating the "felquists." Now the stock exchange and several corporate headquarters had been bombed, including those of Canadair, which manufactured and maintained the air force's CF-104 Starfighter nuclear strike aircraft. More and more rhetoric emerged through alternative media outlets that included a pirate radio station operating somewhere in the

Laurentians. Printed flyers were widely distributed calling for violent revolution, general strikes, and massed violence on a par with or accompanying the huge anti-Vietnam and Civil Rights demonstrations in the United States.[1]

Building A-114, CFB St Hubert

Colonel David Enfield trudged through the snow towards what appeared to be a disused building nestled in the heart of the Forces Mobile Command headquarters complex at Canadian Forces Base (CFB) St Hubert located near Montreal. As a liaison officer to the Royal Canadian Mounted Police and numerous Quebec provincial and municipal police agencies, Enfield probably knew more about the problem than any one organization and that was the reason for his presence in building A-114.

There was a special visitor today. The Minister of Justice demanded a briefing. The man did not dress like a cabinet minister, though he affected a superior attitude and tone. Pierre Elliott Trudeau wanted answers and he deflected Enfield's pleasantries: "Let's get on with it. I have to brief Cabinet this afternoon."

"You are aware, sir, that we have directed our efforts towards determining the level of international support for the FLQ."

"Yes, yes, of course."

"Our signals intelligence stations are usually used to provide us with early warning of a Soviet nuclear attack. Fortunately the Arctic station at CFS[2] Alert was able to catch several French diplomatic conversations. Similarly, the station at CFS Bermuda scooped up the communications between several merchant vessels and points ashore."

"Where?"

"Algeria, mostly; Cuba to a lesser extent. We believe that there are FLQ personnel aboard these ships. Our allied sources, particularly the Americans, are still sensitive about Cuba and take great pains to keep an eye on Castro's crew."

"It is, of course, no surprise that we have received nothing from the French about Canadians training in Algeria," Trudeau mused, "particularly after the shit that came out of de Gaulle's mouth."

Enfield continued as though he had heard nothing. "We are losing our picture of the FLQ that is already based in Canada. They have a cell structure, probably modeled on that of the FLN in Algeria. We even caught one group with a copy of the movie *Battle of Algiers*."

"Yes, I've seen it," Trudeau said impatiently. "Its *cinema verite* tone is matched only by its usefulness as a training film for guerrilla and terrorist groups."

"Well, they're getting nasty. The Montreal police have lost three informants. One was found dead with his genitals stuffed in his mouth, the other was crushed inside a cement mixer. The third just disappeared.

Our information is drying up and that is our primary weapon against these people. We don't want to resort to the same methods used by the British in Cyprus or Palestine. Our society cannot handle that level of brutality. Yet we cannot permit a home-grown FLN or Mau-Mau to destroy what we have built here. We need guidance on how to handle this one."

Trudeau's flight to Ottawa was brief. On arrival, he was immediately escorted to the East Wing to a special Cabinet sub-committee meeting. Pearson was interminable when it came to procedure, Trudeau reflected. It was too chaotic, not enough reason. This was no way to confront the FLQ. The PM was still basking in his Nobel Peace Prize and believed that anything could be settled through rational discussion. Yet Pearson indicated he would stay on for another term. The rumours were all wrong. Pearson was re-evaluating his image and had even employed the media theorist Marshall MacLuhan to assist. "Pearsonmania" was in the offing once he dispensed with that stupid bow tie and the affected academic lisp. He was not interested in hearing about a bunch of bomb-throwing anarchists in Quebec. There was little Trudeau could do convince the PM that a crisis was building.[3]

Quebec City

The MV *Champion* docked in Quebec City. Under the Citadel, a Vauban monstrosity overlooking the Old City, Pierre LeBlanc evaded the incompetent police observation and rendezvoused with a man with a dramatically turned up collar, his face hidden in the shadow of the building, a man who carefully cupped his cigarette when he lit it. In a modulated continental French, he asked LeBlanc: "Are we ready? How many?" LeBlanc's reply in colloquial Quebecois was affirmative: "The strike is set. The weapons are dispersed. We await one last cadre from Algiers. Then we can move."

"What about the Cuban element?"

"We have had no word as of yet."[4]

At that point, the Canadian destroyer HMCS *St Laurent* was in the process of intercepting a trawler off the coast of Nova Scotia. There was concern that the Soviets were using their fishing fleet covertly to support their forward-deployed submarines off the North American coast, a suspicion that was proven when the Navy deliberately tracked, harassed, photographed, and played chicken with the trawlers during Operation Grand Banks. This time, it was different. The target ship had no flag and was proceeding at dusk for the coast. It was also unresponsive to orders from the *St Laurent's* captain, who then ordered two 3.5-inch shots across the bow.[5]

"1800010367
To: CANCOMARLANT
From: HMCS ST LAURENT
Subject: Intercept of Trawler JOSE MARTI

a) Subject vessel boarded after two (2) hour pursuit.
b) Three (3) Cuban nationals apprehended: MARTINEZ, SANCHEZ, and RAUL. All claim diplomatic immunity.
c) Subject MARTINEZ does not fit physical profile of Spanish-speaking Caribbean native. Believe MARTINEZ is a citizen of east bloc nation.
<msg ends>"

Montreal, Quebec

The Montreal-based FLQ cells quietly swung into action in the late spring and early summer of 1968. Like any revolutionary terrorist organization, all cells operated independently of each other, except in extraordinary situations when Le Committee deemed it necessary. A propaganda cell at McGill University was short of funds, therefore a team was assembled to rob banks. Part of the money went to a third group which established two safe houses in a downtown row housing complex. Yet another drew on monies supplied from an offshore account in Liechtenstein to fund a select group of union leaders. Within days, Montreal was shut down. The students were on the streets, the transport trucks, busses, and taxicabs would not perform their duties, and the police were on strike. Premier Bourassa was forced to ask the Chief of Defence Staff for Aid to the Civil Power.

For those at Mobile Command HQ in St Hubert, this request was disconcerting. The Canadian land forces were structured primarily to deter a Soviet attack on NATO's Central Region in West Germany. One brigade group with its nuclear weapons was positioned there, with two earmarked mechanized brigades based in Canada prepared to deploy when war was declared. The other brigade group was an airportable formation for use in the defence of North America against Soviet airborne or amphibious incursions. As Canada had no de-colonization problem like the French, Belgians, Dutch, or British, there was no need to maintain a specialized counter-insurgency force.[6] The Americans were having enough problems adapting to Vietnam. Pearson would not permit funds for altering the role of the armed forces to participate alongside the United States in that adventure. Instead, excess funds were used in an elaborate scheme to improve the economic potential of Quebec. Pearson and others believed that the Quebecois could be bought off like any other Liberal Party crony. Didn't Lyndon Johnson think he could negotiate with Ho Chi Minh like he was just another senator or union leader?

Canada Press, Paris, October 16, 1968: "President de Gaulle assassinated. France in turmoil."

Associated Press, Paris, October 18, 1968: "Left-leaning 'Government of National Reconciliation' formed in France: Promises end to Cold War and increased co-operation with USSR."

Reuters, Washington, DC, October 18, 1968: "High-level diplomatic sources reveal French leadership infiltrated in 1940s by communist movement."

Associated Press, New York, October 19, 1968: "Defecting French military and intelligence leaders land at La Guardia. Claim Moscow is behind coup."

"Top Secret (Zed Plus)
To: Minister of National Defence
From: Chief of the Defence Staff
19 Oct 68
Ref: special information

Dear Colleague,
    My liaison officer in Washington has passed on information about the situation in Paris. As you can gather from your diplomatic counterparts, the situation is not as fluid as the journalistic community portrays it and the Soviets have by now gained significant leverage in French affairs. The Americans suspected for some time that the existence of the Sapphire espionage ring was not deception, though they did not trust their source one hundred percent due to his overly emotional involvement. Our sources tell us that members of Sapphire already constituted what amounted to a covert skeleton leadership group and were immediately deployed to take control. It is equally clear that all members of Sapphire are committed communists, some even having membership in the party dating back to before the Second World War. How they slipped through the screening process established in cooperation with The Org (Ghelen's organization) in West Germany is anybody's guess. CIA analysis passed to me suggests that France now constitutes a national security threat to Canada and any francophone nation not yet under communist control. We can expect that the range of subversive tactics that we have seen employed in Algeria will now be directed at us. The further weakening of NATO as a result of these recent events is cause for concern and may embolden individuals or groups to commit further acts which further Soviet aims.
    Sincerely,"[7]
    One of the NATO-tasked battalions was on standby in Quebec to assist with civil emergencies. The French-speaking 2nd Battalion, The Royal

22nd Regiment, or "Van Doos", was brought in to Montreal to take over from the police.

Corporal Michel Drapeau was standing on a street corner with his 10-man infantry section. Looting had broken out the night before and the quick reaction force company was deployed to contain the rioting, which was in the process of being mopped up with CS gas and riot batons. A ¾-ton army truck drove by loaded with troops carrying FNC1 assault rifles.

"Who're those guys?" asked Private Guy Lamontagne.

"Don't know. Are they from C Company?"

The truck stopped and the men jumped out to form a line facing a group of about 100 demonstrators. Before anybody could do anything, the five men raised their rifles and fired into the crowd. Blood flowed into the gutters and people scattered. Drapeau and Lamontagne fell to a burst of sub-machine-gun fire from behind.

Canada Press, Montreal, June 13, 1968: "Canadian troops kill 14 demonstrators, wound 30. Mass rioting broke out yesterday night as automatic weapons were fired into a crowd of peaceful demonstrators outside McGiU University. Two soldiers were subsequently beaten to death by the rampaging mob."

Ottawa, Canadian Forces HQ

"What the hell happened?" demanded the Justice Minister. Enfield lit a cigarette before replying.

"They were members of an FLQ cell which infiltrated a Militia unit. So they had the training on the weapons, knew military protocol, uniforms, the works. It gets worse. The armoury was emptied and we have no means of tracking the weapons. There are rumours of guerrilla training camps in the Laurentians and we have deployed CF-5 recce aircraft to find them, but without the imaging pods they can do very little."

"Pods?"

"Yes, sir," Group Captain Mallory piped up. "We asked for them in the last defence budget, but with the cuts and the drawdown in preparation to redeploying from Europe, acquisition was not authorized by your government."

"What is the situation in Montreal?"

"In effect, the provincial government has lost control of the downtown core. Bourassa will not authorize the deployment of more forces to break up this hedgehog. The police are not trained or equipped to handle it. He can't make up his mind."

"Prospects?"

"If we don't intervene now, they will *get* stronger, they will gain more sympathy, and we will be unable to dislodge them from this built-up urban area."

"But we have a large army, tanks, air support."

"Sir," Enfield said patiently, "We don't have the capability to conduct this sort of warfare. Tanks and air strikes are blunt instruments. We need a scalpel. The Prime Minister indicated in his last budget that we were to convert to a lightly-armed peacekeeping force and dispense with mechanized warfare. Neither capability can be used in this environment. The Americans have Special Forces to deal with this sort of thing, as did the French in Algeria and the British in Malaya. With the sparse budget and the selection of one type of mission for our forces, we are unable to operate across the spectrum of conflict. We have little flexibility which in turn limits the Government's options."

"Why can't you just take one of your infantry groups and re-train them?"

Enfield's infinite patience was almost at an end. "Sir, it takes *months*, maybe *years* to develop such a capability. We haven't the time. If we commit troops to this role, they might pull it off with improvization, but the chances are we'd plant a lot of Canadian boys in the ground."

Canada Press, Montreal, June 25, 1968: "'Commander Une' from the 'Montreal Liberated Zone' calls on federal government to recognize Quebec sovereignty."

Globe and Mail, June 27, 1968 (Montreal): "Bulgaria, Cuba, and Guinea call upon Canada to 'free Quebec' in UN session."

Toronto Telegram, June 28, 1968 (Hull): "Black Guard group kills family of four in Gatineau, claims revenge for 'Frog criminal actions' against English-speaking community."

Calgary Albertan, June 30, 1968 (Quebec City): "English-speaking residents of suburb driven away as homes burn: 50 die in flames."

"1 July 1968
Top Secret (Canadian Eyes Only)
To: Minister of National Defence
From: Secretary of State for External Affairs
Ref: special information

Dear Colleague,
    Thank you for your kind letter of June 30. The interception and analysis of French diplomatic traffic indicates that the French will be supporting a motion in the UN General Assembly to recognize an independent Quebec. They also plan to introduce a motion in the Security Council for a UN peacekeeping force to be deployed along the Ottawa River to 'separate' the English-speaking 'terrorist forces' from the French-speaking population. Their plan envisions a force more along the lines of the 1960-64 UN operation in the Congo rather than

a 'thin blue line' mission like UNEF in the Sinai. Keep in mind that the ONUC force acted more as a counter-insurgency force than a peacekeeping force: the Indian Canberra bombers and Irish light armoured units were used against anybody interfering with the central government. In this case, it is clear that any UN-led force operating in Canada will be used to further the agendas of those leading and participating in the force. Other SIGINT intercepts indicate that a number of states have been suborned by Paris into committing to the so called 'ONUCAN' force: Senegal, Mauritania, Gabon, Cameroon, Chad, Cuba, Yemen, Romania, and Indonesia. We believe that the Senegalese will act as the Paris puppet on this one by 'offering' to lead' ONUCAN. Yours,"[8]

Ottawa Citizen, July 7, 1968: "Where is the PM?"

Calgary Albertan, July 8, 1968: "Strong action demanded now, says Alberta Premier."

New York Times, July 8, 1968: "Why Canada matters: A report from our special correspondent."

"July 10, 1968
Top Secret (Canadian Eyes Only)
To: Secretary of State for External Affairs
From: Minister of National Defence
Ref: more special information

Dear Colleague,
    With the absence of any clear direction from Cabinet or the Prime Minister, it is critical we meet as soon as possible. A Supplementary Radio System intercept collected by our SIGINT station near Baden-SSllingen, West Germany (you will recall we moved our nuclear strike aircraft there after de Gaulle insisted we withdraw from our bases in France by 1966) indicates that rehabilitated OAS (that's 'Organisation Armee Secrete') terrorist personnel were infiltrated into Quebec last spring. It was, apparently, march or die for them. The intercept came from a station located at our now closed RCAF base at Grostenquin, France. It was logistical in nature, but it is the first clear evidence of direct French complicity. Please handle the information source discreetly as we do not want to compromise it. On another matter, I understand the Justice Minister is taking a firmer hand in things. Watch him carefully, my friend.
    Yours,"[9]

CFS Lamacaza, Quebec

The air force security team was shivering in the dank gloomy night. Canadian Forces Station Lamacaza had to be one of the most isolated stations south of the 51st Parallel and its personnel equally as bored as any of those serving on the Distant Early Warning Line in the Arctic. Lamacaza, however, had a different purpose. Airman John Forbes removed the magazine from his Sterling SMG and checked the action for the thousandth time. His two German shepherd companions whined and growled at each other softly. A twig snapped in the tree line on the other side of the double fencing festooned with razor wire. A swishing sound followed by a loud bang echoed over the compound as a paraflare illuminated the proceedings. Momentarily blinded by the light, Forbes dropped to one knee and pulled the SMG's stock to his shoulder. The dogs barked furiously. Four subdued "bloops" were heard in rapid succession.

The first mortar round missed but the second landed on the 150ft long rectangular roof of the shelter which in turn exposed its contents to a third and then fourth round. The cocooned Bomarc anti-bomber missile's solid fuel detonated, hurling the body containing the W-40 nuclear warhead through the side of an adjacent shelter into another Bomarc and the control surfaces into the air. One sliced through a missile technician, brutally ending his short 20-year life.

Forbes let the dogs loose and joined the other nine men sweeping the woods. FNC1 fire rained down on the team as they were caught in an ambush. Forbes and another man, Downs, opened up with short bursts, keeping the barrels on target. Men were screaming and commands shouted in French dominated the frenzied discourse. The dogs were upon some felquists as Downs and Forbes caught up with three wounded adversaries. As one of the fallen raised a 9mm Browning pistol, Downs emptied the remainder of the SMG's magazine into his chest.

"From: Northern NORAD Region, North Bay
To: CinCNORAD, Cheyenne Mountain Complex
BENT SPEAR

a) 447 SAM Sqn attacked by unknown elements.
b) Missile status: eight (8) CIM-66 missiles destroyed, six (6) damaged, fourteen (14) functioning.
c) Special Ammunition Storage Site NOT, NOT, compromised.
d) Functioning missiles not operational due to contamination by nuclear materials scattered around the site.
e) Fifteen (15) personnel KIA, forty-six (46) WIA. Opposition forces: five (5) KIA, null (0) WIA. Heavy weapons captured.
f) Station commander has declared CFS Lamacaza non-operational for NORAD duty.
<msg ends>"[10]

Canadian Cabinet Security Committee: July 13,1968

Justice Minister: "Where is the PM?"

< deleted from recording >

SSEA:[11] "The US State Department has issued us a formal request through the Permanent Joint Board on Defence. The McGovern transition team wants to deploy American forces to Canada under the auspices of the Ogdensburg Agreement of 1940."

Finance Minister: "We have no choice. We can't handle this on our own now."

Justice Minister: "Oh, bullshit."

Defence Minister: "CinC NORAD is going berserk. There are only ten Bomarc sites, two of which we control, and the destruction at Lamacaza leaves a huge gap in the air defence system. We don't have the resources to cover the gap, since we drew down the number of manned interceptor squadrons last year. This compromises NORAD's ability to deter and defeat a manned bomber attack against critical industrial areas and SAC bases. This in turn compromises Strategic Air Command's ability to carry out its mission, which is fundamental to the deterrent strategy of NATO."

Chief of the Defence Staff: "We are in a stalemate. We deployed two of our available three brigade groups to Quebec and they control access to Montreal, but not the core of the city itself, nor the airbase at Lachine. CF-101 Voodoo interceptors control the airspace; they already shot down an unmarked transport that tried to get into Lachine with Eastern-bloc weapons on board. We lack the manpower we require for fighting in built-up areas. As you will recall, the Militia is seriously undermanned and five years ago training shifted to National Survival rescue missions, not combat missions. The airportable brigade group is our strategic reserve. It was in the process of converting to an airmobile formation with helicopters, but those machines have not yet arrived, nor have the pilots been trained. A paradrop into the city would be suicidal, like Arnhem in the last war. We estimate that it will take several weeks to mount an operation to retake the city."

SSEA: "Our diplomats in Moscow believe that the Soviets may soon call upon the communist world for a multinational force of transport aircraft to 'relieve the besieged city of Montreal,' sort of a reverse Berlin Airlift."

Finance Minister: "This is shocking. What would the Americans do?"

Minister without Portfolio: "Can we negotiate? Perhaps develop some form of joint sovereignty like the British and the Palestine Mandate? Or Cyprus?"

Justice Minister: "Look where that got them."

Chief of Defence Staff: "Sir, we recommended against the deep cuts to the armed forces, but we were cavalierly ignored. These are the consequences of a lack of preparedness. We insisted on having the capability and the numbers to fight across the spectrum of conflict, but you people denied us the resources. Our critical front line role with NATO in Europe was and is the keystone of our strategy in the Cold War and rightly so. Other armies are able to handle multiple missions, but you didn't want us to, particularly after the TV footage of how the Americans are fighting in Vietnam. What would you have us do?"

Justice Minister: "We can bring back our forces stationed in West Germany."

Chief of Defence Staff: "With all due respect sir, to do what? The CF-104s are equipped with nuclear weapons. We can't use those here in this situation. 4 Canadian Mechanized Brigade Group is equipped with Centurion tanks, Bobcat armoured personnel carriers, Bobcat self-propelled artillery, and Honest John nuclear rockets. It is designed to deter and defeat a Soviet attack against NATO in Europe, not crawl down sewers and alleys in downtown Montreal. SACEUR tells me that if we withdraw this formation from Northern Army Group, his defensive plans in that region will lack credibility; he has no other formations available, and the Soviets might exploit that. I recommend leaving it in place."

Defence Minister: "The intelligence coordination centre confirms that the revolution is spreading into the Quebec hinterland. We no longer have the propaganda resources to counter that since the CBC[12] facilities in Montreal are all in the hands of the rebels. We need to act now."

Minister for Health and Welfare: "What are the options?"

Clerk of the Privy Council: "I had my staff develop some ideas. May I present them?"

Justice Minister: "By all means."

Clerk of the Privy Council: "There are three. First, we can request UN assistance under Article 51 to pre-empt the French proposal. The problem is that they have their hooks into the Chinese and Soviet reps on the Security Council and are ahead of us in that game."

Agricultural Minister: "That would be ironic: asking Greece, Turkey, Egypt and Israel for a peacekeeping force...

Clerk of the Privy Council: Quite. "There is the American option: we can request assistance under the terms of our bilateral defence relationship in the Military Cooperation Committee and Permanent Joint Board on Defence."

Justice Minister: "Once in, they might not leave. It would cause irreparable damage to our national psyche which is predicated on the fact that we are not American."

Clerk of the Privy Council: "We could also ask for assistance under NATO Article 5: An attack against one is an attack against all. Or the Commonwealth."

Health and Welfare Minister: "Somehow I think that Ghana, Malaysia, New Zealand, and Australia wouldn't be crazy about deploying troops to Canada for the long term, particularly in the dead of winter."

Agricultural Minister: "What about Rhodesia? South Africa?"

< comments deleted >

Postmaster General: "Nigeria is dealing with a separatist problem now with Biafra. Perhaps we could learn something from them."

< comments deleted >

Justice Minister: "The NATO option has promise. It keeps the Third World out of our affairs, it counterbalances predominant American power, and NATO is predicated on the UN anyway as a regional organization under Article 51. Let the Europeans come to our aid for a change."[13]

Canada Press, Brussels, July 14, 1968: "Canadian Ambassador requests NATO assistance to repel attack on Canadian sovereignty."

Associated Press, Brussels, July 16, 1968: "Canadian requests for collective defence fall on deaf ears: How soon they forget."

Ambassador Cadieux was furious and his first secretary knew it. "Those bastards!" he swore as he launched a glass ashtray across the room, "80,000 Canadians die for the protection of Western Europe in two world wars and they *want to debate it?*" The ashtray shattered against a framed Tom Thompson print on the wall.

"Well," his assistant noted, "We do have backing from the UK and the Americans. We can put the arm on the Dutch and maybe the Belgians: we helped them out in West New Guinea in 1962 and in the Congo in 1960. They owe us. Write off the Scandinavians. And Portugal, since we didn't support them joining the Alliance in the first place. Forget Greece and Turkey: neither is impressed with us over Cyprus in 1964 and 1967. As for Italy and West Germany, the Canadian people will probably balk at allowing former Axis power troops on our soil. Italy isn't too crazy about this anyway."

"20071967
To: SACEUR
From: CFHQ/CDS personal
Ref: Canada's NATO Commitments

> This message is to inform SHAPE that 4 Canadian Mechanized Brigade Group will be withdrawn from NATO's Central Region within one week. Furthermore, the other two brigade groups dedicated to SHAPE'S Strategic Reserve are as of this point removed as earmarked NATO forces. The ACE Mobile Force commitment provided by two Canadian battalion groups to Norway and Turkey is also withdrawn.

We deeply regret these moves but the nature of the national emergency in Canada and the unwillingness of NATO nations to come to our aid dictates this action. 1 Canadian Air Division will remain in Europe as it constitutes 23 percent of SHAPE'S aerial nuclear striking force in the Central Region.
<msg ends>"[14]

"21071967
To: Canadian Minister of National Defence
From: SACEUR
Ref: Canada's NATO Commitments

The withdrawal of 4 CMBG will open a serious gap in the main defensive position of NORTHAG. With little or no warning Warsaw Pact forces have the capability to attack in the I (British) Corps with a minimum force of five divisions. By moving Warsaw Pact forces forward, this capability would be increased to 12 divisions. Should forward forces not be capable of containing an attack, a withdrawal to more favourable main defensive positions would be mandatory. 4 CMBG is tasked with organizing this position. Without this force in prepared defensive positions, the forward units in contact would not be capable of being reinforced to allow orderly transition to the main defensive battle. This could increase the likelihood of the early use of nuclear weapons.
<msg ends>"[15]

CFB Trenton, Ontario

The first troops from West Germany were arriving by Yukon strategic transport at CFB Trenton, Ontario. It would be some weeks before the vehicles, artillery, and heavy equipment showed up and until that time 4 Canadian Mechanized Brigade Group's personnel were crammed into every nook and cranny in eastern Ontario with their personal weapons and equipment. They replaced the men from 2 Canadian Infantry Brigade Group, who were then deployed to re-take the St Lawrence Seaway so that American shipping from the Great Lakes could gain access to the Gulf of St Lawrence and thus the Atlantic.

The base at Trenton was overcrowded. The Quebec People's Militia (QPM) had overrun CFB Bagotville airbase north of Quebec City the preceding week. It was only by sheer luck that the nuclear MB-1 Genie air-to-air rockets for the CF-101 Voodoos were evacuated in time by American C-141 Starlifter transports. Most of the Alouette Squadron escaped, but their ground crews were not so lucky. After a pitched battle, the base security force was overrun by superior numbers and most of the base was seized intact. The NORAD-tasked radar stations in the region were also abandoned, which left a huge hole in radar coverage behind the DEW Line.

If the Soviet bomber force attacked, NORAD would be unable to direct interceptors against them until they were much further south. By that time they would be in range of the SAC bases at Plattsburg AFB and Griffiths AFB in New York, or Loring AFB in Maine.

The officers and men from the 1st Battalion, Royal Highland Regiment of Canada (The Black Watch), were quartered at CFB Kingston, east of Trenton, almost half way to Montreal. Captains John Llambias and Deryk Gravelle pondered their lot. The Yukon flight had been bone jarring and sleep had been impossible. Several gin and tonics at the Vimy Officer's Mess eased their pain. The Watch were without their Bobcat APCs and were adapting to light infantry tactics once again.

"What's the word? Where to? Straight downtown?" Llambias asked.

"You still know those Int people?"

"Yeah, but they're tight lipped as usual."

"So what is B Company training for?"

"We keep loading onto the Hercs, fly around a bit at night, and then land at some old British Commonwealth Air Training Plan airfield near Gananoque, pour out and run. Nobody knows nothing."

The colonel stalked in. "Gentlemen, it's on. Return to your platoons. We are on two hours notice to move as of now."[16]

Gravelle and Llambias were loaded into separate C-130s. Their men lounged the best they could around several jeeps equipped with 106mm recoilless rifles. After a sickening drop, the Hercs thumped down. As the engines screamed and brakes screeched, the ramps were down and the men of 1 RHR of C poured out into a dark occasionally studded with green tracer fire. The former RCAF station Lachine, in the process of being converted to an international airport, was on the southern outskirts of Montreal. Gravelle and his men, assigned to seize the terminal buildings, roared up on their jeeps and engaged the FLQ fighters with 106mm fire at near point-blank range. The bulky infrared gear, some of it mounted on the weapons with reams of black tape, gave them the advantage.

Two FLQ-manned 40mm Bofors guns posed serious problems, however, once their stunned crews recovered. A Buffalo transport in the process of landing was turned into a smoking ruin on the runway, as were the 30 men aboard. Llambias' platoon had an SS-11 ATGM mounted on a jeep. The gunner brought the specially stabilized binoculars up to his face and gripped the joystick. "Firing now!" The French-made anti-tank missile peeled off the rail mounted on the back of the jeep. The shaped charge made contact with the makeshift shield of the Bofors (they were scrounged from a naval depot and destined for one of the Navy's aircraft carriers) and detonated with a thump, destroying the crew with the gun.

As day broke, the men of the Black Watch surveyed the situation. They held the field and its facilities. There had been no felquists in the area beyond those who were manning Lachine, and all of these had been killed or captured. A throng of Montreal suburbanites blocked the main gate, but they were dispersed with machine-gun fire directed over their heads. Anybody who threw a rock was shot to deter further aggressive activity.

Gravelle was talking to Captain Theo Heuthorst, one of the Here pilots: stray machine-gun fire had severed several of the aircraft's vital organs and it was stranded for the time being.

"What have you heard?"

"The Dutch have flown in a marine battalion. They're holding the Ottawa-Hull area to free up troops for Montreal. The Americans moved parts of the 82nd Airborne Division to Plattsburg and mobilized the New York, Vermont, Maine, and New Hampshire National Guards to patrol the border. I was talking to a C-141 crew after the Bagotville affair. They tell us that there aren't enough American forces, that they're so committed to Vietnam, Laos, and elsewhere, that its going to take time for them to put something together. There's a lot of rioting in Los Angeles and Detroit. The US Air Force wants to solve the whole Quebec thing with fighter-bombers, but Ottawa won't let them use napalm or any of the other assorted weapons they're employing in Southeast Asia."

"What about the British? We hear they're in New Brunswick."

"Yeah, we caught that, too. They're stretched pretty thin as well: all over the Persian Gulf, Northern Ireland, Biafra, and Malaysia. I saw some at Fredericton when we dropped off 1 Canadian Guards at CFB Gagetown. They looked like airborne guys, but they had a beige beret, not a maroon one, and it had this dagger with wings on it. We heard from the Argus antisubmarine patrol boys that they bagged a Soviet submarine trying to land shit to the FLQ forces operating near Quebec City. 5 Brigade was evacuated from CFB Valcartier north of Quebec City. The insurgency seems to be centred around Montreal, or so the CF-5 jocks say. We hear weird stuff, like the Soviets sending in a special team to strip the radar sites near Bagotville and get int on our air defence system. Or that they've given the Fclquists chemical weapons or worse..."[17]

The roar of jet engines drowned out Heuthorst's words. Without warning, five C-l4ls landed in succession and taxied to the unfinished hangar area. Men wearing camouflaged uniforms and sporting green berets with a Trojan Horse insignia ran up to Gravelle and Heuthorst.

"I'm Major Tannenger. Who's in charge of security here?"

Heuthorst gawked as several unwieldy objects were extracted from the insides of the C-14ls and then moved into the hangars. Llambias met some of the Special Forces personnel in the makeshift ops room. "Bear any burden, eh?" he grinned. They gave the thumbs up.

Within hours, a complete US Army Ranger company had been flown in. Centurion tanks and Lynx reconnaissance vehicles from 8th Canadian Hussars moved in from their staging areas near Oka and secured the

Lachine perimeter. Brigadier-General David Soper briefed the senior officers commanding the activities at the airport.

"Gentlemen, this is the outline plan for Operation Grab Bag: the seizure of the political leadership of the separatist movement and the destruction of the FLQ/QPM command complex. Intelligence sources indicate that they are co-located in the Queen Elizabeth Hotel in downtown Montreal. The combined US—Canadian force, using the element of surprise, will proceed by air, secure the operations zone, raid the offices and extract or kill all personnel on the fourth and fifth floor. Any obviously foreign support or liaison staff are to be captured for interrogation. A ground force based on a truck-mounted Dutch parachute battalion will proceed from CFB St Hubert east of Montreal to the hotel and extract the prisoners. Detailed orders will follow within the hour. I know there isn't the usual amount of planning time, but the target is fleeting and the opportunity must be seized. Go prepare your men."

The objects delivered by C-141 were US Army helicopters, a mixture of UH-1 Iroquois and AH-1 Cobra gunships. The Cobras were equipped with 20mm and 7.62mm Gatling guns, while the Iroquois were stripped down for speed. The force flew off just before dawn, low over the suburbs and swooped down on the QE hotel. Things started to go wrong immediately. The FLQ, it was later discovered, were equipped with experimental SAM-7 shoulder-launched surface-to-air missiles. Examples had been used by the Viet Cong against American forces in Vietnam, but security prevented wide distribution of the knowledge. In minutes, the radio net was jammed with reports of "Iroquois down!"

Several squads were scattered all over the area. The survivors regrouped and stormed the QE to find that most of the FLQ leaders had evacuated. Cobras prowled the urban canyons looking for targets, but were unable to find any masses of enemy forces for their weapons. The Dutch, however, had a tough time. They were ambushed trying to get to the downtown core by FLQ teams armed with RPG anti-tank weapons and masses of civilians hurling Molotov cocktails hastily made from the Esso and Shell gas stations along the route. After suffering heavy casualties, the Dutch withdrew into another ambush and, after losing more men, eventually limped back to St Hubert. Gravelle's platoon scored a success, however. A team of three Algerian advisors was apprehended, while the Rangers caught a Cuban who claimed his name was Chabot. Moving from alley to alley, the force's remnants were eventually extracted by helicopter from the roof of a hockey rink.

In the boiler room of the Lachine terminal building, one of the "Algerians" broke after hours of intense interrogation. "I am Major Pierre Langois of the French Army... "he gasped. Langois proceeded to spill hi guts into a microphone for the benefit of the intelligence unit's reel to reel tape recorder.

"5 August 1968
Top Secret (Canadian Eyes Only)
To: Justice Minister
From: Minister of National Defence
Ref: LANGOIS interrogation

My dear colleague,
    The following points emerge from the interrogation:
    1) A French covert unit which included OAS persons committed the murders in Gatineau and elsewhere. The Black Guard organization does not exist.
    2) Soviet Bloc equipment is trickling past our naval forces but not in large quantities.
    3) The FLQ has expanded its cell structure to Metis areas in Manitoba and Acadian areas in northern New Brunswick.
    4) The QPM continues to expand guerrilla operations in the hinterland but does not have enough trained manpower even to conduct small unit operations. The blockade prevents them from acquiring enough heavy weapons to equip such forces.
    5) Former Militia personnel have been consolidated into three light infantry battalions and possess enough equipment and ammunition to conduct effective defensive operations in Montreal. Another battalion is in Quebec City.
    Sincerely,"[18]

Canadian Cabinet Foreign Affairs Committee: August 15,1968

Secretary of State for External Affairs: "Our attempts to use the Langois transcripts in the North Atlantic Council to force NATO members to censure France have failed. We cannot, obviously, use the taped recordings..."

Justice Minister: "Clearly, no..."

Secretary of State for External Affairs: "The McGovern administration is in the process of extricating itself from Vietnam and trying to maintain peace in the continental United States. The demonstration in Washington, DC, yesterday required an entire infantry brigade to contain."

Minister of National Defence: "We are hearing disturbing things from our counterparts in West Germany. Some bright light in the Bonn government named Egon Bahr is proposing the eventual unification of East and West Germany after a warming up period he calls Ostpolitik. We understand that there are many who support such a move."

Secretary of State for External Affairs: "Our embassy in Bonn confirms this. Furthermore, our intelligence sources in West Germany tell us that there was a secret meeting between representatives of the West German government and the Soviet Union. We can only speculate about what this means, but it will mean the end of NATO as we know it."

Chief of Defence Staff: "West Germany about to go, France gone, the Scandinavians questionable, Turkey and Greece at each other's throats over Cyprus. Italy marginalized by its revolving door government. The Americans distracted... That leaves us, the Dutch, Portuguese, and the British."

Justice Minister: "Is your briefer here yet?"

Chief of Defence Staff: "He was delayed. The transport he was on was hit by anti-aircraft fire coming out of St Hubert."

Colonel Enfield: "Gentlemen."

Chief of Defence Staff: "Please continue, Colonel."

Colonel Enfield: "Discussions with the Americans in the Military Cooperation Committee have given us a better appreciation of the situation. Word came through this morning that Bonn has ordered the withdrawal of all NATO-tasked forces from West Germany."

< shocked gasps >

Unidentified: "Shit!"

Colonel Enfield: "The American view (Administration and Joint Chiefs of Staff) is that we no longer have a credible deterrent system in place. First, the deterrent forces in the NATO Central Region, with the withdrawal of the Canadian Brigade Group from NORTHAG, are no longer able to defeat a Warsaw Pact attack and would have to resort to theater nuclear weapons' use."

Chief of the Defence Staff: "So? We have that capability."

Colonel Enfield: "Bonn will no longer permit the use of nuclear weapons on its soil and is trying to revoke strike plans which include dumping about 100 MT-yield weapons on targets in East Germany. There are other problems. The destruction of NORAD-tasked air defence facilities in Quebec compromises the ability of the continental air defence system to protect the SAC bombers in the short term. This degrades the strategic nuclear deterrent, which we need to back up any military action we take in Europe. In short, we don't have the means to deter Warsaw Pact actions in Western Europe and the Mediterranean. Intelligence projections suggest that Moscow is going to move on Prague and crush the 'socialism with a human face' experiment there. They could just as easily take those forces and direct them into West Germany if Bonn 'invited' them in."

Justice Minister: "So: we are faced with Fortress North America with its British outpost near Europe. Remarkably like 1940?"

Chief of Defence Staff: "Yes, it is, isn't it?"[19]

Associated Press, Berlin, October 17, 1968: "A Neutral Germany Reunifies, with Soviet Security Guarantees."

Reuters, October 17, 1968: "North Atlantic Treaty Organization Dissolves."

Reuters, October 20, 1968: "Greece signs mutual defence pact with Soviet Union, Turkish forces invade Cyprus."

Associated Press, October 21, 1968: "Italy, France and Spain invited to join European Peace Community in Berlin."

Staff Sergeant Bob Dolan and his team from Hereford worked their way slowly through the forest in the hills north of Hull. The Australians were operating to their west and he was concerned that there be no "blue on blue" action. Fratricide would screw up this very important mission. The SAS were leading the final stages of Operation Shelf Life, designed to wipe out guerrilla activity north of the capital. Using the techniques he learned in Malaysia when operating against the Indonesians, Dolan was able to identify two enemy company group areas. Air strikes were called in on the largest group because it was located in several buildings. The CF-5s rolled in and dropped napalm, which made that group of guerrillas "combat ineffective." The Quick Reaction Force, which consisted of a company from Deryk Gravelle's Black Watch battalion flown in by Iroquois choppers, swept in on another and made short work of them in a sustained firefight.[20]

Far, far to the east, the Centurion tanks of the 8th Canadian Hussars and the Fort Garry Horse supported the Queen's Own Rifles in vicious house-to-house fighting in Montreal. An American mechanized brigade from the 23 rd Americal Division was making slow progress on their right flank and a breakthrough was desperately needed. New units had been raised and trained: the 2nd Canadian Sikh Battalion from Toronto was deploying to the eastern townships to root out FLQ activity there, while The Oka Rangers, a special operations unit consisting mostly of native North Americans, provided critical reconnaissance information for their efforts.

It would be a long, savage fight.

The Reality

Practically all of the American and British literature dealing with counter-insurgency and counter-terrorism ignores the fact that Canada was probably the only NATO country which disrupted and destroyed a cell-based revolutionary terrorist movement before it could cause serious damage to the polity. Canadian planners believed that the FLQ and its related support structures were progressing through a four-step revolutionary programme that would progress from political mobilization to open armed conflict. Canada's strategy was to disrupt the transition from urban terrorism to small-unit operations in the hinterlands. The sudden mass deployment of the armed forces in 1970 to support intelligence and police operations in Quebec administered the *coup de grace* to a revolutionary effort which started in 1963.

In addition to carrying out an ambitious seven-year bombing campaign, kidnapping a British diplomat and murdering a Cabinet minister, the FLQ infiltrated the Militia to get training and stole vast numbers of military weapons including anti-tank weapons and assault rifles. An FLQ attack against the nuclear weapons facility at CFS Lamacaza was disrupted before it could be executed. Some FLQ members were, in fact, trained in Algeria by the FLN, and de Gaulle gave public moral support to that enterprise. At the height of the 1970 crisis, an Arab terrorist cell was intercepted infiltrating Canada. The Black Guard group did exist. American covert military support to Canadian Army operations was also a factor in the 1970s' operations.

If, however, the FLQ had significantly more political and diplomatic support from external sources, particularly a destabilized and alienated France, the situation would have been very different. France herself was in a great deal of turmoil at the time and the list of reasons is nearly endless: Algeria, American dominance of NATO strategy, the Berlin and Cuban crises, nuclear weapons command and control, the exclusion of the United Kingdom from the new economic relationship in Europe. It is clear that the social dislocation generated during the 1960s was widespread in Europe and North America and did not necessarily need an abundance of direct support from the Soviet Union. Indirect support, however, in the form of training, propaganda, diplomatic manipulations and the right circumstances could produce a situation benefiting the Soviet Union far beyond its expectations or planning. It would only take the will to exploit such a situation. Linking the French situation with Soviet aims could have easily produced the catastrophe depicted herein, if it occurred at a critical time coincident to developments in Quebec.

Author's note. Bruce Powe (under the pseudonym Ellis Portal) generated a similar scenario in his well-written and fascinating but unjustifiably obscure 1968 novel *Killing Ground.* My take on events, though similar in some ways to Powe's, differs significantly in the effects of such a crisis on NATO, NORAD, and the Canada-US relationship. I have also drawn on my knowledge of Canadian national security policy formulation and military capabilities during the Cold War era, including recent access to declassified Cabinet and intelligence sources.

Bibliography

Black, Eldon, *Direct Intervention: Canada-France Relations, 1967-1974*, Carleton University Press, Ottawa, 1996.

Bosher, J.F., *The Gaullist Attack on Canada 1967-1997*, McGill-Queen's University Press, Kingston, Ontario, 1999.

Lisee, Jean-Frangois, *In The Eye of the Eagle: Secret Files Reveal Washington's Plans for Canada and Quebec*, HarperCollins, Toronto, 1990.

Maloney, Sean M., *War Without Battles: Canada's NATO Brigade in Germany, 1951-1993*, McGraw-Hill Ryerson, Toronto, 1997.

Maloney, Sean M., "A Mere Rustle of Leaves: Canadian Strategy and the 1970 FLQ Crisis," *Canadian Military Journal*, Vol. 1 No. 2. Summer 2000, pp. 73-86.

Porch, Douglas, *The French Secret Services: A History of French Intelligence from the Dreyfus Affair to the Gulf War*, Farrar, Strauss and Giroux, New York, 1995.

Powe, Bruce, *Killing Ground: The Canadian Civil War*, Peter Martin Associates, Toronto, 1968.

Notes

*1. I would like to thank Major-General John Grodzinski of the Directorate of Corporate Memory for access to valuable primary sources used in the production of this study.

2. CFS: Canadian Forces Station.

*3. See Peter Archambault, Between Faith and Reality: The Impact of Ayn Rand on Canadian National Security Policy (Toronto: University of Toronto Press, 2008), pp. 232-45.

*4. I am indebted to my student Jason Blake for this insight into Afro-Caribbean political connectivity during the Cold War from his unpublished PhD dissertation: "Death to Truth: The Untold Story of Cold War Africa."

*5. Michael Hennessy and Michael Whitby, Uncle Louis's Destroyers At War: The St Laurent Class from Design to Dismemberment, 1950-1990 (Ottawa: Queen's Printers, 2010), pp. 231-34.

*6. Richard Martin: "The Origins of Canadian Stabilization Operations: Licking the Coin, 1955-1975," unpublished PhD dissertation, Royal Military College, 2005.

7. For more on Sapphire, see Porch, *The French Secret Services*, pp. 410-17.

*8. National Archives of Canada, Manuscript Group 666, volume 107 file: "Political Violence in Occupied Quebec."

*9. *Ibid.*

*10. As quoted in David A. Rosenberg's "Operation RIVET: Arleigh Burke, Nuclear Weapons, the FLQ Crisis, and the Collapse of NORAD," *International Security*, Vol 900 No. 4 Winter 2006, pp. 392-96.

11. Secretary of State for External Affairs: Canada's equivalent to the Secretary of State or Foreign Secretary.

12. Canadian Broadcasting Corporation: Government-run propaganda department like the British BBC, but not as insightful and much more prone to bias.

*13. The full version of this transcript, which included blood and coffee stains, was sent to the author anonymously in a brown envelope. A version with sections redacted by Access to Information officers from the Ministry of Truth also acquired by the author conforms to the brown envelope version.

*14. National Defence, Directorate of Corporate Understanding, RG 200, file "NATO and Canada."

15. This quote is based on part of a real message sent by SACEUR (General Andrew Goodpaster) to Canada's Minister of National Defence (Leo Cadieux) in 1969. In reality it contributed to preventing the pull out of Canadian forces from NATO commands in Europe. See Maloney, *War Without Battles*, Chapter 4.

*16. John Llambias and Deryk Gravelle, *Up Yer Kilt! The Black Watch Goes to War 1951–69* (Vanwell Publishing, St Catherines, 2006), p. 450 and its sequel, *If It Isn't Scottish, It's Crap! The Black Watch Goes to War 1970–2001* (Vanwell Publishing, St Catherines, 2008), pp. 8–25.

*17. As quoted in Scott Robertson's in-progress unpublished monograph: "Strike Hard, Strike Sure, Strike Now, Or Else: The RCAF and the FLQ War." (Directorate of Corporate Memory, 2003).

*18. Interview with Brigadier-General G. Ohlke, Directorate of Counter-subversion and Defender of the Faith, 23 May, 2005.

*19. This transcript was located in the McGovern Papers manuscript group at the McGovern Commemorative Library and Shrine, file 1970. The usefulness of Canada's critical and important relationship to the United States during the Cold War was violently questioned by representatives of the moribund US diplomatic historical establishment during a Temple University conference in the spring of 1998. The author was present for the exchange and instrumental in demonstrating that such negative views were patently false and based on an arrogant and narrow-minded conception of North American affairs.

*20. Andy Maloney, *Bravo Uniform Lima Lima: The Untold Story of the SAS in Canada, 1969–1975* (Winged Dagger Press, Lausanne, 2004), p. 112.

6
A FRATERNAL WAR
The Sino-Soviet Disaster, 1968

Forrest R. Lindsey

"We will not conceal [that] we are seriously concerned with the fact that differences which have arisen are constantly becoming deeper and the scope of the questions under debate is constantly widening, while the sharp public polemics are assuming forms impermissible in relations among Marxists-Leninists."
Chairman Mao Tse-tung, Peking Review, November 29, 1963[1]

Sergei Efremovich Ivanov was in a hurry. A short, white-haired man with a cigarette in his stained hand and a perpetual stooped-forward posture, he moved with little grace to collect his materials and get to the parking lot where his driver awaited him. In less than an hour he was expected to present to the full Presidium and the Central Committee a definitive prediction of American responses to a set of Soviet courses of action. Ivanov was no stranger to these upper echelons of Soviet power since he had been uncannily accurate in his assessments of American intent in the past. From his office in his branch of the Committee for State Security, he had correctly framed the American responses or lack of responses to potentially dangerous international situations many times before and each time he had provided exactly the correct assessment. Each time he was rewarded with yet another step upward in rank and another office closer to the Kremlin. His kind of prescience was rare and the decision makers of the Soviet Union kept him close by, so close that he had not spent a weekend at his *dacha* with his family in nearly a year. Crisis tended to follow crisis lately as the Cold War waxed and waned. Today the rumors of war were again in the wind and the clear, unvarying accuracy of Ivanov's analyses was needed.

The United States of America and its allies, the member nations of NATO and SEATO, had formed a formidable block to Soviet power since just after the end of the Great Patriotic War. On the surface, they appeared to form an unbreakable wall around the Soviet Union, the Warsaw Pact countries and their socialist allies. However, various episodes, starting with the posturing around the blockade of West Berlin, then the ineffectual threats against the suppression of the Hungarian counter-rev-olutionaries, then their withdrawal of intermediate range nuclear missiles from Turkey in the face of Soviet missiles in Cuba, demonstrated that the capitalist powers were weak. The final *piece de resistance* was America's removal of its military advisors and aid from Vietnam and the unopposed success of the communist revolution there. Ivanov had already made his mark before this, but it was his flawless prediction that President Johnson would refuse to commit American ground forces to a war in Vietnam that guaranteed his fame. With this assessment, the Soviets moved to ramp up their support of the forces under Ho Chi Minh and, surprisingly quickly, the Saigon regime was overrun.

A unified and grateful People's Republic of Vietnam placed the superb port facilities at Cam Ranh Bay, Da Nang, Haiphong, and Vung Tau at the disposal of the Soviet fleet and the positioning and rapid growth of Soviet power in that sector gave effective control of the waters of Southeast Asia and all of the vital traffic that flowed through them.

A powerful socialist Vietnam was very helpful to the revolutions in Indonesia, Laos and Kampuchea, and soon after the red flag rose over Saigon successful new movements, augmented with first-rate arms and experienced advisors, overthrew the capitalists in all these countries.

For the first time, a warm water year-round set of ports sustained the Soviet Navy and the fleet grew to support its new responsibilities. Con-trol of the Straits of Malacca gave control of the connections between the western Pacific and the oil of the Persian Gulf. This, in effect, meant that the growing power of the Japanese and South Koreans was checked. It also meant that Australia and New Zealand were unimportant to the overall equation of world power and most importantly, America and its alliances were firmly excluded from nearly half of the world.

The present situation was an annoying side effect to this new order-ing of socialist strength. The People's Republic of China, which had been a close ally of the Soviet Union during the days of the Korean War, was undergoing the throes of a Cultural Revolution. In the process, hundreds of thousands of Chinese had died and hundreds of thousands more Chi-nese were displaced or in prison. The festering border conflicts between the Soviet Republics and China were gaining in violence and a steady reinforce-ment of the troops in these desolate places was taking place. The anti-Soviet propaganda of the Mao regime had gotten more and more strident and incidents between fleet elements of the two socialist powers occurred weekly as naval forces met each other in the narrow waters around Hainan Island and the Spratleys, and many other places. Of all things, the gains enjoyed by the Soviet government and its many allies had proven to exac-erbate the tensions between Mao's China and its socialist brothers.

To himself, Ivanov admitted that he had been surprised about Johnson's decision not to oppose the Vietnamese revolution. His predecessor had introduced American military advisors to assist the Saigon regime and had spent a lot of money propping up that set of leaders. Once Kennedy had been killed, Johnson reversed his policies and withdrew all direct support of the Vietnamese puppets. For an area that was so critical to American strategy, it was surprising to see them hand it over so easily.

Like many Russians, Ivanov privately admired the Americans—they were brash and imaginative, and like the Soviet Union, their country was a mixture of many disparate peoples and cultures and had been started from a relatively new beginning. There were more similarities than differences and even as a committed communist he had watched with admiration as American industry and science had grown. All the same, they lacked even the most fundamental sense of what it takes to survive as a major power, to lead, to stay in position. A major power has to demonstrate will, strength, and courage. As in the animal world, a nation unwilling to face dangers to itself, to sacrifice, will rapidly fall to the mercies of the stronger. And as in the animal world, mercy is nothing to be depended upon.

The Americans, he had concluded, had lost the revolutionary fervor they used to have and, while they had become comfortable and rich, they had developed feet of clay. They had no shortage of money to spend, such as in the so-called Marshall Plan for Western Europe and no shortage of propaganda to dispense about freedom but they were reluctant to expend themselves for their expressed ideals. A fatal flaw.

Clearly Communism was the inexorable future, exactly as Marx had said. This had proven to be a system with the strength and the ability to sacrifice itself for its ideals. That was the kind of system that would gain and keep power. Now the question seemed to be, who would lead the socialist nations to the future, the Soviet Union or Mao's China?

In the back seat of his Chaika,[2] Ivanov organized his notes and prepared briefing materials. The Western alliances, particularly SEATO, were e. itially emasculated in the face of Soviet naval positional superiority. Ai. ican naval forces in the region were unquestionably large and capable, part 'arly in their ability to move aircraft carrier battle groups far from their ?s in the Philippines and Japan but they were too scattered and too far awi o influence Soviet naval moves in Asia quickly. The estimates put togethei ' the Committee's naval experts assessed American response times to > approximately one to two weeks for carrier battle groups to arrive in tL "outheast Asian area. The American Polaris ballistic nuclear missiles can. in their submarines were a significant capability and an ever-present t it but they were essentially useless without a clear will to use them.

The question 1 'd to answer for the assembled members of the highest organs of Soviet p>. • was whether the United States and its allies would intervene in the p >ed operation to seize and subdue the People's Republic of China.

The Maoist clique had become a grave danger to the progress of socialism and the schism that had developed had grown from an embarrassment and a wasteful diffusion of power to an increasingly dangerous focus of conflict within the communist movement. China had formerly devoted most of its efforts to campaigns against its own people but lately China had refocused its propaganda against Moscow and it was only a matter of time before greater confrontations would begin. The time to decide the direction for the Socialist world and to eliminate the growing distraction of Mao and his perversion of communist doctrine was now.

The Soviet leadership had decided to strike the head of the snake now, to drive across the Mongolian frontier and use their assembled combined arms armies to surge rapidly south to split and disorganize the People's Liberation Army (PLA), and isolate and seize the Chinese capital, Peking. To do this, the Soviets would need quietly to move large forces from their positions in the West opposite the NATO armies and to take those forces and all of their supporting equipment and munitions the thousands of miles to the Chinese frontier without being detected.

The Chinese had one really massive weapon to confront the Soviet Forces: inexhaustible supplies of fighting men.[3] The three advantages that the Soviets had to offset the Chinese manpower were modern, well-equipped maneuver forces, allies surrounding China (India, Vietnam, North Korea) and large stocks of tactical nuclear and chemical weapons. The first advantage would provide the necessary upper hand with the Chinese forces if surprise were maintained. The second would give the Soviets contingencies if the initial phase did not go as well as planned (plus some potential for alternate avenues of attack and support). The last advantage of special weapons would have to be employed if the situation turned somehow to favoring the Chinese and they were able to bring their enormous advantage in manpower to bear.

Would the Americans use this opportunity to strike an Eastern Europe that had been weakened to support the Chinese operations? Would the Americans use their organs of intelligence to let the Chinese know what the Soviet forces were about to do? Would the Americans and their allies assist China to deepen the wedge between the socialist camps? These were the serious questions that faced the Soviet leadership as the armies detrained along the Amur River in the Mongolian wasteland.

The stage in the Great Hall of the Kremlin was framed with a huge bas-relief of stylized workers reaching upward with massive hammer and sickle. This imposing display made Ivanov feel small and insignificant as he approached the podium before the assembled leadership of the greatest power on earth. When he opened his notes and his first transparency was displayed on a giant screen, Ivanov forgot his initial discomfort and focused on the substance of his briefing: the Americans would not interfere. Through slide after slide, he laid out the rationale for his conclusions.

TheAmericans were irresolute, unprepared, and comfortable. The Americans would view the internecine war between the Soviet Union and China as a potentially advantageous event in which two enemies would bloody themselves without American losses. Since America did not have any contacts with the Chinese regime, it was unlikely that America would reveal the Soviet intent to the Chinese if they discovered it. The Americans and their allies were not positioned to interfere and could not get into position in time. The NATO forces in the West were unlikely to attack when the main Soviet armies were moved because of Western qualms against initiating attacks and the lack of unity among the allies for this type of action. They would certainly fear the strong resistance that the remaining Warsaw Pact forces, augmented with tactical nuclear and chemical weapons, could provide. Lastly, the American strategic nuclear "deterrence" forces were useless to prevent Soviet action, since that threat was neatly counterbalanced by equal or greater Soviet capabilities. The West, with the United States at the center, was neatly stalemated.

At the end of his presentation, Ivanov was startled to hear applause and looked up from the podium to see hundreds standing and clapping. The die was cast.

China was not unaware of the proximity of greater action by its Soviet neighbor. Chairman Mao had directed the Chinese people's and the Party's attention to the revisionist and imperialist tendencies of the Brezhnev— Kosygin government while deploying the PLA in greater numbers in the most likely paths of intervention. All the same, while his intelligence agencies detected greater numbers of Soviet troops moving towards the border, the most likely reason seemed to be to impose the usual Soviet dictates with a larger force to back them up. Mao still had work to do to eliminate the fractious elements within his own government to assure the continuation of his own vision for a socialist future. His vision was fixed on regenerating China's revolutionary zeal by eliminating his internal opposition and once that process was complete, driving across the Taiwan Straits to eliminate the Kuomintang traitors once and for all.

Forward!

"We shall not conceal it: watching all these maneuvers by the Chinese leadership, we, like all the Marxist-Leninists of the world, are justifiably alarmed at the dangerous path along which the Chinese leaders are dragging their great country."

M.S. Suslov, to the Plenum of the Communist Party of the Soviet Union Central Committee, February 14, 1964[4]

Thus it was, that on May 13, 1968, the massive Soviet attacks along three fronts into China stunned China and the whole world.

The initial portions of the Soviet attack went together like the parts of a fine Swiss watch. The critical mountain passes were secured by parachute reconnaissance or helicopter-borne battalions and the PLA security forces were overrun or bypassed as if they were not even there. The main portion of the attack used the doctrine that had served the *Red Army* so well during the latter half of the Great Patriotic War. Armored forces closely supported by the frontal air forces and heavy barrages of divisional artillery crushed the Chinese forces that stood in their way. The *Pacific Front* had the heaviest going, from its attack jump-off positions out of Vladivostok, driving through difficult and canalized terrain through Changchun then seizing the critical road and communications hub at Fushun/Mukden. The *Central Front* drove the long way from its staging areas at Ulaanbaator in the Mongolian People's Republic, south-southeast along the main railroad like a dagger across the deserts towards Peking. The *Western Front* started out from Frunze in the Kirghiz Socialist Republic and followed the path of the ancient Silk Road, driving straight east past Alma-Ata virtually unopposed for hundreds of miles as it headed for the "back door" to the central areas of China.

The plan was simple, straightforward and quintessentially Soviet: pin the PLA in position, defeat the forces in detail, use masses of supporting arms to find or make an opening to move to the next pockets of resistance. Using these three forces to drive individually towards Peking ensured that one or all would trap the Chinese leadership in place for a quick and decisive defeat of Mao and his clique. Once Peking had been taken and the troublesome Chinese government was removed, Moscow had little doubt that for all intents and purposes, the war would be over. With a new and more cooperative socialist China, the conflict with the capitalist powers could resume apace from a single, unified communist family.

In war, no operational plan, no matter how well thought-out or capably carried out, survives its first contact with the enemy unaltered. This operation was no exception to this rule. The People's Liberation Army was aware of its imbalance *vis-a-vis* the Red Army and had long ago determined that the best way to deal with that imbalance was through trading distance for time, then bleeding their invaders through a thousand cuts. The *Pacific Front* force succeeded in securing the Shenyang road junctions but found itself slowed and ambushed through the tough mountainous terrain to the southwest. The size advantages of a larger force can be negated and even overturned if that force has to push through single-lane roads and steep canyons. The PLA commanders in this sector used a combination of cunningly conceived artillery ambushes and mined hillsides to make the Soviets pay for every yard of ground gained. The onset of heavy spring rains augmented the efforts of the Chinese defenders and caused the momentum to bog and then disappear as armor-heavy forces dealt with obstacle after obstacle.

The *Central Front* force ran into less opposition from the PLA but was bogged down nonetheless by the difficult ground it had chosen as its axis of advance. The Mongolian deserts are some of the most barren and difficult pieces of ground on earth, and vehicles, even good military vehicles, do not hold up well over long distances over that kind of ground. Tracked vehicles had to rely on wheeled transporters to carry them for the extended distances (since tracked vehicles use large amounts of fuel and break down frequently on long road marches) but the primitive roads would not support the great numbers of wheeled vehicles that were required. The advance slowed every time the roads were blocked by broken down or mired vehicles and new routes had to be made.

Slowed vehicles that bunch up around an obstacle in open areas have a special nightmare—air attacks. The pilots of China's Peoples' Liberation Air Force (PLAF) were able to break through the Soviet air cover as the ground forces penetrated deeper into Chinese Mongolia and they wrought havoc on the massed vehicles spread out and stopped in the open desert. Columns of black smoke marked the places where the PLAF had gotten through, guiding the next waves in against more of the columns.

The inability of the Soviets to overcome these obstacles was rooted in another factor—the lack of operational experience in the forces. The rates of advance on the *Pacific* and *Central Fronts* should have been as fast or faster than their predecessors over these same routes in 1945 during the August Storm campaign against the Japanese. The difference was that the *Red Army* of 1945 had extensive combat experience, seasoned and talented commanders, and efficient staffs. The *Red Army* of 1968 was a peacetime force, largely made up of recently mobili2ed reserve divisions from Central Asia, Siberia, and the Far East, with only a small portion from the cutting edge of divisions from the *Group of Soviet Forces Germany (GSFG)*. The peacetime Soviet forces had an enormous amount of dead wood in their upper officer ranks, the product of the Soviet system's relentless pull towards mediocrity. And it showed.

Combat drills designed for the well-metalled roads and gentle fields of Western Europe were a poor fit for this new theater of mountains, defiles, wild forests, and swamps. The enemy was also not the one around which Soviet combat doctrine had been designed. The skills of the Chinese infantry in this environment, on the other hand, were a perfect fit. The techniques of close combat, ambush, camouflage, and deception were employed in terrain which was ideal to hide masses of their stoic and relentless infantry. The Chinese learned quickly that massing large numbers for an attack was suicidal, since they would be struck by overwhelming Soviet artillery and air strikes. Instead, the Chinese commanders learned to infiltrate their forces into positions, then concentrate them quickly for a surprise attack, then melt away quickly to strike again. These tactics allowed them to bleed and stall the Soviet advance while

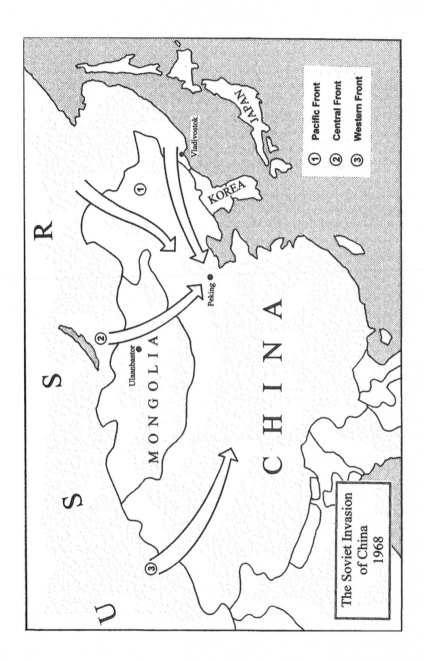

The Soviet Invasion of China 1968

other forces preyed upon the extending Soviet lines of communication. The end result was a deadly parity without a decisive outcome and at a great cost in blood.

Of the three forces, the *Western Front* had relatively smooth sailing. No appreciable organized opposition, good rates of advance, and no casualties to speak of. It was moving through sparsely settled areas with few military forces. The few that were in the area pulled back and out of the way, monitoring the progress of the Soviet columns but not providing any great obstacles. The only enemy the *Western Front* faced was time. The long distances took time to overcome and Moscow's timetable required fast victory and fast resolution before their opponents in the capitalist world took advantage of the USSR's distraction with China.

The *Soviet Navy* was doing the best of all and, from its first contact with the Chinese Navy, it made short work of the minesweepers and coastal patrol craft it encountered.[5] The naval leadership eagerly sought a greater role and recommended an amphibious landing in the vicinity of Shanghai. This idea was considered briefly but the armed forces staff was getting too occupied with the rapidly expanding problems of the fronts.

The rest of the world was watching. Most of the United Nations called for immediate cessation of aggression but Moscow and its satellites blocked any resolutions that called for their withdrawal. The United States' and its allies' first reaction was as Ivanov had predicted, to view the Sino-Soviet war as an internecine squabble that had gotten ugly but could also have benefits. The biggest dangers for the NATO and SEATO allies were the greater power that the Soviet Union would have if it were successful in its conquest of China and the potential for this war to overflow to the rest of the world. There were debates in the US Congress and the respective parliaments of its allies, there were increases in defense spending, and there were increased deployments of forces to Germany and Japan but in the main, Ivanov was accurate as always. The Americans and their allies would not interfere.

The war continued for several months without taking Peking or even getting much closer. The main mass of the PLA had been brought to bear against the three Soviet axes and the fight had devolved into slow and deadly attrition as summer reached its full heat. Casualties were heavier than anticipated but the Chinese were in a better position to sustain them. They had the interior lines of communication to bring up massive replacements. They also had much greater numbers to call from. The Soviet forces were being bled steadily as they tried to find openings to pursue a mobile war where they could triumph. Each new opening led to another ambush, which led to yet another static front and yet more punishing casualties. Because the distances were so great, Soviet *Frontal Aviation* squadrons could not remain on station very long and when the skies were empty of Soviet aircraft, the planes of the PLAF were raking the Soviet positions with bombs and rockets.

As the weeks dragged into months and the conclusion of the war became less certain, and the pressure of the long exposure to the possible actions of the capitalists started to weigh in, the Soviet leadership took the direction that they had wanted to avoid but could no longer do so. The front commanders received the code word that they had been begging for, the word that authorized them to begin to employ chemical weapons and tactical nuclear weapons. The first nuclear attacks were delivered using FROG[6] tactical rockets against frontline PLA formations while the rear support areas were attacked with persistent nerve agents using aircraft spraying methods. The Chinese forces were staggered by these attacks and the Soviets were able to exploit the devastation they caused to gain significant ground, for a short while. The leadership of the Chinese forces did not hesitate to give their front-line commanders the clearance to begin their own nuclear attacks on Soviet forces. The door had been opened and the war had entered a new and more desperate phase.

As the Chinese and the Soviets traded 10-kiloton strikes,[7] against each other, the world began to suffer along with the combatants. In each nuclear blast, the products of the explosion, including the irradiated debris from the ground, soared upward to the highest reaches of the atmosphere. When it reached those altitudes, the radioactive isotopes of iodine, strontium and americium, and bits of remaining fissile material circulated and spread over every square mile of the Earth's surface. Throughout the world, high altitude sampling aircraft began to sense the presence of these deadly products, confirming what the seismic readings had been telling the scientists since the first moment those weapons had been fired: the war had begun to be a nuclear war. The particles settled to the Earth with the rains and where they touched, they were ingested by plants and animals and humans. For tens of millions of people, many completely innocent of the war or the development of atomic weapons or any blame at all, their lives were brutally shortened by the falling particles from someone else's fight. Where the nations of the UN had been disturbed by the events of the last several months, genuine panic was spreading. Even nations that had been supporting one or the other side were calling for an immediate cessation of hostilities. It was too late. The casualties had been too catastrophic, the losses too grave, and complete victory only seemed to require one more good strike. The Soviet government sent orders to the Strategic Rocket Forces to prepare to target the major cities of China for a knockout blow. The same orders were communicated at nearly the same time to PLAF bomber forces to plan an attempt for a long-range one-way attack against their hated enemies in Moscow.

In Maryland, just a few miles north of Washington, DC, the National Security Agency had intercepted the coded texts from both sides and with the greatest urgency possible notified President Johnson and the Joint Chiefs of Staff of their contents. The Sino—Soviet War had hit a phase that had been postulated to be possible but was not believed to be plausible. Yet it was here, now—a true major thermonuclear exchange was about to take place. The war had reached a point that could not be ignored. The next stage would involve unthinkable death tolls in China and around the world. The madness was about to spread beyond the theater of operations of a couple of communist thugs to their neighbors and bystanders and even to the self-focused United States. The information was instantly communicated on secure channels to the NATO leadership and emergency staffs met deep in Cheyenne Mountain, Colorado, to develop contingency war plans, while President Johnson met with his National Security staff to open the hot line to Moscow. The Soviets must be convinced to stop their war and any further nuclear detonations at all costs.

The collective judgment of the free world leaders was that the Sino-Soviet War was past any hope of containment or settlement between the parties. The UN had been impotent to direct a solution and the situation had developed very rapidly to an exceptionally dangerous state. India and Pakistan had gone to full mobilization, as had the Republic of China in Taiwan and North and South Korea. Japan was in desperate straits, as it was in the path of the majority of the downwind radioactive products and was already suffering its first casualties. Japan was requesting more US troops for its defense and the Diet was meeting to consider suspension of its constitution in order to assemble powerful Japanese armed forces once again. Europe was mobilizing, too, as the communist powers increased their levels of alert. The direct equivalency between the major powers had apparently nullified the threat of a major nuclear exchange, but it seemed that no one had seriously considered the possibility of a conflict between putative allies evolving into a general nuclear war. Nonetheless, it was a fact and it was the situation that threatened the world in the late summer of 1968.

It was clear to Johnson and the NATO leaders that the Chinese and the Russians were not going to slow down on their own and that all of the diplomatic pressure from the United Nations was not going to affect a thing. LBJ had called Brezhnev on the hot line but was told, in effect, to mind his own business. The collective wisdom of his cabinet and the key members of Congress amounted to scaling up the US and NATO Defense Condition (DEFCON) readiness alert levels to prepare for potential threats against the US or Europe or the West's Asian allies. That made a certain sense, since the elevation of the alert status would put the major defense forces in the proper positions for an adequate response if one was required but, more importantly, it sent a signal to both sides that the US and its allies were ready to get moving if the dangers began to head in their direction. This situation had the White House working late, seven days a week and rankled LBJ because he should by all rights be campaigning for his reelection right now. The Republicans had nominated Richard Nixon and he never underestimated the political skills of Tricky Dick. It did not feel like the right thing to do, but he followed his advisors' recommendations and issued the orders to bring the NATO alliance to DEFCON 2,[8] War Alert.

The news that the Americans and their allies had mobilized their military forces to high alert ran through the Soviet *nomenklatura* like an electric shock. The Soviets never trusted the West—and this was a perfect example of Western perfidy. The Soviet Union was in an important and difficult struggle with China and the West was showing its true colors by threatening war. Well, so be it. If the capitalist world was ready to risk fighting the combined might of the socialist powers, they would get what they deserved. The Soviet Union had withstood the most modern and capable enemy in history, fascist Germany. It had withstood the worst that the Nazis could deliver and it could withstand the worst that the capitalists could send, too. Sergei Efremovich Ivanov was summoned to the Kremlin late that evening to explain how this turn of events could happen, given his predictions a few short months before. In the meantime, the lights in the major cities of the Soviet Union were out and the atomic shelters were stocked and exercised as the Soviet government and the long-suffering Soviet people prepared for the worst. To match the actions of the capitalists, the Kremlin issued orders to raise the readiness of Strategic Rocket Forces that were dedicated to American and European targets and to ensure that the long-range Tupolev 95 squadrons were at their highest state of preparedness. Remaining Soviet naval forces had sortied from Murmansk, the Baltic, Petropavlovsk, and of course, from the Vietnamese ports in preparation for the worst.

Confrontation

"Our enemies have always made the same mistake. In my lifetime— in depression and in war—they have awaited our defeat. Each time, from the secret places of the American heart, came forth the faith they could not see or that they could not even imagine. It brought us victory. And it will again."
President Lyndon Johnson, Inaugural Address, 20 January 1965[9]

The intelligence agencies of all the major powers listened in awe as the situation rapidly escalated. As soon as President Johnson was notified of the latest series of escalations, he reluctantly matched the movements of the Soviets with his own. The Atlantic Fleet sailed from Norfolk and Charleston and Mayport and the Pacific Fleet sailed from San Diego and Pearl Harbor and Subic Bay and the Strategic Air Command kept its fully-armed B-52s just minutes away from their fail-safe points. Carrier battle groups approached the Western Pacific and no one had any illusions that this mobilization would end up well.

President Johnson attended to his part of the worst world crisis in history and none of his staff could tell him what he had to do to stop this thing. He had the hawks in his NSC and the Congress telling him to "Blow the hell out of 'em, before they have a chance to do it to us." He also had the doves from his party telling him to back off and sit this one out. He did get one idea from a professor at Harvard to approach Brezhnev at a personal and confidential level to assure him that the US and its allies did not want war. The professor even offered to help Brezhnev approach the Chinese to reach a cease-fire and to help broker a political solution between the communist powers. The reason Johnson paid any attention at all to this professor was that everyone he called said that this guy was one of the best. He had to try everything and anything, so he sent a classified message to the embassy in Moscow to expect a Doctor Kissinger within 24 hours and to do everything they could to set up a meeting between Brezhnev and this Kissinger as soon as possible. Johnson wanted to see him to meet him face to face before he left but there was no time. He wondered if Kissinger was a Democrat or a Republican.

When the Chinese and the Soviet leadership received word of the West's escalations, their plans to conduct major nuclear strikes against each other were delayed, to watch the capitalists and to be ready. Thus the war had bogged down again as both sides dealt with massive casualties and huge areas of contaminated ground. The weapons that were supposed to decide battles were superb at killing people but formed large obstacles to movement when they were used. The persistent nerve agents had the viscosity and evaporation rate of motor oil and the areas that had been sprayed were lethal for months when anyone's skin or lungs came in contact with the smallest part of the poisons. The really difficult part was that the presence of those poisons was not obvious and it took slow, laborious procedures to determine which areas were actually contaminated and which really were not. Both sides used prisoners of war to facilitate the decision process.

The nuclear residual danger areas were much worse. Weapon development to that point had been necessarily rapid and, while the weapons were powerfully destructive, they were also enormously inefficient. The residue of fissile material was scattered for tens of thousands of square miles and in combination with the radioactive products of the explosion itself, made the areas deadly for centuries to come.

Kissinger was conducted from the embassy to the Kremlin by special convoy of limousines and was taken directly to meet Secretary Brezhnev, Premier Kosygin and the closest staff members. After courtesies were exchanged, Kissinger got to the heart of his mission. With just Brezhnev, Kosygin and the appointed interpreter, Kissinger laid out a proposal to broker a cease-fire and disengagement conducted by the NATO and SEATO representatives in complete secrecy from the rest of the world.

If Brezhnev approved, they would approach the Chinese government directly and would arbitrate the issues to be resolved to effect an honorable disengagement for both sides. He also offered to get an aid package from the West approved to help restore the damage sustained by the parties. Best of all, he offered a new relationship with the Soviets, initially kept secret except to the highest levels of government, as part of this offer. Brezhnev had no reason to trust this professor or to believe that he could pull off a deal like this, yet this approach appeared to offer a chance to bring the world back from the brink of total destruction with no more losses than they had already sustained. Best of all, this deep-voiced professor grasped the Soviet need for privacy, for an under-the-table deal was the sort that they trusted the most. Time was critical; Brezhnev agreed to Kissinger's plan and passed orders to the Strategic Forces to reduce their defense posture slightly.

The initial success of Kissinger's mission electrified the Johnson State Department and the President himself. The go-ahead to fly to Shanghai had been obtained through trusted sources within China and, only a few short hours later, the professor was on his way to meet with Chou En Lai and the senior members of the Chinese Communist Party. The same technique worked for them and, within hours, the first cease-fire orders were issued and the armistice negotiations begun. The world did not know how it had happened, but little by little things began to return to normal. The fighting stopped and stayed stopped and the naval and air and strategic rocket forces returned to the posture of lethal vigilance that they had assumed months before. US and allied teams of experts worked with the Chinese to monitor and decontaminate the sites where the nuclear and chemical weapons were used and financial aid was quietly approved and disbursed to pay for rebuilding and rehabilitation. President Johnson did not benefit from Kissinger's mission, however. Instead he was handily defeated in the 1968 elections when it was revealed that Kissinger had been advised by none other than Richard M. Nixon, the Republican candidate and now the President of the United States. The relationships started by that fateful mission reverberated for years to come and eventually caused the dismantling of the mechanisms that put the world on the edge of instant destruction.

In the lowest levels of the Lubyanka Prison, Sergei Efremovich Ivanov had much to contemplate. Like any other member of the Soviet leadership, he well knew how quickly one could rise to the heights and just as quickly descend to the cell he occupied now. It did not make any difference that, after all, he had been right again. The problem was that he was seen as supporting the devastatingly poor decision to attack China. All of those who had not covered their tracks well enough were designated as Traitors to the Revolution and he had not covered any tracks at all. In the quiet of that small cell, late at night, he allowed himself to admire those unpredictable Americans. It was hard to be an expert about people who did not follow a consistent path!

The Reality

Of course, the United States did get deeply involved in trying to stop the "National Liberation War" in Vietnam. This ended in 1975 in victory for the Vietnamese communist forces and an apparent victory for communism itself. What really happened, however was that "comfortable and sheltered" Americans spent eight long years defending an ally against the North Vietnamese and the combined efforts of the Soviets and the Chinese and all of their allies and, in doing so, lost 56,000 of their best young men in the process. This message was not lost on the communists or the rest of the world; it said that Americans were tougher than they looked; it said that Americans were willing to expend their children in a prolonged, miserable fight to protect an ally. Most importantly it told the communists that these National Liberation Wars—externally supported civil wars—were expensive and inconclusive and not worth pursuing in the future. There were no more after Vietnam. There were proxy wars, such as in Angola with Cuban mercenaries, and there was even a direct intervention in Afghanistan but no more National Liberation Wars. In the end, it was the determination of American fighting men in Vietnam that stayed in the appraisals of the will of the United States and when Presidents Nixon and Ford and Reagan kept up the diplomatic pressure on the Soviets and the communist world, it was the image of the courage of those young Americans that stayed in view.

That, in the end, is how a major power should show itself to the world.

Bibliography

Erickson, John, *Soviet Military Power,* Royal United Services Institute, London, 1971.

Garthoff, Raymond I., *Soviet Military Policy, A Historical Analysis,* Praeger, New York, 1966.

Griffith, William E., *Sino-Soviet Relations 1964–1965,* MIT Press, Cambridge, MA, 1966.

Hazard, John N., *The Soviet System of Government,* University of Chicago Press, Chicago, 1964.

Hinton, Harold C, *The Bear at the Gate, Chinese Policymaking Under Soviet Pressure,* American Enterprise Institute for Public Policy Research, Washington, DC, 1971.

Hudson, G.E, Lowenthal, Richard, and MacFarquhar, Roderick, *The Sino–Soviet Dispute,* Praeger, New York, 1961.

Jackson, W.A. Douglas, *The Russo-Chinese Borderlands, Zone of Peaceful Contact or Potential Conflict?,* Van Nostrand, Princeton, NJ, 1962.

Pretty, R.T., and Archer, *D.H.R., Jane's Weapon Systems,* London, 1968.

Tanner, Henry, "Moscow is Quiet," *New York Times,* October 16, 1964.

Notes

1. Hinton, Harold C., *The Bear at the Gate*.
2. A top-quality Soviet limousine that was only available to top Party leaders, available in black, black or black.
3. Estimated as 150 million men of fighting age available for call up, 3 million men under arms as of 1967. Source: *jane's Weapon Systems 1967*.
4. Hinton, Harold C., *The Bear at the Gate*.
*5. There are unconfirmed intelligence reports that the Republic of China's Navy took advantage of this confusion to settle scores with a number of escaping Chinese vessels.
6. Free Rocket Over Ground, an effective but indifferently accurate truck-transported artillery rocket with chemical or nuclear or conventional warheads. The 'accurate' part is probably not all that important with the nuclear warhead.
*7. Estimated yields, based on DOE seismic station data. US Department of Energy Report, *Radionuclide Contamination of Soil Samples, Northwestern China*, Washington DC, 1971.
8. DEFCON from *DEFease CONdition*. The various levels are as follows: DEFCON 5 is normal peacetime operations; DEFCON 4 is heightened intelligence and security readiness; DEFCON 3 is increased force readiness; DEFCON 2 further increase in readiness, but less than maximum; DEFCON 1 is maximum readiness. See www.fas.org/nuke/guide/usa/c3i/defcon.htm
9. Source: Bartleby.com at www.bartleby.com/124/pres57.html

7
TO GO BOLDLY IN AMONGST THEM
The Invasion of North Vietnam

Kevin F. Kiley

"Take what your enemy holds dear and he will be amenable to your will."
Sun Tzu Wu

"The sense of duty makes the victor."
Vegetius

"In order to smash, it is necessary to act suddenly."
Napoleon

"Gentlemen, the enemy stands behind his entrenchment, armed to the teeth. We must attack him and win, or else perish. Nobody must think of getting through any other way. If you don't like this, you may resign and go home."
Frederick the Great before the Battle of Leuthen: December 5, 1757

Somewhere over Laos: January 21,1970

Colonel Arthur "Bull" Simons sat in the back of the HH-53 helicopter going over the mission in his head, wondering what had gone wrong. The troops, pilots, and the air support had been magnificent. Everyone had done his job. The only screwup had been his. His helicopter had landed in the wrong compound, a look-alike, 400 yards from the actual target. That error was quickly rectified by immediately taking off and landing in the correct compound, after "conducting business" where they first landed. That the prisoners had been moved without American intelligence assets finding out had not been the mission commander's fault.

Almost immediately after landing in the lookalike compound, Simons and his support group found themselves in the middle of a mass of enemy troops, over 200 of them, running around the compound wondering what had landed in the middle of it. Not wasting time, the American raiders had opened fire, with small arms and miniguns from the helicopter, shooting down or scattering all of the bad guys in moments. When little or no return fire was taken, the bird had immediately lifted off and continued the mission. They had landed and deployed in the correct target area within minutes.

What was puzzling to Simons was that there was no way those people in that first compound were Vietnamese. For one thing, they were too big. They could have been Chinese, but he doubted that. They were still too tall. He was convinced they were Europeans, and that meant either Russians or East Germans. Also, as far as he could discern, they had not effectively returned fire either because they were too shocked or most were not armed. Probably the latter. There was no resistance at the Son Tay Prison Camp either. North Vietnam might be a hollow shell militarily. It just might be. He had to make some phone calls and see some people when he got back home.

The Pentagon: January 29,1970

Bull Simons made his way to the office of an old friend, who was now the Vice Chief of Staff of the United States Army. Simons had an idea, and he had not talked to anyone about it. This was going to be the first go round of this one. The Vice Chief of Staff and he went back a long ways, and he was asking a Big One to see him like this. It was unofficial, it was quick, and the Chief of Staff, who did not like Simons, and the feeling was mutual, would not have liked what he had to say. The Vice Chief might not like it either, but at least he would listen. What Bull Simons wanted was a meeting with the President. He probably would not get it, and he just might go out of here ordered to retire, but he had to try. Young men were dying in rice paddies and jungle in South Vietnam, fighting a war the country did not want to win and was busting a gut to get out of. His idea just might accomplish both tasks much sooner than anyone expected. Win or lose, this was his last mission anyway. It was time to retire; he was just getting too old for this kind of fun and games.

Office of the Vice Chief of Staff, The Pentagon: January 29,1970

"Bull, are you out of your mind? You can't believe for a minute that the President will buy this. Kissinger will laugh you out of the White House and then both you and I will be relieved for being a couple of smartasses, of just being plain naive, or both."

"Sir, you know I'm not out of my mind. I'm telling you they don't have enough stuff on the ground in North Vietnam to stop a sick cat. The whole damned North Vietnamese army is in the South, or in Cambodia, waiting for us to leave. We can do this if we have the guts for it."

"That's the whole point, Bull, the political will does not exist. I believe you, the Chief of Staff might believe you, and undoubtedly the President will. They just won't do it."

"Aren't they planning to invade Cambodia anyway in April?"

Shocked, the Vice Chief of Staff shouted: "How the hell did you find out about that? Wait," holding up his hand and looking away: "Don't tell me. If you do, then I'll have to fire somebody for not keeping his damned mouth shut."

"Sir, this will work. You know it will. We have to do it for one reason: Those boys fighting and dying in that godforsaken country for the past nine years. If we quit, and that's what it looks like we're going to do, then it's all for nothing and we've broken faith with our own people. We can use the Cambodia thing to mask what we really want to do. It will suck them down into the south, while we walk in their front door."

"You're preaching to the choir, Bull, and you know it. Don't you think I know that? It makes me sick to think about it."

"Then, Charlie, do something about it. What do you think you have those four stars for? We owe those troops and their commanders to do something to end this mess. And end it with a win. At least we ought to try."

"Dammit, don't you ever talk to me like that—you know me better—don't you ever say anything like that again, not to me!"

Ignoring the outburst, and standing up to his full height, wearing his Alphas and all his myriad ribbons, Bull Simons came to attention and stated very slowly and succinctly: "Sir, I request permission to see the President of the United States on a matter of national security."

"Permission granted you sonofabitch. Maybe it's time we both retired and went fishing."

"Are we going to tell the Chief of Staff?"

"Hell, no. He wouldn't listen to us anyway. Besides, he's on leave, and that gives us an excuse, as I'm acting Chief of Staff."[1]

The Oval Office: January 29,1970

"Come in, gentlemen and sit down please."

The President of the United States, an abrupt, somewhat ill at ease, and much shorter man than the two soldiers, beckoned them in to the Oval Office. The two soldiers sat together on one side of the coffee table, the President and his National Security Advisor, Henry Kissinger, on the other. Just as they sat down, the door opened from the outer office and the Army Chief of Staff and the Chairman of the Joint Chiefs of Staff marched tight-lipped into the room. The Chairman's face was blank and did not demonstrate the open hostility the Chiefs did.

The Chief of Staff and Chairman both nodded to the President and Kissinger, and the Chief gave the Vice Chief and Colonel Simons an icy, irate look that told of his great displeasure at the two of them going over his head. His withering glare told them: "When we get out of here you're through."

"Now that the entire cast is assembled," the President said: "Perhaps, you could tell us what this is all about?"

"Sir," the Vice Chief began: "Colonel Simons has two things for you. One concerns the security of the United States and the other is a proposal."

The President and his advisor both looked at Simons simultaneously. "They call you Bull, don't they Colonel?" the President asked.

"Yes sir, they do."

"OK, then, Bull, let's have it."

"Sir, as you've undoubtedly been briefed on the Son Tay mission, I'll forego most of that portion. As you know, my helicopter landed in the wrong compound initially. It was about 400 yards away, and in an identical, from the air anyway, compound. As the aircraft landed and we unassed the bird..." At the "colloquial" use of normal service language, the Chief of Staff groaned and rolled his eyes. Bull Simons looked at him in disgust. "As we unassed the bird, Mr President, we ran into an enemy compound full of about 200 personnel running out of barracks, shouting and starting to shoot. There were only 20 of us, so we opened up as soon as we got off the bird and did not stop firing until there was no one moving in the compound but us. The miniguns on the bird did most of the work. The ground was literally covered with dead and dying, and we immediately started checking bodies until the aircrew screamed at us to leave. We got on the aircraft and left to continue the mission. We were not on the ground more than five or six minutes."

"Anyways, on the way out, after the mission failed because we did not find any of our POWs..."

At that, the Vice Chief interrupted: "Bull, it was not an operational failure..."

"Sir, we did not do what we set out to do. Therefore, it was a failure." He turned back to the President, who looked at Colonel Simons with new respect.

"As we sat in the bird on the way out, two of my men came to me with documents. As you are undoubtedly aware, sir, Special Forces personnel are required to have at least a working knowledge of another language. Most of those who went on the raid spoke at least passable Vietnamese. I had one Russian and two German speakers, all fluent, on my bird. What two of them brought to me almost gave me a heart attack." He grinned: "I'm old enough, anyway. They had searched a few bodies and found some identification on two of the people we killed. If the documents are authentic, and I have no doubt they are, we killed one Russian two star and an East German colonel, who also worked for the Stasi. They were advisors, and the East German at least was helping to interrogate our men."

At that revelation, even the jaw of the Chief of Staff hit the floor. The Chairman retained his look of composure and did not say anything.

"Where are these documents, now?" asked the President. "Right here sir," and Bull Simons pulled open his attache case and gave the documents to the President. He held on to them for a moment or two, one in German, and the other in the Cyrillic alphabet of the Russian language, and then handed one to Kissinger. "Here, Henry, you read German, tell me if it's as Bull says it is."

Kissinger did as he was asked, read over the document, gave it back to the President, nodded, and said in his slow, deliberate, and accented English: "It's as he says it is, Mr President. We'll have to check this for authenticity, but I don't see why it wouldn't be."

The Chief of Staff was furious. He exploded, momentarily forgetting where he was. "Colonel Simons, you are guilty of a breach of security. Why in hell did not you turn these over to the proper channels for analysis, as per proper procedure?"

"If I had, general, they would have been buried somewhere and not put to good use. Some chairwarming sonofabitch would find them in ten years and wonder why we did not use the information to our advantage—again"

"And you know how to do that better than the intelligence people do you?"

Smiling slyly, he said: "Sir, I'm here aren't I?"

At that the Vice Chief stifled a guffaw, even the National Security Advisor let go of a slight smile. The Chairman kept his poker face and gently grabbed the Chief of Staff's arm, reminding him where he was. The Chief of Staff sat back in his chair fuming, glaring at Simons.

The President looked at Simons with a grin: "OK Bull, you've made your point, I think. What is it you want?"

"Sir, these documents prove the Russians and the Soviet bloc are actively aiding the North Vietnamese. This may also hint that the Chinese are out of the loop." The President and Kissinger exchanged glances, noticed by both Simons and the Vice Chief. The Chief of Staff was not paying attention any longer. He continued: "If that is so, we don't have to worry about intervention from the Chinese, who hate the Vietnamese anyway, and the feeling is more than mutual, if we invade North Vietnam."

"WHAT!" the Chief of Staff shouted, coming out of his chair: "Are you out of your mind? There is no way we are going to invade North Vietnam. We are in the process of withdrawal and turning the war over to the South Vietnamese! The press would have a field day even knowing we were discussing this topic. Do you want more riots and demonstrations in the streets?"

"We already have that, sir, so this won't change the situation much, now will it? At least we know the score in that respect. Most of them work for the North Vietnamese anyway," Simons shot back.

"As for the South Vietnamese, they will promptly lose it if we don't finish it. Withdrawal, or any other term you want to use, sir, is just a very polite way of saying selling out, cutting our losses, and going home. As for the press and the protesters, they can go screw themselves."

"You listen to me Simons..." then the Chief of Staff remembered where he was. The Chairman calmly said: "Sit down, general, please." The Chief of Staff looked at the President and stammered: "I beg your pardon, sir." The room became very quiet and you could have heard a pin drop. The President said nothing about the altercation, but turned to Simons and said very calmly: "You said you had a proposal, Bull."

"Yes sir, I do," and lifted a thin manila folder out of his attache case. "Sir, I've spent the last few days coming up with an outline for an OPLAN to invade North Vietnam. Sir, we all know the North Vietnamese Army is in the south. They may have a training division in the north, plus support and anti-aircraft troops, plus Russian support troops and advisors. Maybe 10,000 all told. If we invaded, we'd win in a walk and they'd be caught with their pants down. They cannot redeploy their army faster than we can take the north if we do it right. They don't have the strategic mobility, or the tactical mobility for that matter, that we do. The Ho Chi Minh Trail is a one-way road, and with our present policy of staying out of Laos and Cambodia, they get a big freebie. We could do it with five divisions, three more to follow on, and have the Marine divisions in the south attack across the DMZ on the same day. We could use the proposed Cambodia invasion as a strategic ploy to occupy most of their troops in the area while we take Hanoi and Haiphong, and, if we're lucky, most of their government. Endex. Then we dictate peace terms in Paris around their damned decoupage table. The Russians and the Chinese can kiss our ass. We present the world with a fait accompli."

"When would you want this to go?" asked a now very interested President. The Chairman was paying very close attention now.

"Sir, you cannot be serious?" an almost hysterical Chief of Staff shouted. "This is insane. Think of the political backlash and the protests that will happen from the far left!"

"You mean like we already have, general?" the President asked ruefully.

"Sir, this won't work, it's too dangerous, the Russians and the Chinese won't stand for it..."

"Screw the Russians and the Chinese..."

"Bull, easy now," said the Vice Chief calmly.

The President looked at the Chairman and the Vice Chief very cold-eyed and dead calm. "Gentlemen, did you know about this?"

The Chairman, with a thoughtful look slowly said: "No sir, I did not."

The Vice Chief, however, said: "Yes sir, as of this morning, and I concur with Colonel Simons one hundred percent. We can do this and it will work. The air and naval assets, with the exception of amphibious shipping, are in place already. Logistically, we can support it from Cam Ranh Bay and Da Nang. They don't have a pot to piss in up North, and we'll get strategic surprise, maybe even tactical surprise. We have special operations teams in the North, and along the Chinese border. It's quiet and the information we get from them concurs with Colonel Simons' analysis. It's worth a shot."

The Chief shook his head resignedly: "You cannot rely on uneducated and ignorant Montangard tribesmen for reliable information."

"Oh really?" the Vice Chief countered: "They know what a man with a gun is, and they can count. Besides they have Americans with them, senior NCOs for the most part, unless you think they're ignorant too. That was your problem when you commanded over there—you wouldn't listen to reliable information from reliable, loyal sources and that's why you got caught with your pants down in January 1968," the Vice Chief shot back.

"You sonofabitch!" the Chief of Staff said. "You knew this, went over my head, and are now trying to get the country involved in a major war. I'll have your request for retirement on my desk first thing in the morning."

The Vice Chief looked his boss straight in the eye. "We're already involved in a major war, general. I'm prepared to do that and so is Colonel Simons. What do you think they pay us for? Both of us are sick and tired of all the political garbage. We are involved in a major war. Up to now it hasn't been run effectively or with the object of winning. This might do it."

"General, you're relieved. Report to my office immediately."

For the first time, the Chairman of the Joint Chiefs of Staff spoke. "If anyone is going to retire, Bill, it's going to be you. You may report to your quarters as you clearly cannot control yourself. Consider yourself relieved." Shocked at the turn of events, the Chief gathered his hat and briefcase and quickly left the room. "Good riddance," Simons thought.

"Gentlemen," the President interrupted, "It might be a good idea if we all calm down." He did not contradict the Chairman's last, and only, statement. "We have been looking for a way out of Vietnam, and this may be it. Personally, I'm tired of war protesters, dead American servicemen coming home in boxes, and hearing unending nonsense and garbage on the news of how evil and imperialistic we are. This will catch everyone, including the news media and the anti-war movement, flatfooted."

"Has the Secretary of Defense been brought in on this?" All three remaining soldiers shook their heads. Kissinger spoke up: "He's out of town on leave, fishing I think, Mr President." "Good. I'd like time to digest this. General, schedule a meeting with the Joint Chiefs, but don't tell them what it is about, except that it is critical to National Security. And tell Mrs. Woods[2] that she can 'retune' the electronics now." The President gave a rueful grin at the last remark to the Secretary of State as he got up and walked towards the door to the outer office."

As the President reached for the door handle, he turned to the three soldiers: "Gentlemen, you are dismissed, and don't discuss this with anyone until I give you the word."

As they made for the door, the President added: "By the way, Bull, you're being promoted to brigadier general. General," he said looking at the Vice Chief: "You're now the Chief of Staff of the Army, and general," looking at the Chairman: "I concur with your decision regarding the former Army Chief of Staff. Good day, gentlemen."[3]

JCS Conference Room, The Pentagon: February 4,1970

"Good Morning, gentlemen," the brigadier general briefing the Joint Chiefs of Staff began, This is the order of battle and general OPLAN for Operation Olympic..."

I hardly believe it, thought the new Chief of Staff of the US Army, but we're really going to do this. We even named it after the canceled invasion of Japan in War II. I don't think Bull actually thought we'd get this far, but we sure did. We really have to pull this off or it will be the largest crisis the country will face since the Civil War. If we win, though, it will solve a lot of problems.

"... Gentlemen, do I have any questions?" the briefer concluded 20 minutes later.

"No, Fred, thanks. You've covered it completely and did not waste time. That's why they call it a brief." The Chairman of the Joint Chiefs of Staff smiled at his own wit. More seriously, he turned to the other general officers, and the key civilians, the Director of Central Intelligence, the Deputy Director of the FBI for Counter-intelligence, and the Secretary of State, and, of course, the Secretary of Defense.

"Well, it's a go. We invade on June 6. June 14 was lucky for Napoleon; maybe June 6 will be lucky for us. The orders relieving General Abrams of command in Vietnam were sent this morning. There was no explanation. I'll meet Creighton when he gets here and calm him down. He's the ideal commander for this operation, but he won't know until he gets back to Washington. His Deputy can take over what will be a somewhat depleted Military Assistance Command Vietnam (MACV). The ARVNs [South Vietnamese Army] will not be told until the morning of June 6. Their operational security sucks."

Turning to Brigadier General Simons the Chairman said: "Bull, you're going to run the clandestine operations."

"Yes, sir."

"Well... ?" "Sir, we already have ten teams in the proposed invasion area."

"I thought it was twelve?"

"It was, sir, until last night. We lost contact with two of the teams near Haiphong."

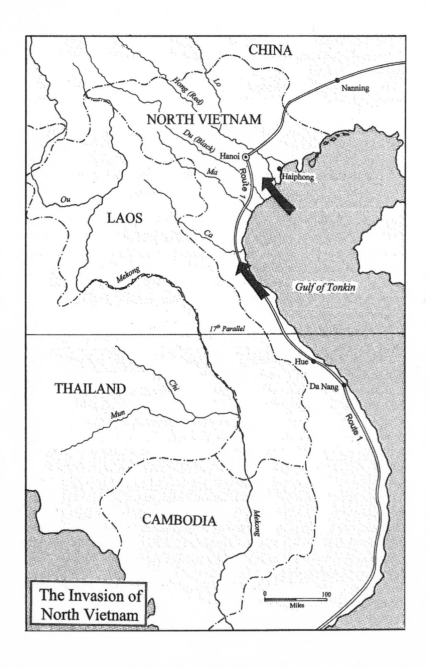

The Invasion of
North Vietnam

"Hell!..."

"Sir, to be blunt, we're going to lose a lot more before we're done."

"I know, Bull, but it still gets to you."

"Yes, sir, it does."

"But maybe this time it'll work and put an end to the mess."

"Let's hope so, for all of our sakes and that of the country."

The Director of Central Intelligence gave a quick rundown on Eastern Europe and the Company's assets in the Far East. There were no indications that the Russians were catching on. Key personnel were being ordered out of Europe and going either to home bases or to units that would be staging in Okinawa. He finished with: "There is a considerable communist element in Okinawa that we will have to keep an eye on and be aware of. However, as that has been a staging area before, we are going to pass it around that units coming out of Vietnam will stage there before coming home. For the short planning period, that ought to work."

Next came the FBI Deputy Director. "The concerns we have at home are the two anti-war groups, the People's Committee for Peace and Justice and the National Peace Action Committee. Both are in bed with the North Vietnamese and are actively aiding them in their war effort.[4] We are going to discreetly," he gave a small, sly grin, and then continued, "arrest their key personnel at the beginning of June to shake up and confuse those two organizations so that their effort to support the North Vietnamese gets disrupted and they are more concerned with getting their 'comrades' out of jail than spying and passing information to the enemy. We have operatives in both organizations with enough credible evidence to hang those assholes. When the invasion succeeds, we intend to indict them for treason."

The Secretary of State was next. "As you know, we have been in contact with the Chinese seeking some type of rapprochement for some time, hopefully leading up to a meeting between Mao and the President. The Chinese, it appears, are as eager for it as we are. From our contacts, we are convinced they will not interfere in this endeavor."

The men around the table looked both impressed and relieved. That was a major concern to all, and now the Chairman of the Joint Chiefs was reminded of a maxim of George Patton: Never Take Counsel of Your Fears. He then stood up and went to the screen and quietly and politely asked that the OPLAN schematic be put up again. "Gentlemen, I'll be quite honest. If this had come to me first, I would have not only said no, but hell no. And I would have been wrong. This operation has to succeed. The Spartans used to have a saying, actually, it was the Spartan women, when the men went to war: 'Come back with your shields or on it.' We should all keep that in mind. We have an opportunity here, and we need to take advantage of it. A positive result might make the world a different place. Failure is unacceptable, and is not an option. The word is a firm go from the White House. Congress is not being told until the first wave is on the ground killing bad guys. It's time to take the gloves off."

Turning to the newly promoted Brigadier General Simons, the Chairman said: "Bull, you have done the country a great service at considerable personal risk. You have my personal thanks for what you have done. You have shown all of us what we should have done earlier. It would have saved the country a lot of heartache." Looking at the rest of the grim faced senior officers around the table, he said: "I hope we kick their ass all the way to Thailand."[5]

Orders went out to *MACV,* recalling a furious General Creighton Abrams, who handed his duties to his more than competent Deputy, reminding him that the Cambodia operation was to have the highest priority. His temper and disposition worsened on the long flight home, and was more than ready to burst out as he made his way to the office of the Chief of Staff to report. Not bothering to knock he made his way into the inner office past the office staff who did not dare say anything to Abrams, as they had seen his temper in action before.

Slamming the Chiefs door behind him, violently enough to make the office staff wince, he demanded why he had been relieved with no explanation. The Chief calmly asked Abrams to sit down and have some coffee, and then he very quietly asked him how he would like to command the expeditionary force that was going to invade North Vietnam in June.

There were not too many things that would render Creighton Abrams dumbfounded. This one did.

"Come again, Charlie?" Abrams asked with a ridiculously stupid look on his face.

"I said, Creighton, would you like to command the expeditionary force that is going to invade North Vietnam in four months?"

"You're kidding right? This is a joke, and not a very good one?"

"No, it's a reality. Didn't the Chairman meet you at the airport?" Abrams shook his head. The Chief of Staff continued: "The President gave his approval last week, and the units designated for it are listed in the briefing papers you neglected to pick up from Colonel King on the way in. The Navy units, especially the amphibious ships, have already sailed for Japan and Okinawa. We're invading on June 6. The Cambodia invasion will go ten days earlier. I'll ask just one more time, are you interested?"

Then the Chiefs face broke into a huge grin as he handed Abrams a cigar, followed by an offer of "refreshments." The two old friends then looked at each other and smiled conspiratorially.[6]

The units designated for the invasion were the 173rd Airborne Brigade (Separate), the 11th Armored Cavalry Regiment, the 101st Airborne Division (Airmobile), the 1st Cavalry Division (Airmobile), the 82nd Airborne Division, and the 2nd Marine Division (Provisional), and the 3rd Marine Division (minus). The 2nd Marine Division (Provisional) would be made up of the Headquarters of the 2nd Marine Division stationed at Camp Lejeune, North Carolina, taking the following units organic to that division: the 6th Marine Regiment, an infantry regiment, and the 10th Marine Regiment, which was the division's organic artillery regiment. Two infantry regiments would be attached to it after it arrived in Okinawa, one from each of the Marine divisions in Vietnam. The 4th Marine Regiment and the 9th Marine Regiment would be pulled out of South Vietnam early, and be sent to Okinawa.

The ARVN 1st Cavalry Regiment would participate in the invasion of Cambodia in place of the 11th Cavalry Regiment. Ostensibly, the 11th Cavalry would be redeploying; in reality, it was going to the DMZ to participate in the invasion of the North. The ARVN Marine Division would replace the 3rd Marine Division in I Corps along the DMZ, and the ARVN Airborne Division would be General Davison's reserve for Cambodia. None of these units would be told why they were moving, only that they were. Too many big mouths and ears among them.

No units were going to be pulled out of Europe to participate. The units chosen for Olympic which were already deployed in Vietnam were quickly announced as being designated as part of the President's already planned 150,000 troops reduction for the year. They would be pulled out as entire units, go to Okinawa to retrain and re-equip as well as get replacements, and then stage and embark on US Navy amphibious shipping for the trip across the South China Sea.

Three divisions from the continental United States were designated to be prepared to move to the Far East as follow on to the invasion if needed: the 1st Armored Division, the 3rd Armored Division, and the 5th Infantry Division (Mechanized). Hopefully, they would not be needed. If they had to deploy to Southeast Asia it would mean the invasion was in trouble. They would not even start to move until after D-Day on June 6.[7]

XVIII Airborne Corps Headquarters was deployed immediately to Okinawa and would control the 173rd Airborne Brigade, 82nd Airborne Division, and the 101st Airborne Division. Another corps headquarters, designated II MAF, taken mostly from Camp Lejeune, would control both the Marine Divisions and the 1st Cavalry Division. Don Starry's 11th Cavalry Regiment would be attached to the 3rd Marine Division.

The 11th Cavalry Regiment and the 3rd Marine Division would attack across the DMZ separating North and South Vietnam, and proceed as quickly as possible up Highway 1 on the coast. The 173rd Airborne Brigade would parachute two of its battalions in the vicinity of Hanoi to establish an airhead, the rest of the brigade and the 1st Cavalry Division would reinforce the airhead and head for Hanoi. The 2nd Marine Division would conduct a seaborne assault across the beaches south of Haiphong, while one of its regiments, on four LSTs, would take Haiphong harbor by a *coup de main*. The 82nd Airborne Division would be the force's reserve, to be committed on order.

Prior to this combined effort, Brigadier General Simons would lead a heliborne force of approximately 200 special operations troops to Hanoi and attempt to take the Politburo somewhat intact. This would leave the North Vietnamese virtually leaderless. A massive air and sea bombardment would precede the invasion by 90 minutes.

The Parrot's Beak, Cambodia: May 30,1970

The major units designated for the invasion of Cambodia were the 1st and 9th US Infantry Divisions, supported by all available artillery assets not already allocated to the invasion of the North. The 1st ARVN Cavalry Regiment would screen both units to the north to provide early warning of *NVA* units coming into the area to oppose the invasion of the communist sanctuaries. *COSVN, the Viet Cong* headquarters, was located in the Parrot's Beak, and was a major objective, as were the known communist base camps and supply dumps, but the real objective was to draw as much of the *North Vietnamese Army* as far away from the DMZ as possible. After that, *it* was an economy of force mission, to allow the invasion to succeed nearly unopposed up north, and catch the *NVA* between the northern invasion force and the rest of the US Army and the ARVN.

The invasion was launched behind a massive air and artillery bombardment, and it caught the *NVA* by surprise, both tactically and strategically. The two American divisions quickly overran enemy supply dumps, capturing huge amounts of weapons, ammunition, and supplies, and inflicted heavy casualties on the unsuspecting enemy units. Going faster and farther into Cambodia than expected, the Americans surrounded the *COSVN* area, capturing it on the second day of the invasion, and with it, most of the political infrastructure that had been based there. This, coupled with the immense losses the *Viet Cong* had suffered in their 1968 Tet Offensive, finished off the *Viet Cong* as a viable political and military force in South Vietnam.

The surprised North Vietnamese rushed their closest units to oppose the invasion, but committed them piecemeal, to be torn up suffering heavy losses to the superior firepower of the American and South Vietnamese units. Fresh units had to be pulled out from other areas of South Vietnam and Cambodia to reinforce the battered remnants in the Parrot's Beak, finally halting the American advance on June 3- MACV ordered battalions from the 25th Infantry Division and the 23rd Infantry Division to reinforce the allied effort, and the ARVN Airborne Division was also committed to the Cambodian operation. The *NVA* became desperate, pulling units from wherever it could to stop the allied effort, and its losses in men and material were mounting dangerously. By June 5 the entire Parrot's Beak had been cleared of all North Vietnamese resistance, and their losses were staggering.

Allied intelligence tracked the new units being moved to support those in the invasion area, and allied air and artillery hammered them savagely. At the end of the first week of the invasion, an equivalent of seven North Vietnamese divisions had been committed to stop the allied invasion, and casualties in some units had reached a staggering 70 percent. Average losses in all units exceeded 35 percent. Their orders from Hanoi were to hold at all costs and eject the Americans from Cambodia regardless of the price.

Meanwhile, on June 1 an American naval squadron quietly took up station outside the Cambodian port of Sihanoukville, the main port in Cambodia through which the North Vietnamese funnelled supplies into Cambodia, and then into South Vietnam. Ostensibly "neutral" shipping, in actuality Soviet merchantmen bringing war supplies for the North Vietnamese, were stopped and turned away. The supply of weapons, equipment, and food coming into Cambodia by sea suddenly dried to a trickle and then stopped.[8]

Guam: 2100, June 5,1970

The first B-52 bomber rumbled down the runway, slowly building up speed to lift its huge load from the earth to the sky. The internal bomb bays of each of the huge aircraft were filled to capacity with 500lb bombs. Additionally, each of the monsters had external loads of the same lethal weapons slung under its wings. As the bombers picked up speed and started to lift off the runway, the long sleek wings literally started to flap, oscillating majestically up and down under the weight of the external bomb loads, giving each aircraft the look of a gigantic bird of prey, which, in effect, each of them was.

They were going in three plane groups, an "arclight strike," to North Vietnam to bomb strategic targets in the Hanoi and Haiphong areas. They would carpet-bomb their targets, leaving whatever they hit nothing but a pockmarked ruin. As one witness described such a raid, they did not have to hit their target, just get close to it to neutralize it.[9]

The bomber crews knew nothing of the planned invasion, just that their new air offensive against the North was to force the North Vietnamese to get serious at the conference table. The air portion of the invasion, dubbed Linebacker II, was an all-out air effort against North Vietnam. Air Force aircraft from Thailand, as well as Navy and Marine aircraft from US Navy aircraft carriers in the Tonkin Gulf were also flying sorties in this new offensive which would continue until the North Vietnamese cried "uncle." The aircrews were told the gloves were off and that Washington was serious. They would see later if their efforts were worth it or not.

By the time the B-52s returned to Guam, the American assault force would be ashore in North Vietnam.

Over North Vietnam: 0300, June 6,1970

"Wild Weasel" was their nickname, and they were F-105 Thunderchief two seat fighter-bombers, affectionately called "Thuds" by their crews. They were armed with an impressive array of electronic detection equipment as well as Shrike anti-radar missiles as their payload. They were SAM hunters. They went into the night to ferret out the North Vietnamese anti-aircraft sites for destruction by allied aircraft. They hunted alone, and their job was to get the North Vietnamese, and the Russians who also manned anti-aircraft sites in the North, to light up their target acquisition radars and fire at them. It was exciting, lonely, dangerous, and very deadly.

Within striking distance, but out of radar range of the SAMs, the strike force which would actually launch the ordnance against the targets waited for the call from the Weasel. Tonight, the strike force was made of Air Force F-4s, and they had worked with this particular Weasel before.

Lieutenant Colonel Sam FitzHugh, and his backseater Major William Morrow, were expert at playing the game. Shot down once, they had still been successful in every Weasel mission they had flown. Skirting the hills and flying low, periodically popping up long enough to provoke a radar contact, and usually the missile that went with it, they were carefully scanning the darkened terrain below, looking for the telltale missile blast.

"Come on, Luke, time to come out and play with Daddy," FitzHugh spoke conversationally into the microphone. Morrow chuckled, and then shouted "missile launch" as the alarm beeper went off in the cockpit. FitzHugh immediately took the Thud into a steep dive; the missile veered, and then went into the aluminum chaff that FitzHugh had released behind them, exploding harmlessly. "Target acquired, ordnance launched," came in from the strike leader, and both FitzHugh and Morrow watched satisfied as the SAM site was hit and neutralized.[10]

"One down, three to go," muttered Morrow as FitzHugh turned the aircraft towards the next target. All over North Vietnam the same thing was happening to the enemy anti-aircraft network. The gloves had indeed come off.

Outside Haiphong Harbor: 0400, June 6,1970

The four LSTs carrying Battalion Landing Team 2/6 (Reinforced), flying Soviet naval ensigns and having their running lights rigged as merchantmen silently glided towards the entrance to Haiphong harbor. Their mission was to land at the quayside in the harbor, disembark the three Marine battalions crammed into their flat-bottomed hulls, and attempt to capture and hold, relatively intact, a portion of the port until relieved by ground forces.

The four captains had been told that their ships were expendable and to get the Marines ashore at all costs. The harbor must be taken and held. There would be air support once it was light, and reinforcements should be there by 1800 on D-Day, but the section of the harbor seized by them had to be held at all costs. They must not get sunk until all the Marines and their equipment were ashore.

There was a flotilla of four destroyers close by in case they got into trouble on the way in to the approaches to the harbor, but once inside, they were on their own. They were to enter the harbor at H-90 and hoped to land their troops by H-60. Then they had to hold until relieved.[11]

The Gulf of Tonkin: 0430, June 6,1970

The USS *New Jersey* was steaming on station with its escort of destroyers and cruisers, taking up, with its battle group, its fire support position. The battleship was at general quarters, sailors manning its three immense turrets, the deadly 16-inch naval rifles having been checked and rechecked for the upcoming fire support mission the *New Jersey* and its battle group had been assigned. All hands were more than ready for this mission, for which they had trained endlessly for the past month.

Off its port quarter, the USS *Newport News,* a heavy cruiser fitted with 8-inch guns, was turning into the wind, getting onto its station, its naval rifles not having the range of the huge guns on the *New Jersey.* The destroyer escort screen was dividing up between the two larger ships, to protect them from the light craft, especially torpedo boats, that the minuscule *North Vietnamese Navy* was known to possess.

The battle group's fire support mission was to suppress enemy radar and anti-air assets along the three preplanned air corridors leading into North Vietnam.

On the bridge, the captain of the *New Jersey* turned to his gunnery officer and the navigator: "Bring her on station." "Aye, sir," answered the navigator, giving the helm order to the pilothouse. Slowly, and with great dignity, the World War II battleship turned into the wind and ran parallel with the Vietnamese coast. The ship's gunnery officer looked at the captain and said: "Do you think they're ready for this one skipper?" Grimly shaking his head the captain answered: "They're about to get an education."

Commands went down from the bridge to the main battery, the huge turrets rotating, the guns elevating like the snouts of some primeval beasts, sniffing for their prey as they methodically and majestically turned to port. When they were at the required bearing, the gunnery officer told the captain: "Safe and ready sir." The captain looked at the young gunnery officer and grinned: "You may fire when ready, Gridley."[12]

The "Hanoi Hilton": June 6,1970

The helicopters swooped in low over the city in the predawn darkness, the natural stillness broken continuously by American air raids, the explosions of dropped ordnance ripping through the constant noise of the helicopter engines. The concussion of the B-52 raids on the helicopters was terrific, the birds being thrown around in the sky, the pilots pulling hard on the controls to bring them back to their selected route in to Hanoi.

Aboard the lead aircraft, Bull Simons was going through the mission checklist in his head. Their objective was the notorious North Vietnamese prison, dubbed the Hanoi Hilton, where the greater majority of the American prisoners of war were being held. The raiding force was built around the veterans of the Son Tay raid, augmented to 200 with carefully selected and screened volunteers, most of them from other Special Forces units. Not only would they have to overcome all resistance in the prison to free the prisoners, they would have to hold until the helicopters could come back to pick them up, as the closest landing zone was 500 yards from the prison in a park, and they could not loiter in the capital after putting the landing force on the roof of the prison and several adjoining buildings. This was going to be a rough one.

They were going to be just as heavy losses, if not heavier, for the other two special operations missions that were taking place simultaneously with this one. The other two targets were the Defense Ministry and the Politburo. The missions were going to be snatch missions, in that people were going to be taken, alive or dead, and brought out again. The mission profile was very low—five helicopters and 24 men per mission. One of the helicopters was flying in empty to take the prisoners back with it.

What they wanted was the Politburo and General Giap, with as many of his staff as they could cram on the Huey. Both groups were known to meet early in the morning while it was still dark in order to avoid the American air raids, at least most of them. Both groups would land on the roof of their respective buildings, head downstairs and kill or capture their respective targets. That would leave the North Vietnamese leaderless. Casualties were expected to be heavy but for targets like these it was worth it. Even if they killed all of the bad guys it was better than nothing. Bringing back prisoners, though, was highly encouraged.

Simons, sitting close behind the cockpit of the Huey, was alerted by the pilot as the objective approached. Pointing to the pilot where he wanted the bird put down, Simons turned to the grim-faced young men of his team, and gave them the thumbs up sign. Grinning slightly at their response, he removed the headsets and put a green beret on his head as the bird landed on the roof of the Hanoi Hilton and his men exited the aircraft, weapons at the ready.[13]

LZ X-Ray, near Hanoi, North Vietnam: H-30
Brigadier General Hal Moore, commander of the veteran 173rd Airborne Brigade, was in the first stick of the first C-130 aircraft that would begin dumping its cargo of paratroopers from the brigade into the skies over North Vietnam. As a battalion commander in the 1st Cavalry Division in 1965, Moore had fought the first significant American ground action of

the war against North Vietnamese regulars. They were a tough, veteran, and skilled enemy, and although Moore had been briefed that resistance should be minimal, he was not taking any chances.

If this was going to be a Cakewalk they would soon find out, but Moore had briefed his four battalion commanders that this might be the hardest fight they had ever had. Harder even than the famous Dak To fight in November 1967, when the 2nd Battalion of the 503rd infantry, one of the brigade's four airborne infantry battalions, was awarded a Presidential Unit Citation.

They were jumping into the enemy's heartland just outside his capital, and Moore expected resistance to be savage. He did not care that the entire *North Vietnamese Army* was in the south. When had the intelligence wallahs been right so far in this messed up war. At least they were doing the right thing, invading the North, and the brigade was up for it. They should have done this two and a half years ago after Tet 68. Better late than never.

Moore looked at his watch, and then turned to look at the two lights, the green one that would go on when it was time to jump. The jumpmaster, whom Moore had known for years, grinned at him and gave him a thumbs up. He would jump last, after the stick was out the door.

Suddenly, the jumpmaster pounded Moore on the back, pointed at the open door of the C-130 and yelled "GO!' into his ear. Moore flung himself from the aircraft, feet and knees together into the blackness of the North Vietnamese morning, as his parachute was torn from its pack by the static line. It was a combat jump and they were at 500 feet.

Although they wore two parachutes, the second one being the reserve in case the primary failed, it was a superfluous gesture. If the main parachute did not open from that height, there was not enough time to deploy the reserve manually. To Moore's intense relief, his main parachute opened perfectly, and he descended quickly, but safely to the ground. Once again, he had maintained his promise to be the first one of his unit to go in.[14]

The DMZ: H-Hour, June 6,1970

The leading elements of the 11th Armored Cavalry Regiment crossed the DMZ exactly at H-Hour, racing up Highway 1 into North Vietnam. There was token resistance, which was quickly brushed aside, the artillery bombardment at known enemy locations being more effective than they had initially planned. The air bombardment had also done its job as promised, and the troopers were fully into North Vietnam making their way to their initial objectives along the coast.

Behind them, the 3rd Marine Division was clearing enemy elements that had been bypassed by the cavalrymen. The intelligence reports had for once been close to correct, there was not enough here to stop a sick cat, and the cavalrymen and Marines were neither cats nor sick.

At the same time the 2nd Marine Division was landing unopposed on beaches south of Haiphong, while the 1st Cavalry Division was air assaulting two brigades simultaneously into Hanoi and its environs, followed as soon as possible by its third brigade, taking only as long as necessary for the helicopters to fly back to the assault ships and refuel, rearm if necessary, and reload with more troops.

The airhead was held at first by the four battalions of the 173rd Airborne Brigade, but when the 1st Cavalry Division landed and took over the perimeter, the four infantry battalions of the 173rd moved out to seize its objective, which was Hanoi. It was followed by two brigades of the 1st Cavalry Division. Heavy equipment and weapons were flown into the airhead later that afternoon, and by 0600 on June 7, all of the assault units were on the ground, the initial objectives were seized, and there was fighting in downtown Hanoi.

The 2nd Marine Division linked up with its battalion in Haiphong harbor at 0300 on June 7. The lead battalion had suffered minimal losses in its assault, although one of the LSTs had been sunk by fast gunboats of the *North Vietnamese Navy*. As the battalion was landing, the commander of the destroyer flotilla had disobeyed orders and gone into the harbor on hearing the LSTs were under attack, and had scattered or destroyed all of the North Vietnamese naval units in the area. Thereafter, they had supplied close in fire support to the Marines who had beaten off one determined North Vietnamese assault, and a few minor ones that had gone nowhere. Haiphong was secured.

Simons' raiders took and held the Hanoi Hilton, but they were trapped when available *NVA* units moved against them. They lost heavily defending the prisoners, but held against determined efforts to retake the prison. They were finally rescued when the 2nd Battalion of the 503rd Infantry from the 173rd Airborne Brigade broke through to them at 1300 on June 7. They captured both East German and Cuban interrogators in the prison who were later identified by many of the prisoners as those who had ordered them to be tortured.[15]

The 101st Airborne Division was brought in to the airhead after the 1st Cavalry Division, and it was this unit that fought the largest battle of the invasion. The North Vietnamese recovered their wits by noon on D-Day, and all support and training units were hastily organized to begin counterattacks on the afternoon of June 6. To the Americans' surprise, they had armor—Russian PT-76s and old T-54/55s which initially caused heavy losses to the 101st. Artillery batteries engaged in gunfights with North Vietnamese armor, sometimes at point blank range, the artillerymen giving as good as they got.

US airpower struck back swiftly, hitting the North Vietnamese assembly areas, and going in low and close to knock out *NVA* armor. The North Vietnamese took half the airhead before they were done, and casualties in the 101st were unusually heavy. However, with the final repulse of this *NVA* counter-attack early on June 7, the last organized resistance in the Hanoi/Haiphong area ceased.

Both Hanoi and Haiphong were declared secured at 1200 on June 10. The Marines and cavalry men fighting their way up Highway 1 linked up with the troops in the north at 1900, June 12. They had encountered no significant resistance from the North Vietnamese, overrunning SAM sites and isolated units piecemeal, the cavalry bypassing them and the Marines mopping them up.

Long Range Penetration and Ranger teams had been inserted into Laos along the Ho Chi Minh Trail ten days prior to the invasion. What Colonel Simons had said was true—it was a one-way road, and that road was south. They had watched as more troops and supplies were carried south to support the *NVA* in Cambodia and South Vietnam. As the air offensive picked up, that steady stream slowed to a trickle. On June 10, ARVN Marine units were sent into Laos to cut the trail permanently. The *NVA* units south of them were hopelessly cut off.

The two raids into Hanoi to capture the Politburo and Defense Ministry were both successful, but at heavy cost. The mission at the Defense Ministry met the most resistance. Over half of the raiders were killed or wounded, but General Giap was captured and flown out immediately to the fleet. Joining them were Pham Van Dong and Le Due Tho, leaders of the North Vietnamese government after the death of Ho Chi Minh. The North Vietnamese snake was effectively decapitated.

Denouement

The *NVA* found itself to be cut off in South Vietnam as a result of the naval blockade and the successful US invasion. Suffering very heavy losses to General Davison's invasion force in Cambodia, with no hope of resupply or reinforcements, it surrendered to the Americans and South Vietnamese in August 1970.

The campaign slashed the North Vietnamese jugular so quickly that the Soviet Union had no time to react. Thousands of Soviet, Warsaw Pact, and Cuban military and civilian personnel had been captured along with very embarrassing documentation. The US made the most of this propaganda windfall and promptly sent most of the Soviets and their friends home. China made the required anti-Western noises but also chose to emphasize that Soviet attempts to outflank China had failed and clearly noted that US forces had left a wide buffer zone along the Chinese border that they had not entered.[16]

The North Vietnamese delegation to the Paris Peace Talks signed, with little choice, a peace treaty with the Americans and South Vietnamese in December 1970. By the treaty, the independence of South Vietnam was guaranteed and the North Vietnamese Army laid down its arms and was repatriated to the North on a schedule that would conclude in December 1971. A United Nations observer and peacekeeper force was put into North Vietnam by the treaty. Nonetheless, the United States, on the Korean model, remained effectively in charge. Chinese opposition to this arrangement was muted in the fanfare of the clearly anti-Soviet Sino-American Treaty of Shanghai that resulted from the historic meeting of President Nixon and Chairman Mao in early 1972.

The Reality

Unfortunately, there was no invasion of North Vietnam, for which there were two opportunities: after Tet 68 and again after the Son Tay raid in November 1970 (not in January as portrayed in this chapter). The *North Vietnamese Army* was largely in the South and could not have deployed in time to stop an invasion. The political will, however, did not exist to end the war in that manner. There was concern over Chinese intervention/ interference, which undoubtedly was a factor in the decision not to invade. The American participation in the war was ended with the signing of the peace treaty in Paris in 1973, after the North Vietnamese were decisively defeated in the Easter Offensive in the spring of 1972.

The United States did invade Cambodia in April 1970 in the Parrot's Beak region. Large quantities of supplies were captured and heavy losses inflicted on the North Vietnamese. *COSVN* was not found or taken, unfortunately.

By the peace treaty, the existence and independence of South Vietnam were guaranteed. After the United States had withdrawn its troops and air power, the North Vietnamese waited until 1975 to invade and conquer South Vietnam, in direct violation of the 1973 treaty. While there had been great howls of anguish from the radical left in the United States over the US involvement, as well as violent anti-war protests during that period, the immense silence after the fall of South Vietnam from those same sources is noteworthy.

Bibliography

Burkett, B.G., and Whitley, Glenna, *Stolen Valor: How the Vietnam Generation was Robbed of its Heroes and its History,* Verity Press, Dallas, TX, 1998.

Palmer, David, *Summons of the Trumpet: U.S.-Vietnam in Perspective,* Presidio Press, San Rafael, CA, 1978.

Schemmer, Benjamin F, *The Raid,* Harper and Row, New York, 1976.

Stanton, Shelby, *The Rise and Fall of an American Army: U.S. Ground Forces in Vietnam, 1965–1973.*

Time-Life, *The Vietnam Experience,* Boston Publishing, Boston, 1986.

Notes

*1. Simons, Arthur, Into the North: The US Invasion of North Vietnam (McGill, New York, 1975), p. 45.

2. The President's secretary, of Watergate fame, or infamy, whichever you prefer.

*3. Simons, Into the North, p. 56.

4. Burkett and Whitley, Stolen Valor, p. 112.

*5. Simons, Into the North, p. 97.

*6. Abrams, Creighton, Memoir of an Invasion (Patton Press, Fort Knox, KY, 1974), p. 29.

7. The available units in Germany had to remain in place for the NATO commitments. There was considerable worry over the status quo in Europe at this time. The Russians had invaded Czechoslavokia in 1968. Units in the US were not at full strength or readiness. Some, such as part of the 82nd Airborne Division, and the 101st before it deployed to Vietnam, were used for riot control duty.

*8. Abrams, Memoir of an Invasion, p. 121.

9. This little gem was uttered by one of the Marines who served with the author in Saudi Arabia and Kuwait one evening when we were watching a B-52 strike into Kuwait. Interesting, to say the least.

*10. FitzHugh, Samuel R., Wild Weasels (Collins, London, 1980), p. 221.

11. This scenario was presented by the author in a staff planning course in the early 1980s, though the objective in the exercise was not Haiphong. To put it simply, it was not well received by certain higher ranking personnel.

12. This was the famous command issued by Commodore George Dewey to the captain of his flagship, the USS Olympia, that began the Battle of Manila Bay on 1 May 1898.

*13. Simons, Into the North, p. 289.

*14. Collins, Tom, The Last Combat Jump (Venable House, New York, 1990), p. 147.

*15. Most of the captured interrogators were killed in the subsequent North Vietnamese counter-attacks on the Hanoi Hilton. Simons, Into the North, p. 331.

*16. Herrington, Stuart, The History of Soviet Involvement in the War in Southeast Asia (Schlaeger Books, Boulder, CO, 1985), pp. 237–42.

8
FIRE AND ICE
Sixth Fleet versos *Fifth Eskadra,* October 1973

Wade G. Dudley

A Poem

"Some say the world will end in fire, others say in ice," murmured the young officer, shrouded in the darkness of a moonless Mediterranean night. "What's that, sir?" asked the tired petty officer standing at his side, both taking the air at the taffrail of the USS *Aubrey* after a long shift in the Combat Information Center (CIC). Lieutenant Rick Gadsden considered his answer as the guided missile destroyer furrowed the sea, one of three consorts to the cruiser *Little Rock,* flagship of the United States' Sixth Fleet. Why had those lines come to mind? Perhaps it was the running lights of the Russian warship shadowing the American task force, a vivid reminder of the Cold War in which Gadsden had lived his entire life. Perhaps it was some memory of his first six months at sea, cruising on Yankee Station—a vision of flaming engines as Intruders launched into just such a night to deliver a payload of death over North Vietnam.

"Just an old poem about the cold of hate and the fires of passion." The sailor chuckled: "Well, I can't think of anyone that I hate right now, and passion's gonna have to wait until we get back to Athens." Both laughed—the fleshpots of Athens were well known and beloved by the entire fleet—and headed for their too warm bunks and a few hours' sleep. "By the way, sir, happy birthday." Gadsden had forgotten that the newborn day, October 6, 1973, marked his having survived to the ripe old age of 24. Neither man knew that before the moon had again run through its phases, both would be baptized in fire as the ice of a war grown cold quickly melted.[1]

Ice and Fire

Following World War II, the clash of political ideologies backed by the militarism developed during years of constant conflict forced nations into one of three increasingly armed camps. The Western Bloc, those nations that (more or less) embraced the principles of democracy and capitalism, looked to the United States for leadership. That nation had emerged from World War II as a true superpower: highly industrialized, tremendously wealthy, and the only possessor of the atomic bomb with its fearsome destructive capability. The Eastern Bloc, most members having been rapidly indoctrinated in the joys of communism after Soviet occupation in 1945, carefully watched Russia (formally the Union of Soviet Socialist Republics) for its cue. The USSR's sheer land mass, tremendous military-industrial base, and its development of an atomic weapons' program in the late 1940s guaranteed its place as the world's second superpower.

A third camp, that of non-aligned nations, constantly dwindled over time. In an increasingly bipolar world, its axis drawn through the United States and the USSR, neutrality was dangerous. Neither the American CIA nor the Russian KGB had scruples about toppling a government and replacing it with a more pliable regime. Besides, both powers were more than willing to trade money and weapons for allegiance to their cause. What matter if the image on the coin was that of Washington or Lenin, or if the weapon was stamped Kalashnikov or McDonnell-Douglas? If these gifts came with ideological price tags, so be it: rallying cries were always needed and "Free the working class" worked as well as "Pay the working class more" in most situations. So, one by one, Third World nations abandoned their cries of Pan-Africanism and Pan-Asianism to militarize and take their proper place as card-carrying, gun-bearing capitalist lackeys or communist dogs (take your pick, remembering that the status could change based upon the origin of the next monetary donation or shipment of weapons).

This bipolar world was one of often unreasoning hatred firmly based in the almighty opposites of capitalism and communism, of democracy and totalitarianism. No middle ground existed. Witch hunts and purges proliferated on all sides, generating a howling fear which only increased existing hatred. By the early 1970s, it was as if humanity was locked in ice, a very Cold War.

But this Cold War was not without its flames. The price of admittance for a Third World nation was often paid, and willingly so, in blood. From the hills of Greece to the jungles of Malaysia to the mountains of Peru, men and women waged civil wars for political control of their nations or settled old scores with their neighbors using weapons and funds provided by one or both superpowers.

One popular conception of the Cold War presents it as a clash of surrogates—the United States and the USSR struggling vicariously on third world battlegrounds. If so, the great puppeteers were not very accomplished at controlling their strings. In 1950, North Korea's rush across the DMZ disconcerted that nation's supposed Russian masters, while it has never been unusual for Americans to be fired upon by weapons of their own manufacture. Apparently the only thing the superpowers were worse at than "managing" foreign wars was direct intervention. Vietnam and Afghanistan were debacles of the first order, toppling those individuals in power to the right and left, and providing proof positive that entrance into a conflict requires a reasonable strategy for exiting the conflict. Unfortunately, the Cold War, by its very nature, allowed only one possible exit strategy: the complete elimination of the opposition.

By mid-1973, that elimination had not been realized, though certainly an excellent opportunity for a thorough rearrangement of much of the world's topography had been barely averted during the Cuban Missile Crisis of the early 1960s. The strategy of Mutual Assured Destruction (aptly abbreviated as MAD) embraced by both the USA and the USSR promised a most unsatisfactory conclusion if passions ran uncontrolled, so brinkmanship and plausible deniability became the order of the day. Though the wall of ice could be chipped by such endeavors as the Strategic Arms Limitation Treaty (SALT) of 1972 and smoothed by reciprocal visits of dignitaries, it would continue to exist.

But neither superpower reckoned with their client states in the Middle East. There the fire of war burned hot, fed by religious passion and a desire for revenge. There those who dispensed the tools of war so readily in the name of ideology would discover that their world could easily end in fire— the flames of a nuclear holocaust.

Setting the Stage

In March 1971, as President Richard Nixon and his Presidential Assistant for National Security Affairs, Henry Kissinger, struggled to disentangle the United States from its involvement in Vietnam, American congressmen engaged in the yearly fiasco of budget-planning. Their proposed allocations, a direct reflection of public sentiment regarding Vietnam in particular and war in general, stressed reduction of conventional military forces. Projected cuts in appropriations for naval construction, amounting to a billion dollars in 1973, concerned the Chief of Naval Operations, Admiral Elmo R. Zumwalt, Jr. On March 5, he routed a telling memorandum up the chain of command:

> "I find this potential force reduction, in addition to the requirements for broad cuts in planned procurements designed to modernize our forces for the future, to be unacceptable in the face of the Soviet threat... I have informed you repeatedly of my concern for the continuing degradation of Naval capabilities... In my judgment, the end FY '70 forces gave us a 55 percent probability of success if we become involved in a conflict at sea with the Soviet Union... While I judge our naval forces today have only a 35 percent chance in an engagement with the Soviet Union, that level of confidence is reduced to 20 percent based on [new

budget projections}. It is perfectly clear that we are unable to support the fighting of a war overseas by the U.S. or allied forces should the Soviet Union challenge the U.S. for control of the seas..."[2]

Zumwalt's concerns were valid. By 1972, major naval assets of the Soviet Union, on a hull for hull basis, outnumbered those of the US Navy by 820 to 447. The disparity would increase as aging American warships, many built during World War II, made their final journey to the salvage yards. Only in the category of carriers would the Western superpower maintain a clear superiority, and in most potential theaters of operations that superiority could easily be challenged by land-based communist air power.[3]

Far more telling as to the potential for conflict was the increasing number of Soviet ships at sea throughout the world. Between 1956 and 1972, ship-days (days at sea per hull) had increased from 500 to 14,500 in the Atlantic Ocean, from none to 1,900 in the Caribbean Sea, from 200 to 5,900 in the Pacific Ocean, from none to 8,900 in the Indian Ocean, and from 100 to 17,700 in the Mediterranean Sea.[4] In the last named theater of operations, ship-days of the USSR's *Fifth Eskadra* considerably exceeded those of the US Sixth Fleet.[5] Greater Soviet presence at sea also increased the direct confrontations between vessels and aircraft of the two superpowers, ranging from near-misses and collisions to charges of gunfire (hotly denied, of course). Frequently, officers on both sides would simulate attacks on ships and aircraft of the opposite fleets—but only in the name of realistic training. In times of increased international tension, such confrontations tended to be more numerous, with the potential for assuming deadly proportions.[6]

The Nixon White House, very much aware of the anti-militarism prevalent in public opinion, developed a three-prong approach to maintaining political power. Internationally, the Nixon Doctrine called for support of foreign allies without committing American troops. This aid would take the form of both cash and military materials. Meanwhile, Kissinger sought detente—a thawing of the Cold War—through both public and private meetings with communist leaders, most visible in the continuing SALT talks and in paving the way for Nixon to visit Communist China. Domestically, the Nixon approach was far more subtle, at least until federal investigations revealed the Watergate break-in of June 1972. Each of these strands would play a key role in the events of October 1973.

Detente was acceptable to Moscow, as long as it did not give the appearance of weakness within the Soviet Union. Leonid Brezhnev, General Secretary of the Communist Party and leading member of the Politburo (the penultimate governing body of the USSR), had no illusions that any direct military confrontation with the United States held the seeds of nuclear holocaust. Imbedded in the Russian memory was how the Russian Empire had stumbled to its destruction in 1914 by letting the intemperate actions of clients rather than calculation drag it into World War I. Still, the world was a troubled place, and Soviet client states did not always practice restraint. Thus Brezhnev could not have been surprised when, on October 3, 1973, President Anwar Sadat of Egypt informed the Soviet Union that Egypt and Syria planned to employ the weapons supplied by their communist benefactors to settle, once and for all, the "Middle Eastern Question." Realizing that Sadat would attack Israel regardless of Brezhnev's opinion, the Soviet leader began the evacuation of Russian non-combatants from Egypt while warning the Arab leader that his attack must be successful since the Soviet Union could not guarantee full replacement of expended or destroyed material.[7]

The Yom Kippur War

The Arab-Israeli War of 1973 has several names. It is often referred to as the October War, having opened and ended within the same month. Arabs frequently refer to the event as the Ramadan War, as it was fought during that holy month of the Muslim calendar, while Israelis invariably refer to the incident as the Yom Kippur War, since the initial Arab assault came on that Jewish holy day.[8] Outside the Middle East—in that unforgiving portion of the world the events of 30 years past are still quite relevant and daily cry for revenge—the conflict is more often than not simply remembered as the precursor to the Confrontation of 1973.

Regardless of name, history records that at 1400 hours on October 6, Egypt and Syria unleashed a massive assault on unprepared Israeli forces. By the end of the first day of combat, Syrian armor had achieved significant gains along the Golan Heights, the most direct route into Israel, while Egyptian forces had pierced the Bar Lev Line, Israel's strong but undermanned defensive positions along the Suez Canal. Israeli commanders were shocked by the lavishly equipped Arab forces. Most surprising of all were the man-portable Sagger wire-guided anti-tank missiles and the dense concentration of SAM (surface-to-air missile) sites. Israeli armor and air losses quickly mounted, and reserves considered adequate for a repeat of the Six Day War of 1967 suffered rapid depletion. The Israeli government immediately appealed to the United States for emergency military aid.

Despite the knowledge that Soviet shipments of weapons to Arab states had not wavered (freighters stuffed with weapons and munitions had left the Black Sea port of Odessa bound for Egypt and Syria as the conflict began, while an airlift continuously operated through the first days of the war), the Nixon government hesitated. Some sources blame Kissinger for the delay in supporting the only ally of the United States in the Middle East, claiming that he felt a military defeat would make Israel more willing to consider concessions necessary for a lasting peace in the region. Others point to the State Department's unwillingness to face a potential oil embargo by Arab nations. In truth, President Nixon's time was so consumed by the rapidly progressing Watergate scandal, coupled with the cloud of corruption surrounding Vice President Spiro Agnew, who would resign on October 10, that it impaired sound judgment throughout the executive branch.[9] Only late on that same day did the president authorize Operation Nickel Grass, the resupply of Israel by the Military Airlift Command (MAC). He approved the operation's continuance for over a month, until the first seaborne supplies would arrive at Israeli ports.[10]

As events unraveled, a rapid Israeli mobilization allowed counter-attacks against both Syria and Egypt to begin as early as October 8. On the Golan Heights, Israel rapidly achieved dominance. By October 11, its artillery and planes were actually attacking targets inside Syria and an advance against the Syrian capital, Damascus, appeared feasible. Strikes against Egyptian forces in Sinai were repulsed on October 8 and 9 with heavy losses, though they slowed the Egyptian advance and allowed the concentration of further Israeli reserves. By October 10, Egyptian forces had at last advanced beyond the protective umbrella of the fixed SAM sites located on the western bank of the Suez Canal. This allowed Israeli ground forces, strongly supported by air power, to stabilize the front and to begin a series of counter-actions culminating in a massive armor battle on October 14. Tank losses ran over 20:1 in favor of the Israeli forces, shattering Egyptian morale and opening the door to an advance to the canal itself.

The Yom Kippur War did not limit itself to land. In the Mediterranean, an aggressive Israeli Navy quickly achieved dominance despite being outnumbered by a factor of 2:1. The most outstanding action was the Battle of Latakia, fought near the Syrian port of that name on October 7. There six Israeli missile boats engaged and sank a small patrol craft with 76mm gunfire and a minesweeper with a Gabriel missile, then dueled with three Syrian missile boats. Despite the fact that the Soviet Styx missiles employed by the Syrians possessed twice the range of the Israeli Gabriels, effective use of electronic counter-measures (ECM) and chaff led to the destruction of all three Syrian vessels without a single Israeli loss.[11] After this encounter, Syrian and Egyptian vessels kept to port, allowing Israeli boats a free hand in supporting coastal operations.

Strengthened by the now rapidly arriving American aid, Israeli forces crossed the Suez Canal on October 16. By October 21, Israeli armor had advanced to within 40 miles of Cairo while isolating the Egyptian *Third Army* in the Sinai. On the Golan front, despite reinforcements dispatched to Syria by Iraq and Jordan and a threat of direct intervention by Soviet paratroopers, Israeli brigades held positions only ten miles from Damascus. Clearly, if a quick political solution could not be found, Israel's military solution—the total conquest of those countries that had attacked it by surprise—would irrevocably destabilize the Middle East.

The world's leading statesmen had been seeking that political solution since October 11, when the Soviet ambassador to the United States, Anatoly Dobrynin, had broached the subject with Kissinger, along with a stern warning that Russia would commit its airborne troops to Damascus rather than allow the Israelis to capture it. On October 16, Soviet pressure on the United States to curb Israel had increased when Sadat formally requested that the Soviet Union initiate a cease-fire motion in the United Nations. Further pressure on the United States appeared the following day, when members of the Organization of Petroleum Exporting Countries (OPEC) announced an embargo on supplies to Israel and its supporters.[12] On October 20, Kissinger himself arrived in Moscow. The following day, Kissinger and Brezhnev agreed on the text for UN Security Council Resolution 338, calling for an immediate cease-fire followed by negotiations to reach "a just and durable peace settlement in the Middle East."[13] Jointly introduced by the United States and the USSR in the Security Council on October 22, the resolution immediately passed. Kissinger flew from Moscow directly to Tel Aviv to pressure the Israeli government into accepting the cease-fire. Both superpowers felt certain the war would end that same day. Unfortunately, they had reckoned without the Arabs and Israelis.

Within hours of the cease-fire going into effect, the isolated and increasingly desperate Egyptian *Third Army* attempted to escape from its pocket. Blaming the Israelis for the resulting military operations, Brezhnev sent a strongly worded message to Washington. Kissinger immediately pressured his UN ambassador to try again, and another attempt at an armistice was set for October 24. In the hours after the abortive escape attempt, however, Israeli forces had resumed military action all along the Egyptian front, steadily expanding their bridgehead on the Egyptian side of the canal. This time, both sides ignored the UN resolution.

Frustration reigned among the key leaders of both superpowers. In the United States, the frustration was accompanied by the genuine exhaustion of Nixon, whose every waking moment revolved around Watergate, and the globe-hopping Kissinger. Late in the evening of October 24, Soviet Ambassador Dobrynin delivered a message to Kissinger from Brezhnev. In part, it read:

> "Let us together, the Soviet Union and the United States, urgently dispatch Soviet and American military contingents to Egypt to ensure implementation of the Security Council decision of October 22 and 23 concerning the cessation of fire and all military activities, and also of our understanding with you on the guarantee of the implementation of the Security Council decisions. It is necessary to adhere without delay. I will say it straight that if you find it impossible to act jointly with us in this matter, we should be faced with the necessity urgently to consider taking appropriate steps unilaterally. We cannot allow arbitrariness on the part of Israel."[14]

Taken at face value, the first paragraph did little except restate agreements discussed previously with Kissinger, while the second paragraph could easily have been accepted as posturing, especially considering that the Soviet Union had not dispatched troops at a time when those forces would have assisted the Arab states in actually accomplishing their objectives. The failure of the Soviet Union to act unilaterally in recent days should have encouraged Kissinger to seek another bout of diplomacy. Instead, the exhausted leadership of the National Security Council, meeting in emergency session shortly after the delivery of the document, reacted strongly to the threat of intervention. On October 25, at 0025 hours, the White House ordered the military forces of the United States to set DefCon 3 world-wide.[15] No member of the council nor the high-ranking military officers who quickly began to implement the increased alert level could have guessed that within hours their action would lead to a full fledged naval engagement between American and Soviet warships in the Mediterranean.

Sixth Fleet and *Fifth Eskadra,* October 6–24

The conflict that opened in the Middle East found Vice Admiral Daniel Murphy's Sixth Fleet scattered far and wide across the Mediterranean basin. Task Group (TG) 60, comprising the cruiser *Little Rock* (fleet flagship, with Murphy aboard) and escorts, cruised south of Crete. TG 60.1, the carrier *Independence* and escorts, rested in Athens, near the end of a brief, but deserved, liberty run. TG 60.2, the carrier *Franklin Delano Roosevelt* and escorts, had scattered among several Spanish harbors for refit, resupply, and (when the workday ended) recreation. TG 60/61, a ten-ship amphibious group built around the *Guadalcanal* and transporting Marine Battalions 2/6 and 3/6, was anchored in various Greek ports.

Aside from its task groups, several units of the Sixth Fleet operated independently on October 6, such as the five attack submarines maneuvering at various points and Patrol Division 21 (Patrol Gunboat Tender *Graham County* and the Patrol Gunboats *Antelope, Defiance,* and *Surprise)* at Naples, as well as the usual replenishment ships.[16] Air assets, aside from carrier planes, included the crack Patrol Squadron 45 (VP-45) at Siganella, Sicily, equipped with Orion P-3Cs and fresh from winning the coveted Captain Arnold J. Isbell Trophy for excellence in anti-submarine warfare (ASW) operations.[17]

The men and women commanded by Murphy were highly experienced in the arts of war. Vietnam had seen to that. Still, among their number could be found a smattering of newbies and transfers (as well as the combat burnouts) who bore watching and training. Overall, the admiral was happy with his people—it was the "highly experienced" equipment that worried him. Too many of his vessels were approaching the end of their useful lives, and the dwindling naval budget meant that they could not be replaced.

Already, ships were in short supply in every potential theater of war. In the Mediterranean, both simulations and strategists agreed that a minimum of three carriers would be needed immediately in a hot war situation (four carriers if the USSR was joined by its Arab allies). Like it or not, however, he would see that third carrier only when the situation neared an explosion point, and then only at the expense of another admiral's bailiwick. Murphy only hoped that the Russkies did not get the jump on him before he could concentrate his scattered forces.

On the morning of October 6, however, it did not appear that the Soviet *Fifth Eskadra* had any warlike intentions. Most of its surface warships— three cruisers, seven destroyers, and nine frigates or corvettes, along with two amphibious vessels, two minesweepers, and several replenishment ships—were anchored in various ports in the Eastern Mediterranean. Additionally, American intelligence had plotted 16 Russian attack submarines operating in recent weeks, almost evenly divided between the Eastern and Western Mediterranean. Intelligence was also aware that the Soviets always relieved their on station submarines in mid-October, so the number of submarines would fluctuate over the next two weeks, and every effort would be made to identify the newcomers as they transited the Strait of Gibraltar or the Dardanelles. Other indicators, such as air traffic, appeared normal, while the confrontations and day-to-day harassment so common at sea during the Cold War had been minimal for months. Then the peaceful morning of October 6 became a distant memory as the surprise attack on Israel by Egypt and Syria took the commanders of both fleets by varying degrees of surprise (though the officers commanding the separate elements of *Fifth Eskadra* had been warned of the coming attack, they had not been advised of the time and date that the offensive would begin).

In the hours following the attack, several Soviet ships sortied and Sixth Fleet noticed an almost immediate increase in air activity as long-range Tu-95RT Bear and shorter ranged Tu-l6 Badger aircraft, operating from airfields in Hungary, Egypt, and Libya, stepped up Russian reconnaissance in the Mediterranean. Soon, a steady stream of An-22 transports (the largest Russia cargo carriers) flew from Soviet airdromes to airfields in Egypt and Syria, replacing military equipment and munitions expended by the Arabs.

Admiral Murphy immediately requested permission from Washington to concentrate his scattered task groups and move to a position within supporting range of Israel. The response shocked him to no little degree:

"The initial guidance... advised that the United States would maintain a low key, even-handed approach toward the hostilities. To project this attitude, the Sixth Fleet was directed to continue routine, scheduled operations and to avoid overt moves which might be construed as indicating the United States was preparing to take an active part in the conflict."[18]

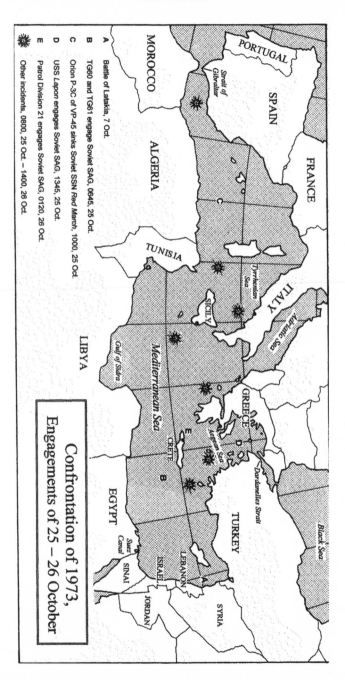

A Battle of Latakia, 7 Oct.

B TG60 and TG61 engage Soviet SAG, 0645, 25 Oct.

C Orion P-3C of VP-45 sinks Soviet SSN *Red March*, 1000, 25 Oct.

D USS *Lapon* engages Soviet SAG, 1345, 25 Oct.

E Patrol Division 21 engages Soviet SAG, 0120, 26 Oct.

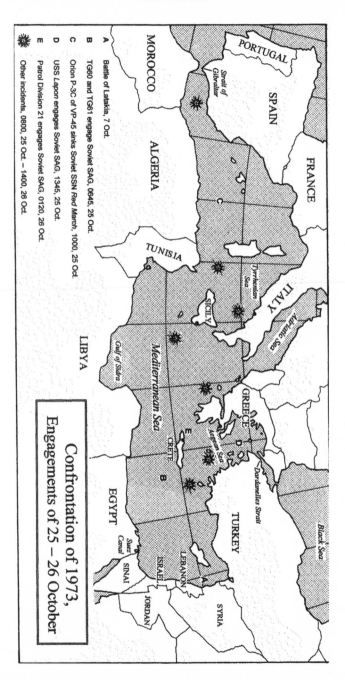 Other incidents, 0800, 25 Oct. – 1400, 26 Oct.

Confrontation of 1973, Engagements of 25 – 26 October

This simply did not make good sense. Was Israel not an ally of the United States? Did anyone in Washington realize that the Soviets were concentrating their forces and would be more than able to do tremendous damage to an unprepared Sixth Fleet with an initial strike? The only positive notes in Murphy's orders allowed him to order TG 60.1 *{Independence* and its escorts) to join TG 60 in the holding area south of Crete but to continue with normal operations throughout the fleet. Under the guise of normality, Murphy increased the tempo of ASW and reconnaissance patrols (for training purposes, of course), ordered TG 60.2 *{Roosevelt* and escorts) to expedite its refit and join ASW exercises in the Western Mediterranean (as close to the Eastern Mediterranean as Washington would allow), and sortied as many replenishment vessels as possible. TG 60/61 finally went to sea on October 9, but only to move to another vulnerable anchorage, at Souda Bay, Crete. At least those ships with their Marines could be kept ready to sail at a minute's notice. Initial steps taken, the admiral could do little except monitor the increasingly dangerous local situation and repeatedly request freedom of action and reinforcement.

On October 9, Sixth Fleet reported that a Soviet submarine tender and a cruiser were shadowing TG 60.1. Such "tagging" was a Cold War norm, but the shadowing vessels were seldom more than an intelligence trawler or a destroyer. The suspected presence of a Russian admiral aboard each of the vessels was also highly atypical. Additionally, several Soviet Foxtrot (attack submarine) contacts had been identified in the vicinity of the task group, and requests by additional Soviet surface and subsurface forces to transit the Dardanelles had been made to Turkey. Washington finally responded to the increasing Russian presence by ordering the carrier *John F Kennedy,* accompanied by three destroyers and an oiler, to leave exercises in the North Sea and to join the Sixth Fleet as TG 60.3. Unfortunately for Murphy, it would not be allowed to enter the Mediterranean. To avoid any appearance of escalation, TG 60.3 would cruise in the Atlantic just outside the Straits of Gibraltar until released by Washington. To make matters worse, as Operation Nickel Grass began, all but four European nations— Holland, Portugal, Italy, and Greece—denied the right of air passage or port usage to American efforts to resupply Israel. Thus Murphy had to create a picket line of destroyers to guide and, if necessary, to succor, the MAC C-5 and C-141 transports involved in the operation. The dissipation of his escorts was unacceptable, especially at a time when the Soviets were obviously concentrating their naval assets, but unavoidable.

Over the next 12 days, as a victorious Israel swept over its Arab attackers and Cold War politics reached a boiling point, Soviet ships continued to enter the Mediterranean while American intelligence officers reported a number of ominous indicators pointing to a Soviet willingness to commit troops in support of their Arab clients. On the morning of October 24,

Admiral Murphy reported a total of 80 confirmed Soviet vessels in the Mediterranean, including 26 surface warships and 16 Foxtrots.[19] The bulk of the surface warships formed three major surface action groups (SAGs). One, composed of *aSverdlov* Class cruiser (four triple-barreled 152mm gun turrets) and a *Kashin* Class destroyer (two twin-barreled 76mm turrets) closely followed TG 60.1, within easy range *of Independence.* A second, and much larger, SAG operated just over the horizon from TG 60.1. Its two *Kynda* Class guided missile cruisers carried SS-N-3 missiles, with a range of 200 miles (though a ship, submarine, or aircraft at the target site was needed to provide targeting data for the SS-N-3s), while the two *Mod-Kashin* and the three *Mod-Kildin* Class destroyers with the SAG had short-range (20-mile) SS-N-2c missiles. This SAG also included four corvettes and various replenishment ships. The final SAG, two *Mod-Kashins,* patrolled off Souda Bay, watching TG 60/61. At least five Soviet Foxtrots hovered near the Crete holding area, and three of them were capable of launching cruise missiles.

In Washington, intelligence sources informed the White House that it "appeared" that Soviet airborne forces had been placed on alert, while all An-22s (the planes needed to transport those forces) had been withdrawn from Arab resupply operations. Soviet pilots were "possibly" flying Foxbats (Soviet first-line air superiority fighters) in Egypt. Five additional Foxtrots were en route via the Atlantic to the Mediterranean, while a cruiser— "tentatively identified" as the *Moskva* (the premier Soviet ship of the day, equipped with helicopters for ASW operations)—and six additional destroyers had declared passage through the Dardanelles and would reach the Mediterranean within 36 hours. Also, the "possibility existed" that Soviet troops in Europe were preparing to move to a higher state of readiness.[20] Then, on the heels of Murphy's solid analysis of Soviet forces within the Mediterranean and the much qualified update by American intelligence services, Brezhnev's letter of October 24 arrived at the White House, and the order to go to DefCon 3 was issued. In the Mediterranean, October 25 began badly, then deteriorated into pure hell.

Sixth Fleet and *Fifth Eskadra,* October 25–26

It took less than 20 minutes for the Joint Chiefs of Staff to initiate DefCon 3 world wide. Much happened in that 20 minutes. In the United States, both Continental Air Defense and Strategic Air Command began repositioning assets and putting additional planes in the air. The 82nd Airborne at Fort Bragg, North Carolina, was alerted for immediate deployment to the Mediterranean, while B-52 bombers in Guam prepared to return home to prep for use in the Middle East. In Europe, anxious commanders recalled troops from leave and began to deploy fully combat-ready units along the Iron Curtain.[21]

Aboard *Little Rock,* Admiral Murphy had been notified of DefCon 3 at 0631 local time. With relief, he noted that TG 60/61, TG 60.2, and TG 60.3 had been ordered to join TG 60 in its holding area at flank speed. Within 72 hours, he would have a concentration of carriers that would allow him to hold his own, at the least, in the eastern Mediterranean. Six destroyers had also been ordered to join his command from the Atlantic and five submarines had surged from Atlantic bases, though it would take these reinforcements as much as a week to reach the waters off Crete. Unfortunately, in the brief minutes that it had taken Murphy to scan the alert order, fire blossomed over his task groups.

At 0600, in the CIC of the USS *Aubrey,* Lieutenant Gadsden had begun running his men through an anti-air warfare (AAW) drill. Such drills were a daily constant during peacetime, and the "blue birds" (training missiles) on the racks offered little danger if an accidental firing command should be issued. Gadsden was quite proud of the efficiency of both his ship and his highly skilled team, as orders to acquire the target and simulate launches of *Aubrey's* SM-1 SAMs came through his headset, transmitted by the officer aboard the *Independence* controlling the entire task group's AAW screen. Certainly Gadsden had no desire to trade places with that officer, who had to integrate AAW ships scattered across a roughly 60-mile circle centered on the carrier.

The *Aubrey's* simulated enemy that morning was an unarmed Soviet Tu-95RT Bear that had been circling overhead for the past four hours, constantly painted by the target-acquisition radar of one or another of the American escorts as it monitored the forces below. At 0631, the destroyer's captain ordered the training exercise secured and for the ship to go to Condition III (wartime readiness). Gadsden immediately ordered the training munitions switched for live birds. At that, a tap on the shoulder marked the arrival of his relief, delayed for half an hour by the drill. Passing over his headset, the young lieutenant made his way to the hatch, planning to take a quick break before checking his men at their Condition III stations. Gadsden whirled as he heard the tense words spoken by his replacement: "I am prepared to fire." Something was wrong, and Gadsden yelled "Verify! Verify!" even as he watched the man toggle two warbirds away. Seconds passed, and his replacement's eyes grew wide as words streamed into his earphones: "My God, they're still playing games over there." The time was 0636.

Destroyer are small vessels. Their crews tend to pride themselves on being as quick to respond to orders as their nimble ships to their helms. Thus the *Aubrey* reached Condition III a full five minutes before the order had made its way through the much larger *Independence* to the officer coordinating the AAW drill. Indeed, that man was still "playing" war-games while live munitions were being racked—and launched—on the destroyer, and since *Aubrey* was at Condition III when the order was received, it was not questioned. In modern war, seconds mean life or death, and the only way to stop a "shoot" order is through direct negation by a superior officer. Still, all was not lost. The SM-ls would take a full minute to reach their target, plenty of time to activate the abort charges in the warhead.

Lunging across the stunned missile officer to reach his console, Gadsden slammed the abort toggles for the warbirds. One bird exploded, pieces falling harmlessly into the sea. The other tracked unerringly, and as a doomed Russian pilot cried in anguish into his throat mike: "They have killed us, the bastards have..." the SM-1 ripped his port wing entirely away.[22] Both Russian and American eyes turned to the sky as the bomber fell from 6,000 feet to impact the blue waters below. There were no chutes.

Accident and coincidence have been the twin plagues of warfare since times no longer remembered. This accident had been of American origin, and upon due consideration, it should not have sparked any more of an incident than any other of the dozens upon dozens of collisions between American and Soviet forces during the Cold War. This time, however, coincidence stalked the bridge of the Soviet *Sverdlov* Class cruiser *Admiral Ushakov*, trailing the American task groups. Its captain, a veteran of years at sea and a capitalist-hating member of the Communist Party, stared through cold eyes at the two cruisers and six smaller warships crowding the waters between the *Ushakov*, its trailing destroyer, and the American carrier just visible on the far horizon. He hated that carrier, a symbol of the unrestrained bourgeois power that dominated the world's seas. Beyond the carrier, already dissipating in the light breeze, a column of black smoke marked the final resting place of a boyish Russian pilot. Tomorrow, in Odessa, a young wife heavy with that pilot's first child would receive a telegram informing her of his death. There was nothing that the captain of the *Ushakov* could do for that wife and unborn child—his daughter, and grandson to be—except give them vengeance and a world free of Yankee imperialists.

At 0645, as the first messages streamed from the Mediterranean to the startled politicians and desk-bound warriors of Moscow and Washington, the *Admiral Ushakov* turned sharply to port and salvoed 12 152mm shells at the *Independence,* while its secondary battery ravaged the closest American destroyer. Confusion reigned through both fleets for vital minutes. The Russian admiral aboard the *Ushakov* could not believe his ears. Why were they firing? Rushing onto the bridge, he tripped over the body of the ship's commissar. Recovering, his eyes flickered across the bridge of a ship at war, a crew finally doing what they had prepared to do for years: ripping the guts out of the damned Americans. The last thing the admiral ever saw was the face of his captain, gripped firmly by the madness born of 30 years of carefully nurtured hate and an instant of loss. In the captain's hand, the pistol that had killed his interfering political officer still smoked.

Then, before either officer could speak, two rounds from the heavy guns of an American cruiser struck the bridge, ending their Cold War in a blast of fire.[23]

Events of the next minutes and even hours in the waters near Crete are hopelessly muddled due to the loss of high-ranking officers and the refusal of the respective governments to release sealed records. From the few published memoirs and numerous interviews with survivors, it appears that the *Admiral Ushakov* became combat ineffective within minutes of the destruction of its bridge, sinking later in the morning with over 600 casualties. Its consort, the *Kashin* Class destroyer, opened fire only when fired upon by two American frigates. Its captain's cries for explanation went unanswered as his ship exploded and sank with all hands some 30 minutes into the action.

In this opening engagement, Murphy's screening forces had lost only one destroyer, though another destroyer, two frigates, and a cruiser had been significantly damaged (casualties totaled fewer than 300 overall). Of course, the relatively light damage to the screen had come at a large price— the carrier *Independence,* on which the Russian cruiser's main battery had been constantly locked, had suffered no fewer than 11 152mm shell hits. Though its power plant remained fully operational, initial reports indicated that the carrier's deck was riddled, its catapults smashed, and fires threatened to reach fuel storage areas. Among its 500 dead and wounded rested the commander of Task Group 60.1 as well as the ship's captain. Except for the planes already in the air, Murphy had lost both his air cover and his main striking arm. This was, of course, only one of many worries for a man who suddenly found himself metaphorically drowning as the ice of the Cold War melted.

Several points held Murphy's attention, even as he reorganized his task groups. The Soviet SAG operating just over the horizon had not yet taken any aggressive action. For the past week, the admiral had kept a strike force of A-6 Intruders and F-4F Phantoms armed with anti-ship missiles in constant orbit around the SAG. Without a carrier to land on, this group would soon need to head for Crete, leaving the Soviets to operate freely. There was also the question of several Foxtrots operating in the area, though no contacts had been reported in the past hours. As for Task Group 60/61, there could be no question of its leaving Souda Bay until the SAG tagging it could be neutralized. Murphy could only hope that the communists would not start lobbing missiles into a (nominally, at least) neutral port. The most important question, however, and the question upon which all else hinged, was this: "Are we at war?"

In Washington, men who had seen far too little sleep and far too much frustration over the past weeks briefed a bedraggled President Nixon on the budding catastrophe in the Mediterranean. Obviously, the Soviets, serious about stopping the Israeli advances in Syria and Egypt, had used the accidental missile firing to justify removing the major threat to convoys of troops and weapons to the Middle East. Kissinger placed calls to the Soviet Embassy as well as to Moscow—none were immediately returned. A frantic call to Israel stressed the need for an immediate cease fire before the war expanded even further. Nixon finally ordered the Joint Chiefs to do whatever they could to localize the situation and to prevent Soviet troops transiting to the Middle East. Meanwhile, Kissinger would try to establish talks with the Soviets.

In Moscow, the events took everyone by surprise. No one had any idea why the Americans had fired on a reconnaissance plane, much less why a Soviet cruiser had attacked an American task force. Were the Americans planning to send troops to Israel? Had their navy actually attacked the Soviet SAG to prepare the way for their amphibious group to move in that direction? Too many questions and too few answers confounded the Politburo. Brezhnev ordered the situation localized while talks could be established with the Americans.

Thus, the messages transmitted to the commanders of Sixth Fleet and *Fifth Ekskadra* from their governments through their respective military hierarchies, though couched in different languages, sounded much alike: "Keep your distance, don't expand the conflict, but don't let them push you around or introduce troops to the Middle East." Unfortunately, there was an awfully large number of planes and ships crowded into the Mediterranean, too many to avoid the occasional shove.

The amphibious transport USS *Iwojima* had entered the Mediterranean on the afternoon of October 24. Its battalion of Marines and their helicopters had been meant to relieve a battalion already on duty with TG 60/61; now ship and men, as well as its two escorting frigates, would reinforce that unit. At 0900 on October 25, the force plowed through the sea at flank speed, bound for Souda Bay, seemingly unaware that it was being stalked.

The skipper of the Soviet nuclear-powered submarine (SSN) *Red March* had received his orders to stop American troops from interfering in the Middle East an hour earlier—he had been tagging the imperialist transport since it transited the Straits of Gibraltar. By 1000, he had positioned his vessel for a perfect shot at the transport and one of the escorts. Then, at the instant that he ordered torpedoes fired, the task group began a puzzling evasive turn. Seconds later, as an American torpedo intercepted his own boat, the captain understood that the target had known about him all along. In the sky above, the crew of *Gloria's Goodies,* an Orion P-3C of VP-45 slapped hands and cheered, having now validated their recent victory in the fleet ASW competition. Over the next 20 hours, VP-45 would add three additional Soviet subs to its tally.[24]

At 1125, the executive officer of the *Independence* informed Admiral Murphy that initial damage estimates, though severe, had been inaccurate.

His fires were under control, enough of the deck to handle landings had been patched, and he expected to have one catapult operating within 20 hours. Including the planes circling the Commie SAG, he could put 28 fighters and bombers back in the air (even if slowly) as soon as the catapult had been repaired. He requested permission to land his air group rather than divert it to Crete, where it could well be denied refueling rights. Murphy concurred—even a few planes would be better than no carrier air until *Roosevelt* reached the area in another 40 hours. In the meantime, he drew his own AAW vessels in tighter, and shifted control of the screen from *Independence* to *Little Rock*.

At 1345, the SSN USS *Lapon* skulked in the Aegean Sea, dodging Bears on Soviet ASW patrol and waiting for the reported *Moskva* SAG to reach its location after exiting the Dardanelles. Since the carrier *Moskva* was an ASW specialist, it represented a grave danger to the *Lapon* and every other American SSN operating in the Mediterranean. *Lapon's* skipper did not know whether to be sad or happy when the SAG appeared on the horizon with a *Kynda* Class cruiser at its center instead of the carrier. He had time to be neither as the escorting destroyers spotted his boat and commenced an attack. Firing in self-defense, *Lapon* managed to sink the cruiser and an escorting destroyer. Severely damaged during the attack, the submarine lay on the bottom for two days before repairs allowed it to limp into Athens. The Naval Unit Citation presented to the vessel the following December was richly deserved.[25]

By sunset on October 25, the situation in the Mediterranean had long passed the stage of "exceedingly tense." In other skirmishes around the basin, *Fifth Eskadra* had lost a submarine, several Bears, and two destroyers. Sixth Fleet had suffered as badly, tallying two submarines, three frigates, and two replenishment vessels lost or presumed lost. Both sides had damaged vessels limping for friendly or neutral ports. Worse, the situation had almost exploded in the Atlantic when a confrontation between an American Task Group and a Soviet SAG off the coast of Norway nearly resulted in an exchange of fire instead of a scraping of paint after two destroyers collided. Across the seven seas, forces of both nations eagerly sought an advantage in a most dangerous game of hide and seek. Meanwhile, diplomats sought to end this meaningless conflict which threatened to end the world in fire.

The politicians spent most of October 25 in the usual recriminations—an admittance of wrong-doing meant an unacceptable loss of face in the game of brinkmanship so often played during the Cold War. In the emergency UN Security Council meeting called for the afternoon and evening of that day, both countries walked out at different times as aides brought in messages of new "atrocities" at sea. Interestingly enough, the loudest cries for an end to the fighting came from Egypt, Israel, and Syria. Not a shot had been fired in the war-torn Middle East that day, and plans appeared to be in order for a permanent cease fire being in place by midday of October 26. Perhaps a nameless Egyptian captain on the Suez front explained the situation best to a reporter from the *Times Post:* "If Soviets and Americans begin to toss nuclear missiles, we [Arabs and Israelis} will have no quarrel remaining for we will all be in Paradise or Hell."[26]

At 2311, the two superpowers finally agreed to UN Resolution 401, which called for an end to hostilities at 0800 (1400 in the central Mediterranean), October 26, disengagement of all forces in the Mediterranean, a three month moratorium on all shipments of arms to the Middle East, and a meeting in Geneva, Switzerland, the following month to determine the causes of the incident. In other words, the ice could begin to reform as the war again grew cold. Decisions made at the eleventh hour, however, often leave time for one last bout of fiery misery.

Bloody Finale on the Wine Dark Sea

As night fell across the Mediterranean on the last full day of the Middle Eastern conflict, Admiral Murphy decided to spring his vulnerable amphibious task group from Souda Bay. Three days earlier, the gunboats of Patrol Division 21 had shifted from Naples to Souda Bay. The mission fell to them. At 0120 on October 26, *Antelope, Defiance,* and *Surprise* exited the bay at flank speed to eliminate the two missile-armed *Mod-Kashins* monitoring TG 60/61 in the Sea of Crete. The skipper of *Antelope,* overall commander of the three-ship unit, remarked to his exec that he looked forward to testing his newly installed RIM-66B surface-to-surface missile system on the "damned Reds." An educated man, he even spared passing thoughts for Homer's description of these waters as "the wine-dark sea," and how the deep, dark Greek red wine looked so much like blood.

Thanks to background radar clutter, the American ships closed to within 20 miles of the Soviet SAG before being spotted on radar. That range closed even further as the *Mod-Kashins* turned to bring their stern-mounted SS-N-2c missiles to bear. The Russians still managed to release missiles first, at almost the same minute as the rapid-fire 3-inch mounts on the gunboats speckled the destroyers with hits. *Antelope* released chaff and held a steady course as it salvoed two missiles at each of the Soviet destroyers. *Defiance,* struck amidships by a Russian missile, slewed to port and began to sink. The remainder of the squadron continued to close the Soviets, who turned to allow their forward twin 76mm turrets to bear. Then the American missiles struck. One of the destroyers disappeared in a small mushroom cloud as a hit ignited sympathetic explosions in its missile magazine. The other seemed to shrug off a single hit and continued to plaster *Surprise* with 76mm fire. In flames, its weapons silent and crew dead or overboard, the small warship coasted to a stop.

Desperately, *Antelope's* skipper held his vessel on a direct course for the remaining destroyer, even after a hit disabled his single gun mount. He saw no options—if the Soviets survived they would fire on the anchorage. Over the address system rang words seldom if ever heard on modern warships: "I intend to ram. All hands gather midships and stern. Prepare for boarding action." There were not enough weapons in the arms locker to equip even a fraction of the men, nor time to distribute them. The crew snatched whatever was to hand: spanners from engineering, cleavers and knives from the galley, a scalpel from sickbay. One petty officer, discovering nothing sharp lying about, ran to his cabin and grabbed a fifth of Jack Daniels. Sprinting on deck, he grinned at his men and took a long pull from the bottle before swearing to "break it over a Commie head."

The *Antelope* struck the Soviet destroyer at an angle, bow crumpling as it embedded itself in the destroyer's engineering spaces. Stumbling, lunging, or crawling the surviving Americans crossed to the deck of their enemy. The cries that filled the night were primal, the product of years of ice-cold hatred released in minutes of hot passion. Even as the joined vessels began to sink, men screamed and hacked and choked and shot each other. Nor did they stop until the blood-red waters closed over them. Hours later, as dawn brought light, the ships of TG 60/61 pulled only two American and five Russian survivors from the sea.[27]

A Poem Revisited

Two men leaned on the taffrail of the USS *Aubrey*. Once they had been young men, but that had ended sometime in the past few days. One, an officer, looked at his watch—0238, October 27, 1973. And things were normal again, as if the world had not changed at all.

"Lieutenant Gadsden, sir?" whispered the petty officer at his side.

"Yes."

"We caused it. Didn't we, sir? All that death for nothing and our ship caused it."

Gadsden considered for a minute, then sighed: "No. I don't think so. Our parents and our grandparents, maybe they caused it when they taught us to hate and fear, and follow orders without question. No. It was just another accident in a long string of human beings having accidents."

"I think I understand that poem now, sir," the petty officer could see that the man beside him had no idea what he was talking about: "The one about ice and fire, sir. Hate—ice—has brought us to this Cold War. But the hate turns hot so quick, and if we can't stop it, then the world will end in fire."

The two exhausted men looked into each other's eyes, and through them to some time a thousand yards and more away, when their world would end in fire or ice.

The Reality

The events of this story, up to and including the DefCon 3 alert of October 25, are true. Fortunately, Sixth Fleet and *Fifth Eskadra* miraculously managed to avoid any direct confrontation while Egypt and Israel, heavily pressured by the major suppliers of weapons in the Middle East (the United States and the USSR) agreed to the cease fire on October 26. The naval stand-off in the Mediterranean between the superpowers did continue for another week, by which time the USSR had superiority in quantity if not quality of warships. But with tensions abating in the Middle East, the situation returned to its Cold War norm by late November.

Lieutenant Gadsden, the petty officer, and the USS *Aubrey* are fiction. The same should be said of the captain of the *Admiral Ushakov* and the crew of USS *Antelope*. That should not be taken to mean that men and ships of their ilk never existed, as many readers who served in the Mediterranean in 1973, or at other times and places, will realize. Could circumstances have combined to make this story, or some form thereof, a reality? Oh, yes. History records numerous accidental discharges of weapons, incorrectly aimed shells, and munitions that exploded at the wrong time and place. In almost every case, however, human error played a part. It is a testament to the training of the navies on both sides of the now defunct Iron Curtain that such human errors were minimized in the Mediterranean in 1973.

Astute readers will have asked themselves one important question as they read this story: "Why did the fictional Confrontation of 1973 not evolve into a nuclear exchange?" There are two good reasons for that path not being taken. First, at no point in my studies of the Cold War have I found a single instance where the politicians of both the United States and the USSR had any doubts that Mutually Assured Destruction would leave no winners on either side. Paranoia does not necessarily lead to suicidal tendencies. Second, it would have been a horrible way to end a story: at this point, dear reader, if you disagree please burn this book to simulate a nuclear firestorm over most of the world's major cities.

Some readers may not be familiar with Robert Frost's short poem "Fire and Ice." First published in *Harper's Magazine* in December 1920, the lines fit so well with the dilemmas of the Cold War that Frost almost seems prescient. Please think upon the following lines as you consider the nature of war, whether hot or cold.

> SOME say the world will end in fire,
> Some say in ice...
>
> I think I know enough of hate
> To know that for destruction ice
> Is also great
> And would suffice.

Bibliography

Aker, Frank, *October 1973: The Arab-Israeli War,* Archon Books, Hamden, CT, 1985.

Hagan, Kenneth J., ed., *In Peace and War: Interpretations of American Naval History, 1775–1984,* Greenwood Press, Westport, CT, 1984.

Hartmann, Frederick, *Naval Renaissance: The US Navy in the 1980s,* Naval Institute Press, Annapolis, MD, 1990.

Herzog, Chaim, *The War of Atonement: October, 1973,* Little, Brown, Boston, 1975.

Israelyan, Victor, *Inside the Kremlin During the Yom Kippur War,* Pennsylvania State University Press, University Park, PA, 1995.

Vego, Milan, *Soviet Naval Tactics,* Naval Institute Press, Annapolis, MD, 1992.

Watson, Bruce W,. and Susan M., eds., *The Soviet Navy: Strengths and Liabilities,* Arms and Armour Press, London, 1986.

Winkler, David F., *Cold War at Sea: High-Seas Confrontation between the United States and the Soviet Union,* Naval Institute Press, Annapolis, MD, 2000.

Zumwalt, Elmo R., Jr., *On Watch: A Memoir,* Quadrangle, New York, 1976.

Notes

*1. Rear Admiral R.A. Gadsden, USN (ret.), *Warbirds Away!* (Callihan Press, New York, 2002), p. 7.

2. Zumwalt, *On Watch: A Memoir,* pp. 337–38.

3. Lawrence J. Korb, "Erosion of American Naval Preeminence," in Hagan, *In Peace and War,* pp. 329–32.

4. Watson and Watson, *The Soviet Navy: Strengths and Liabilities,* pp. 188, 209, 220, 235.

5. Hagan, *Peace and War,* 336. Note that the Russian designation *Eskadra,* like the American term Fleet, is applied to a geographic area of operations rather than a set number of warships, despite that its literal meaning is squadron. It also has a number of westernized spellings (for example: "Estrada').

6. Winkler, *Cold War at Sea,* pp. 177–210.

7. Israelyan, *Inside the Kremlin during the Yom Kippur War,* p. 10.

8. All too frequently, researchers will find "Kippur" rendered as "Kipper," an interesting confusion of historic and gastronomic events.

9. Zumwalt, *On Watch,* pp. 432–34.

10. Http://members.aol.com/SamBlu82/menu7.html.

11. Http://www.us-israel.org/jsource/History/latakia.html; Aker, *October 1973: The Arab Israeli War,* pp. 62–63. The engagement between the missile boats was the first naval battle to feature an exchange of missile fire and the use of electronic counter-measures to defeat incoming missiles

12. OPEC threatened to reduce oil production, thus reducing availability and increasing the cost per barrel, until Israel restored all lands taken during the 1967 War. Though the lands were not restored, OPEC ended the embargo in March 1974 (a clear victory of profit over principle).

13. Israelyan, *Inside the Kremlin,* pp. 136–37.

14. *Ibid.,* pp. 169–70.

15. The alert status of American military forces is defined by five Defense Conditions (DefCon 1–5). DefCon 5 is normal peace time operations, the lowest level

of alert. DefCon 3 calls for military forces to prepare for a potential shooting situation, while DefCon 1 is maximum readiness level.

16. Http://www.gunboatriders.com/theboats/pg86.html.
17. Http://www.navy.mil/homepages/vp-45/prod04.html.
18. Zumwalt, *On Watch,* p. 435.
19. *Ibid.,* p. 447.
20. *Ibid.,* pp. 439–40.
21. *Ibid.,* p. 443.
*22. Gadsden, Warbirds Away!, pp. 111–12. The failure of the second missile to abort has never been explained, though Gadsden noted that extensive testing of remaining stocks of SM-ls by the Navy after the incident revealed "only'" a 0.1 percent chance of malfunction.
*23. Ralucca Boishov, A Family Affair: Wives, Children and War (Free Press, Moscow, 1993), pp. 344–48.
*24. I.M.A. Fakir, Delivering the Goodies: VP-45 in Peace and War (NOVAT Press, Shelmerston, 1987), pp. 183–87. 25.
25. Http://www.usslapon.com/usslapon/citations.html. *Lapon* did receive a Naval
*26. Unit Citation for its efforts in the Mediterranean between June and December 1973, though not for the reasons given here. *Times Post:* "Armageddon" Special Edition, October 26, 1973.
*27. Vassily Chernikoff and Sam Brown, Prepare to Board! We Survived (Truth Press, Washington, 1993).

9
AFGHANISTAN
The Soviet Victory

David C. Isby

The Soviet invasion of Afghanistan in December 1979 proved to be a watershed in the history of the Cold War. The first direct and overt Soviet military offensive outside their perimeter since the 1946 withdrawal from northern Iran, it came at a time when the impact of the second oil shock of the 1970s and the Iranian Revolution alike were both affecting Western economies and the West's relations with the Islamic world. The Afghanistan crisis took place at a time when the West's economies and culture were changing. The West had to learn how to confront the Soviets while standing on this new—shifting—ground.

Afghanistan demonstrated that a superpower cannot fight a small war. The Soviet Union's worldwide interests made sure that the lessons of its war in Afghanistan would have an impact far beyond the mountains and deserts of that war-torn country. The Soviet forces involved were smaller than those of the British in the Boer War, the US in Vietnam, or the French in Algeria. Yet the war in Afghanistan had, in its way, a greater impact on the Soviets than any of those other conflicts had on their participants. Afghanistan came about at a time when the Soviets believed the "correlation of forces" had shifted in their favor, yet when the economic and social costs of the "era of stagnation" were starting to emerge both in the Soviet Union and in their European allies. How Soviet governments made changes in response to this emerging challenge was linked to how they responded to Afghanistan.

Throughout the Cold War participants were continually surprised by the unintended consequences of their own actions. The invasion and continued war in Afghanistan was undertaken for what the Soviets considered modest defensive purposes. Yet because of the extensive problems it created— mobilizing former rivals and creating new ones—Afghanistan brought to a head a decisive crisis of the Cold War. What the US and its allies were willing—and unwilling—to do in response became key for the results of the Cold War.

The Cold War and the War in Afghanistan

The US and its European allies had seen Afghanistan as a peripheral issue in the 1970s. No one projected broader consequences when the April 1978 *putsch* by communist military officers brought Afghanistan to the front pages of the worlds' newspapers. Auden famously termed the 1930s a "low dishonest decade,"[1] but that seems to apply just as well to the 1970s. The mid-1970s Cold War "correlation of forces," to use the Soviet term, was changed by the narrow election, in November 1976, of Jimmy Carter: "a president who is best remembered for alerting Americans to their festering malaise, only to prove incapable of addressing it."[2] He was going to change things. He could not foresee that what he was going to change included Afghanistan.

Carter famously claimed that the US needed to end its "inordinate fear of Communism" and "move beyond the belief that Soviet expansion was almost inevitable but that it must be contained."[3] Carter's 1976 campaign rhetoric showed his belief in instilling what he saw as suitable morality into US policies. He saw this, rather than the Cold War policies of confronting the Soviet Union that he often denigrated, as the key to foreign policy.[4] He pledged to end secret diplomacy and for greater public involvement in decision-making. In practice Carter's commitment to human rights was interpreted, however, as undermining relations between authoritarian governments and the US, even though it was not generally used to confront the Soviet Union for its human rights record.[5] But even when the administration did confront the Soviet Union on human rights issues—as Carter did when he sent a letter to Brezhnev over the treatment of dissident Soviet scientist Andrei Sakharov and when he pointedly received Soviet dissident exile Vladimir Bukovskiy in the White House—he received both rage from the Kremlin and opposition from his own political party. Former presidential candidate Senator George McGovern complained that such actions "look like a reincarnation of John Foster Dulles' attempt to being Communism down by encouraging dissent and revolt in Eastern Europe."[6]

McGovern was wrong, because there was no strategic challenge to Soviet power in the administration. The president was a reflexive supporter of human rights, to be sure, and had no love for tyrants. But Carter was a sentimentalist, and the need for a hardheaded, principled national security strategy was difficult to reconcile both with his worldview and a belief that such a *realpolitik* hangover as a national strategy should co-exist in the morally-based approach he preferred. It would also be a situation-based approach, for Carter felt uncomfortable even with the whole idea of a national strategy.

In this, he had support primarily from Secretary of State Cyrus Vance— a strong proponent of detente but a skeptic on the utility of an overall grand strategy—and also in part from Vance's rival, Zbigniew Brzezinski, Carter's national security advisor. While considered a hard-liner, Brzezinski characterized Carter's policy as a recognition that "the world is changing under the influences of forces no government can control."[7] This meant that no over-arching strategy would be effective. Carter quickly backed down from using human rights against the Soviets and observed: "Our conception of human rights is preserved in Poland."[8] Political allies soon described Carter's policy as "McGovernism without McGovern."[y]

Iran Raises The Stakes

The Iranian Revolution of January 1979 put new importance on the security problems of south Asia and attendant superpower competition there. The turmoil following the sudden abdication and flight into exile of Shah Mohammed Reza Pahlavi, the longtime ruler of Iran and staunch US ally, brought to power anti-American fundamentalist Shiite Muslim clerics led by Ayatollah Ruhollah Khomeini. On November 4, two weeks after Carter had allowed the former shah to enter the US for medical care, 3,000 Iranians—Revolutionary Guards and "student" radicals—invaded the US Embassy in Tehran and seized it, holding 66 Americans, mainly diplomats, hostage. Chief of Mission L. Bruce Laingen and two aides were held separately at the Iranian Foreign Ministry. Khomeini and his supporters repeated demands that the former shah be returned for trial.

It became apparent that the Iranian government would not release the hostages despite a large-scale diplomatic effort. It was unclear whether the hostages were being tortured or readied for execution. However, Carter, facing a re-election battle in 1980, strongly favored a diplomatic solution. Many of his advisors were opposed to the use of force, most notably Cyrus Vance. However, despite this, Brzezinski directed the Pentagon to begin planning for a rescue mission or retaliatory strikes in case the hostages were harmed. Within hours, US Army Special Forces Operational Detachment Delta (Airborne) was on full alert.

This set up the situation for a multi-front conflict for influence on Carter's foreign policy. The 1978 communist coup in Afghanistan had been followed by brutal repression and the systematic elimination of educated Afghans, made possible by an increasing Soviet military presence. This resulted in an escalating anti-communist national rising, bringing the issue of US policy to the fore. Vance opposed any attempt to link Soviet aggression worldwide with the central relationship.[10] Carter himself largely saw the Cold War as limited to Europe. Hence, Afghanistan could not be allowed to disrupt the basic realities of relations with Moscow. And in any case Carter assumed the Afghans could never be more than an irritant to the Soviets. On March 5, 1979 the CIA presented Carter with a series of possible covert actions. On July 3 propaganda support, but not cash or arms, was authorized. However, within months this was changed and monetary assistance was provided and arms were sent from Egypt, Pakistan and elsewhere to the resistance.

Invasion and Reaction

The Soviet commitment to Afghanistan grew throughout 1978–79, with advisors, helicopters, and combat troops being committed to battle. Despite the limited outside assistance reaching the Afghan resistance through Pakistan, the weakness of the Afghan communist government and the growing strength of its opponents led the Soviets to decide on a military invasion. On December 24–25, 1979, the Soviets quickly moved against their Afghan clients, killing the head of state and installing a new pro-Moscow Afghan communist, Babrak Karmal, by 27 December.

Brezhnev personally called Carter on the hot line to assure him of his defensive objectives. But with the American electorate's attention focused on south Asia by the hostage crisis, it appeared that, as in Iran, the US had once again proved to be an impotent and ignorant giant. Carter was furious. He had been photographed in a well-publicized embrace with Brezhnev some six months before. Now he appeared to have been played for a fool. Carter withdrew the ambassador from Moscow. Vance, however, believed the US had failed to understand Soviet motivations, which he saw as primarily defensive.[11] Vance continued to stress that detente and its ripest fruit, the SALT II arms control agreement, were what needed to be preserved, not Afghanistan.

But the Soviet invasion had made Carter receptive to Brzezinski's views and recommendations for a strong response. Carter accordingly authorized the supply of lethal aid to the Afghan resistance[12] and on January 3 he withdrew the SALT II Treaty from consideration for ratification, heading off Senate defeat. On January 7 he announced a grain embargo and then put a temporary ban on US high technology exports to the Soviet Union. On January 20 he announced an Olympic boycott. He acceded to the Senate's demand for a five percent defense spending increase. The US led a debate in the UN General Assembly that voted 104–18 to condemn the Soviet invasion.

On January 23, 1980, the President proclaimed what he hoped would become known as the "Carter Doctrine."[13] He had proposed to say that any attempt by an outside power to gain control of the Gulf would be regarded as "a direct assault on the vital interests of the United States." Brzezinski had fought hard for this language and his views had prevailed. Vance had pointed out that no country in the region would welcome a US base.

For a while, Carter's hard line against the Soviet invasion had widespread support. It boosted him in the polls against both Democratic and Republican challengers. The increase in his polling numbers represented the most dramatic turn-around in the history of the Gallup poll to that date.[14] But, as with so many of the advances of that administration, both the policies and the lead soon started to erode. As early as January, Carter denied that he had changed his views on Soviet behavior.[15] Vance was soon regaining influence.

Much of the impetus for this erosion of the response to the Soviet invasion came from US allies. Europeans were inclined to ignore the invasion of Afghanistan. There was a widespread feeling that this crisis was too distant and involving people that had no impact on their security. France, Italy, West Germany and Japan all opened bilateral trade talks with the Soviet Union in the immediate wake of the invasion of Afghanistan.[16] The Soviets were only too happy to shift from US exports to European and Japanese ones. In 1980 US exports to the Soviet Union were halved, while those from Britain, France and West Germany alone increased by over 30 percent.[17] French policy was seen as so subservient to the Soviets that the domestic press characterized it as "self-Finlandization."[18]

The US did not use its position as head of the Western alliance to mobilize support against these policies. Indeed, on 12 June, Carter told a news conference that he still believed in detente.[19] This made it impossible for Carter to pressure the Europeans to see Afghanistan as a challenge to world security rather than a commercial opportunity. At the same time, German Chancellor Helmut Schmidt flew straight from Washington to Moscow to sign the first pipeline contract with the Soviets.[20] Afghanistan would not prevent cheap energy exports from paying for the Soviet Empire, including its subjugation of Afghanistan. The high technology export ban came off (although higher licensing requirements remained).

Despite their continued economic problems, their seeming success in the invasion of Afghanistan convinced the Soviets that the morale aspects of "correlation of forces" remained in their favor following the US failure to deploy neutron weapons in Europe in the 1970s in the face of widespread opposition and effective Soviet-origin disinformation. The decision, in December 1979, to modernize the intermediate nuclear forces in Europe would be the next target of Soviet policies, modeled on those that had been successful in the preceding years. It appeared that the Soviet occupation of Afghanistan would end up being accepted without imperiling detente as, in the end, that of Czechoslovakia was in 1968.

1980 was an election year. Carter had needed to demonstrate a forceful response to the Soviet invasion of Afghanistan for political reasons and in this he had found strong support from both the Congress and the public. Carter was facing, throughout, a strong challenge from his left in the presidential primaries in the form of Senator Edward Kennedy. Kennedy was running on a platform of redistributive social spending and increased government control that had appeal following two oil-driven shocks to the US economy. Even if US trust in government was reduced due to Watergate and Vietnam, trust in free markets was lower still.

Carter was able to pull off successive narrow victories over Kennedy to win the Democratic nomination and over Ronald Reagan in the November general election. This was the result of a number of factors. The foremost of these was the "October Surprise," the release of the US hostages by Iran before the election in return for undisclosed US concessions. This had followed the final triumph of Vance in Carter administration policy making. He had succeeded in preventing, at the last minute, Delta Force being inserted in the long-planned and rehearsed hostage rescue mission in Iran that had been scheduled for April 24-25 (Brzezinski resigned in disgust). In a crucial late-campaign debate, Carter had succeeded in demonstrating his in-depth knowledge of the details and minutiae of national security while Reagan, having an off-night, appeared old, detached, and out of it. All of these things happened in the days before the election. Indeed, a week before the election, Morton Kondracke, a leading American political journalist had written: "the movement of the presidential campaign suggests a Carter victory."[21] The "October Surprise" of the hostage release and the debate had made it so.

Afgahnistan and the Carter Second Term

Carter's victory was, in many ways, a triumph for the government party over the countryside. Its views were that of the pessimistic in Washington, who saw the lesson of the 1970s as being that the US was in decline. Certainly many Americans had shared this pessimism. Before the Soviet invasion of Afghanistan, Gallup polls recorded that 84 percent of Americans thought the country was on the wrong track.[22] Carter, having gained his second term by playing to this pessimism, had little interest in reversing its direction. Indeed, he did not see that it was reversible. One of the many lamentable things he saw as irreversible was the Soviet military occupation of Afghanistan, even though this was only being enforced by a long and brutal counter-insurgency struggle.

In his second term, Carter was willing to reverse policies that proved to be unpopular with key constituencies even if he had already paid the political price for them. The neutron bomb issue of his first term was a prime example of this approach. Even as a campaigner, he was known for his "flip-flops."[23]

Two key policy decisions that would be effectively—if never explicitly— reversed in the second Carter term were those leading to NATO INF modernization and the provision of aid to the Afghan resistance. Both would be incrementally sacrificed to revive detente and improve relations with the Soviet Union, as would all but rhetorical support for human rights in Eastern Europe and the Soviet Union. In all these cases, Carter found strong domestic approval—no one really was pro-nuclear missiles or pro-Afghan—and gratified the elite media and US allies. None of the US allies, even Britain under Margaret Thatcher, had offered as strong a response to the Soviet invasion as did the US. They were thus in no position to complain when the US response was reversed. After the failures of 1980, Carter acted to remove sanctions from the Soviet Union.

Soviet Policy Changes

With the death of Brezhnev in November 1982 and the rise to power of Andropov as a result, Soviet policy in Afghanistan lost its orientation towards preserving a pro-Moscow *status quo* that would allow the "balance of forces" in the region to reflect Soviet regional dominance. Andropov was unwilling to consider extending the Brezhnev policy that had endured since the initial invasion, that of conducting a limited liability conflict, keeping the number of Soviet troops in Afghanistan limited while also limiting the cross-border operations from Afghanistan, and diplomatic pressure on Afghanistan's neighbor, Pakistan. However, the lack of military and political success in 1980–81, due in part to the continued flow of outside aid through Pakistan, led to an escalation of military action in 1982, including a return to large scale ground offensives, such as the Panjshir V offensive in the spring. Andropov indeed considered a broad range of options for Soviet Afghanistan policy, ranging from withdrawal to large-scale escalation. In the end, he believed that there was too much at stake for withdrawal. Therefore, escalation to conclude the conflict—and prevent a more intensive war that a potential increase in aid flow from the West and the Islamic world in the future might yield—was to be the aim of Andropov's policy.

In the near-term, this was seen by the commitment of additional aircraft and divisions to Afghanistan. This was soon reflected by a change in military action.

The Crisis Shifts to Pakistan

In effect, the second Carter administration redefined the locus of the crisis from Afghanistan to Pakistan. It accomplished this by accepting the inevitability of a regime in Kabul acceptable to Moscow. It saw the value of opposition as being limited to forcing Moscow to accept a regime more nationalist than it would otherwise wish. Despite his support for human rights, Carter was willing to make the world safe for Titoism.

Pakistan saw that it was a likely loser in the second Carter administration's attempts to revive detente. Pakistan had provided a haven for the massive flow of Afghan refugees that had started after the communist coup of April 1978. It had started providing arms and political support for the first Afghan guerrillas soon after that, opening its arms stockpiles for old Lee Enfields and more modern Self Loading Rifles (captured from India in 1965 and 1971).

General Zia ul-Haq, Pakistan's chief of state following a military coup against the failed regime of Zulfikar Ali Bhutto, had famously dismissed an initial Carter aid offer as "peanuts," but after the strong US response of early 1980 had buoyed Pakistan he had worked to oppose the Soviet invasion. What concerned Pakistan in the second Carter administration was not so much its own position, but relations with the Soviet Union. General Zia saw that, whatever aid was being covertly sent to the resistance through Pakistan, the overall trend in East–West relations was towards detente. He realized that the US policy, as originated by Carter and implemented by Vance, would seek to maintain the basic coherence of NATO by making concessions to accommodate European desires for cheap energy and increased trade and by trading away security issues outside of Europe that did not concern the alliance. He realized that the security of Pakistan was, to Washington, just such a peripheral issue. Zia also realized that Pakistan gave the US an opportunity to exhibit its human rights concerns which its goal in reviving detente prevented it from strongly pressing in Eastern Europe and the Soviet Union. Zia realized that, as a military dictator with a poor human rights record, he was a prime candidate to follow the Shah of Iran as a US ally-turned-victim.

Zia also read—it had, of course, been leaked to *The Washington Post*—of Vance's defeat of Brzezinski. He was also a realist enough to know that without a multi-year high-dollar defense buildup—which Carter, by 1981-82, was disinclined to support—the "Carter Doctrine" would remain unimplementable and that this meant explicitly that he could not count on the US to back up Pakistan with its military if the Soviets were to reinforce their troops in Afghanistan and threaten military action against Pakistan. Zia was afraid that this would be the long-term Soviet strategy, coordinated with India. The Soviets would wait for the next India–Pakistan crisis to press Pakistan. India had already detonated a nuclear "device" and was in the process of a large-scale military build-up, bringing in new Soviet-built weapons to replace the older generation, often Western-designed, hardware used in the 1965 and 1971 wars with Pakistan. Pakistan would eventually be faced by a two-front war. Indeed, Pakistan had kept its security focus on the threat from India, especially in the Punjab. Even after the Soviet invasion of Afghanistan, the two weak corps headquartered at Peshawar and Quetta, plus a division-sized force between, sufficed to cover the traditional invasion routes from the west.

To counter this, Pakistan looked to its foreign friends. Saudi Arabia could provide oil and money and leverage in the Islamic world, but little else to counter the threat. China's military credibility was badly undercut by its poor performance in its 1979 invasion of Vietnam. Without US support, Pakistan was risking delayed but inevitable defeat and dismemberment because of its support for the Afghan resistance.

The Soviet forces became more active on Afghanistan's western border near Pakistan. More disturbingly, the Soviets started cross-border airstrikes and special operations against Afghan refugee camps in Pakistan that were also used to shelter resistance fighters. Actions by the US and Pakistan in the United Nations were met by the Soviet veto in the Security Council. Off the record, Soviet diplomats talked of "Israeli rules-of-engagement" being put into effect, that borders would not provide immunity following attacks on Soviet forces and their allies. Pakistan was subjected to increasing Soviet threats, and told that it could not rely on its outside allies to defend it if it were to be subjected to Soviet military action as a result of supporting the Afghanistan resistance.

On the ground, the Soviets also started sending strong signals. Soviet officers were photographed training Baluchi separatist insurgents who had crossed the border from Pakistan in the 1970s. Patrols of the Pakistani Frontier Scouts started to fall victim to well-planned ambushes inside Pakistani territory. There was no effort taken to conceal the evidence, with piles of new-issue Soviet 5.45mm cartridge cases left behind with the bodies. When one ambush—the result of over-confidence—went awry, it left the victorious Tochi Scouts a half-dozen *Spetsnaz* corpses in standard Soviet camouflage uniforms. It was not a message delivered with great subtlety. Andropov placed little value on subtlety.

Pakistan was the target of a "carrot and stick" campaign of overtures from Moscow combined with internal penetration, subversion and terrorism. Offers to provide cheap hydro-electric dams were matched by funding for the many groups inside Pakistan dissatisfied with the Zia regime. Whether this discontent was ethnic (such as the Baluchis who had been suppressed by the Pakistani military in the 1970s), political (such as supporters of the late Zulfikar Ali Bhutto, still seething over his ouster and execution by Zia) or economic (rural Sindhis marginalized by large landowners), all received large amounts of Moscow funding. They also had their leaders taken over the border to Afghanistan or to Moscow to learn the hard disciplines of political warfare: how to manage a cell-based organization, how to operate a clandestine press for a pre-literate peasantry, when to demand elections, and when to open the Moscow-supplied arms cache.

Pakistan's response to this internal penetration was the only one it knew how to do well, internal repression. This led to increased tension with Washington, inflaming the Carter administration's emphasis on human rights concerns and reluctance to be seen backing authoritarian states, however important they might be geo-politically to the United States.

Pakistan was faced with external and internal pressure. It knew it could not count on help from the US above its limited-liability support of the Afghan resistance, continued from the first Carter administration. The Afghan resistance fighters, for all their undoubted bravery and devotion, were poorly trained and organized. The Afghan resistance was extensively divided, reflecting Afghanistan's ethno-linguistic diversity as well as the competition for power between secular leaders, traditional religious figures, and Islamist political movements, both modernizers and revolutionaries. With the US looking for stronger detente, these did not appear to General Zia to be the people who would defeat the Soviet Union single-handedly.

Pakistan also faced a danger that the US could not help it with even if it wished. Pakistan was now home to the largest refugee population in the world, over three million Afghans. With the availability of arms to the resistance, these had the potential to become in Pakistan what the Palestinians had been in Jordan in 1970 or Lebanon in 1975, an armed state-within-a-state, able to launch armed insurrection. Zia had in fact been military attache in Amman during "Black September" 1970 and he was resolved never to see anything like it happen in Pakistan.

Pakistan insisted that it distribute the weapons aid intended for the Afghan resistance. Pakistan's ISI (Inter Services Intelligence) took charge of the process, which it had been involved in from the start on an *ad hoc* basis. It brought to this task a great deal of sympathy and support for the Afghan resistance, but also a limited strategic vision. The Pakistanis realized that whatever happened in Afghanistan was secondary to the balance of forces with India, which constituted the main security threat to Pakistan's continued existence. The ISI also cared little about Afghanistan outside of the areas inhabited by ethnic Pushtuns. Because of the large Pushtun populations in Pakistan's North-West Frontier and Baluchistan provinces, Pakistan wanted both to support these groups and prevent the emergence of a regime in Afghanistan that might revive the call for "Pushtunistan," which included a claim on the territory of Pakistan up to the Indus (Afghanistan had been the only country to vote against Pakistan's admission to the UN for that reason). Groups in northern Afghanistan and in the Hazara Jat received little support.

To address Zia's concerns about the possible emergence of a PLO-like Afghan presence in Pakistan, the ISI would deal only with seven Afghan political parties. Secular leaders—whether military officers or government officials—were discouraged by the ISI. Instead, the parties were led by religious figures, traditional or Islamist. This also reflected the increasing turn towards Islamism as Pakistan began to look to a wider base for international support in its security dilemmas. The Afghan resistance was badly divided going into the conflict with the Soviets. The Pakistanis ensured that it remained so.

Playing the India Card

The most significant Soviet move against Pakistan in 1982-83, however, was being carried out not by cross-border *Spetsnaz* or bombers but by diplomats in New Delhi. The Soviet security relationship with India had been significant since the 1971 friendship treaty. Now, Andropov intended to persuade the government of Indira Gandhi that India needed to support the Soviet moves against Pakistan. India had not seen the Soviet moves against Afghanistan as hostile and had abstained in the UN when called on to condemn the invasion. India had strongly condemned the limited US and Chinese security aid to Pakistan starting in 1980. India was also willing to line up behind the Soviets on issues when there was no cost for doing so, such as in its support for Soviet warships operating in the Indian Ocean or in recognizing the pro-Moscow Hen Samrin regime in Cambodia.

India was not, at first, eager for another conflict with Pakistan. But as deliveries of new T-72 main battle tanks and tankers full of Soviet fuel oil started to increase throughout 1982-83, Indira Gandhi's government began moving towards a military confrontation in coordination with the Soviets.

Motivating India was the continuing concern over Pakistan's work at developing nuclear weapons. It was an open secret that, at its nuclear facility at Kahuta, Pakistani scientists were frantically working to achieve a nuclear capability comparable to the one which India had demonstrated with its first nuclear device. Mutual pledges by both India and Pakistan to avoid pre-emptive strikes on each other's nuclear production capabilities had been considered but had, significantly, never been enacted.

There was also the long-standing Kashmir issue. The remote Siachen Glacier, on the "roof of Asia" where Indian and Pakistani forces were confronting each other at high altitude, started showing up with increasing frequency on high-level briefing maps.

Problems of internal strife were increasing, with a crisis in Assam in 1982, increasing levels of Hindu—Moslem violence and, most significantly, increasing levels of violence in the Punjab, threatening to involve the Sikh population. There was already evidence that Pakistan's ISI had at least contacts with all of these. The KGB found a receptive audience as it turned over a stream of plausible but falsified information that Pakistan was seeking to counter India's increasing conventional military strength with an "asymmetric" approach, seeking to use India's internal divisions against it.

India also had a record of looking to foreign conflicts to deal with internal or external problems, dating back to the years when Indira Gandhi's father, Jawaharlal Nehru, was prime minister. This had been done both successfully—as in the 1961 occupation of Goa—and unsuccessfully— as when India provoked a Chinese military reaction in 1962. But it was 1971, when Indian military action resolved the East Bengal crisis and created the independent nation of Bangladesh from part of Pakistan, that the utility—and efficacy—of military force as both a unifier and remover of problems was impressed on the Indian government in general and on Indira Gandhi in particular. The military, which had been conservative in its willingness to use armed force and reluctant to invest in a large-scale nuclear capability, lost power as part of the security making process in the decade after 1971. They were unable—or unwilling—to put a brake on the move towards war.[24]

In the final analysis, India was willing to prepare to confront Pakistan militarily because it saw domestic benefits—the removal of a future nuclear threat, an improved relationship with the Soviet Union (including increasingly large amounts of basically free fuel and weapons)—and because it did not seem credible that Pakistan's external supporters, the US, China and Saudi Arabia, would be able to intervene militarily. As Indian planning progressed, it was seen as being a limited liability conflict, not intended to destroy Pakistan, as some had called for. Rather, it would remove Pakistan as a claimant to Indian-occupied Kashmir and as a potential nuclear power.[25]

Throughout 1983, the Indian military looked at changing its operational approach to one more likely to yield politically important results in the limited time before international intervention developed the potential to shut down the conflict. Even though the Indians could count on the Soviet veto in the UN Security Council, there was concern that the US would apply pressure that was more likely to be effective than the well-remembered gesture of dispatching the carrier *Enterprise* to the Bay of Bengal during the 1971 War. However, in assessing the second Carter administration, Gandhi realized that the US decision for a "limited liability" relationship with Pakistan led to an inability to deter military action against it.

The Indian Army moved stockpiles towards the frontier. In the 1983 Dig Vijay exercises, the Indian Army looked at the problems of large-scale desert offensive operation with combined arms forces.[26] The Indian Air Force trained with its new Soviet-supplied equipment and weapons. In Afghanistan, the Soviets brought additional supplies and forces forward to Kandahar and Samarkhel, near Jalalabad. Soviet forces made a practice of advancing to the border at Spin Baldak and Torkham and then retiring. By early 1984, however, the forces engaged in these moves—part of the diplomatic offensive against Pakistan—were staying in forward assembly areas rather than retiring to their original garrisons.

The 1984 India-Pakistan War

The 1984 India-Pakistan War followed, like its 1965 and 1971 predecessors, a lengthy mobilization and a failed series of international attempts to reduce tensions. The Soviets ensured that international efforts remained inadequate. It soon became apparent that India intended to strike while the passes to China remained blocked, preventing the Chinese opening a second front to relieve pressure on Pakistan or sending supplies over the Karakoram Highway.

The signs of an Indian offensive led Pakistan to mobilize and plan a preemptive strike of its own. But before it could move, the Indians opened the conflict with an airstrike by MiG-27 Flogger-F fighter-bombers against the Pakistani nuclear facilities at Kahuta and Kamra. The timing of the attack—made before Indian mobilization was complete—managed to secure some element of surprise. The attack, obviously inspired by the Israeli pre-emptive strike against Iraq's Osirak nuclear facilities in 1981, made extensive use of Soviet-supplied air-to-surface missiles.

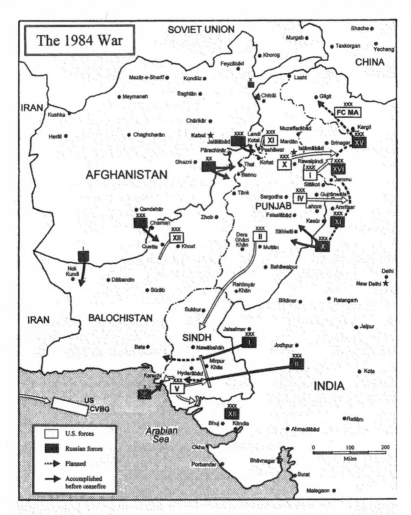

Afghanistan, Pakistan and India: the 1984 War

But the real surprise had been in India's pre-mobilization deployment. In the years 1971–84, the balance between Indian and Pakistani forces had become static, especially in the critical sectors in the heavily populated Punjab, with both sides' major cities, agriculture, industry and transport assets within striking distance.[27] Both sides also had well thought out defense plans, barrier and demolition plans, and fixed defensive positions. This prevented either side from massing a decisive concentration of force that might have been able to secure a breakthrough. The change, in 1983, was that India had decided to shift significant forces to the two flanks of the India–Pakistan confrontation, the far south of the Rajastan desert, and the far north of Kashmir, including the Siachen Glacier.

India concentrated its armored forces in the Rajastan Desert for a rapid advance into Sind, aiming for Karachi, with the goal of holding on against a Pakistani pincer attack in the Punjab.[28] The Indian advance was a two corps operation. The main blow was delivered by I and II Indian Corps. Each was organized with three divisions and together they made a two-pronged thrust in a broad arrowhead formation. This mechanized thrust was backed up by two infantry divisions in reserve. The 54th Air Assault Division was ready to be inserted by airdrop and airlift as required. A brigade was to make an amphibious landing deep in the Pakistani rear, at Korangi Creek west of Karachi. These two corps were initially to advance 150 miles to Hyderabad and then a further 60 miles to the Rahimyar Khan–Reyti line before either consolidating for a push on Karachi or demanding a cease-fire on favorable terms.[29]

Flank security for the main thrust would be provided by two corps, each of two infantry divisions, advancing north and south into Pakistan, to block Pakistani units moving from the Punjab and central Sind from counterattacking.

The Indians planned local attacks in the Punjab, but there the hope was that Pakistani gains could be minimized and that the existing civil unrest would not undercut Indian combat power. It would, however, require that some troops be held back from the front line for rear area protection. The other major thrust, Operation Trident, was a four-division corps operation. Its objective was to occupy the northern area of Kashmir and advance towards Skardu and Gilgit.[30] This would be supported by a brigade-sized Soviet operation to take Chitral and subsidiary specialist units moving across from Afghanistan's remote Wakhan Corridor.

The invasion opened on 1 April. The Indian opening moves were bold and forceful, and presented Pakistan with a significant military threat. What elevated them to the greatest military threat to Pakistan in its existence was the Soviet invasion. Division-sized composite forces of Soviet troops with comparably-sized Afghan communist forces advanced on the two traditional invasion routes into and out of Afghanistan, the Khyber Pass, aiming at Peshawar, and the Bolan pass, aiming at Quetta. A secondary thrust, with a Soviet air assault brigade, moved against Pakistani positions at Wana and Thai. Other brigade-size forces, in the deep south of Afghanistan, moved to cut the rail line to Iran. Soviet aircraft hit Pakistani airbases and reserve units. The KGB unleashed a sabotage and insurrection campaign throughout Pakistan

The International Crisis

The Indian–Soviet invasion of Pakistan presented the second Carter Administration, in its final year, with its greatest foreign policy crisis. Both of the invaders accompanied their military action with a diplomatic offensive that built on years of international groundwork. Both stressed that they were forced into this action by Pakistan's rash actions in Kashmir and Afghanistan. Both compared this to the Israeli incursion into Lebanon in 1982, portraying it as a temporary measure to remove a cross-border threat rather than one seeking the extinction of Pakistan. India stressed its democratic credentials (frayed though these had become under Indira Gandhi's increasingly autocratic rule). Both raised fears of Pakistan's professed Islamic ideology and sought to project the Afghan resistance supported by Pakistan as anti-modern Islamic radicals who held more danger to the West and US interests than did the Soviets and Indians.

Washington was limited in its response. There was a proposal—made before the invasion—to deploy US F-15 fighters and E-3A AWACS radar aircraft to Pakistan, as had been done to Saudi Arabia during the Iran crisis of 1979. This was seen as sending a deterrent signal while being obviously defensive in nature. The general indecision of the administration's approach to crisis management meant that this option was not effectively considered until after the shooting started. Then, it was too late to implement it.

Once again, hesitation and half measures had led to a reliance on diplomatic means that could not be backed up with force—for there had only been a limited rebuilding of US forces in the years following the Soviet invasion of Afghanistan. Even if Washington had wished to intervene militarily, its failure to rebuild its conventional force capability, especially strategic mobility and force projection assets, meant that there would be few viable options if it came to confronting the Soviets, save for a nuclear threat that was not going to be realistic. This administration was also not going to stand up for an ally whose human rights record, military government, and commitment to an Islamic state made Washington highly uncomfortable.

Therefore, Washington made strong diplomatic protests, put forces on alert and deployed the F-15/E-3 combination to Saudi Arabia, where they waited. Two carrier battle groups were sent towards the Arabian Sea. But the real US response would be in, once again, confronting the Soviet move diplomatically as the US had at the time of the invasion of Afghanistan.

On the ground, however, the war was not living up to the potential for successes that the Soviets' diplomatic skills had bought it. The Soviet ground forces were one of the biggest disappointments. The army that was billed as being able to advance on the Rhine at a rate of 100km (60 miles) a day in a future war in Europe found itself ebbing slowly forwards towards Quetta and Peshawar at a rate of well under 10km a day. While the Pakistani Air Force was hard-pressed by Indian and Soviet air strikes on its main operating bases, by operating from dispersal strips it was still able to keep up a strong presence over the forward areas and limit the use of helicopters for close air support, air mobility and resupply which the Soviets and their Afghan allies had counted on.

In the south, the advance on Hyderabad across the Rajastan Desert was not succeeding as well as expected. The two spearhead corps, despite the large supply dumps that had been built-up at the railheads at Barmer, Jaisalmer and Jodhpur, were soon encountering supply problems. The Indian Army was not set up to support a war of rapid movement, especially in its logistics. The corps themselves were advancing—those on the flanks had their own railheads and were doing better—but the logistics support soon started to fall behind. Pakistani air attacks on the advancing armor also proved stronger than anticipated. India had brought fighters up to cover the advance from the airfields at Bikaner, Barmer, Jaisalmer, Jodhpur and Null. Other fighters based at Jamnagar helped cover the southern flank. But each mile the Indians advanced put them further away from their fighter cover and closer to the Pakistanis. The Indian Air Force, always jealous that too-close cooperation with the Army would imperil its independence, had put more of its assets into striking the Pakistani main operating bases.[31]

Pakistan was able to trade space for time. The Pakistanis moved to conserve their forces, not engaging their armored divisions against the Indian economy-of-force defense in the Punjab, but rather shifted them to meet the thrust through the south, while airpower, covering forces, and their own logistics problems attrited and delayed the Indian armored spearheads. Pakistan's small force of AH-1 attack helicopters proved critical on several occasions, decimating Indian mechanized units until suffering losses to their Soviet-built self-propelled air defense weapons.[32] The Indian rate of advance, after repeated ambushes from helicopters and covering forces, slowed as they required thorough reconnaissance before advancing.

The Indian amphibious landing was even less successful. It was supported by a force of over 40 Indian warships, including the carrier *Vikrant*, three missile destroyers, four missile-armed frigates, six corvettes, four minesweepers and large number of amphibious and merchant ships. The force was attacked by Pakistani Mirage fighters armed with Exocet anti-ship guided missiles. Closer in to shore, Pakistani midget submarines operated against the beachhead. However, the Indian forces ashore were soon isolated by Pakistani reserves. As the Indian Navy had to maintain a presence offshore to support the beachhead, this led to a series of naval battles. Most of the Pakistani Navy was sunk, either at sea or, in the case of those ships not operational, in Karachi harbor. However, the Indian Navy also suffered severe losses. The *Vikrant,* damaged by a non-contact torpedo explosion, had to be towed to safety. The Indian amphibious assault— reinforced by airdrops at night—was able to hang on, but at a high cost.[33]

On the northern front, Operation Trident was supposed to reach Gilgit in two weeks by way of Skardu. Limited by the high-altitude winter conditions, it advanced barely a third of the distance in that time, not making it even to Skardu. The Soviet-supplied Mi-26 helicopters that were counted on to support the thrust made sure that Indian forces could advance, but not achieve the high-altitude *Blitzkrieg* that the plan had required.[34] In Northern Kashmir the Indians also advanced slowly.

The Soviet advance was, surprisingly, not much more successful than the Indian one. Even though they were faced by numerically inferior Pakistani forces and could call on superior Soviet airpower, they were unable to achieve their objectives. Part of the reason was that their communist Afghan allies proved no more effective against Pakistanis than they were against other Afghans. The two division-sized Soviet forces were made up mainly of composite units. There were not enough high-quality airborne troops both to spearhead the offensives and keep the lines of communication across Afghanistan open. This latter requirement tied up most of the Soviet effort.

After 12 days of fighting—with ongoing US diplomatic pressure and the threat of an oil boycott of India from OPEC—Pakistan accepted a Soviet-offered cease-fire. The Pakistanis were proud of themselves. Alone, they had held off a massive two-front invasion and kept their major military forces intact. The Indian and Soviet—Afghan forces disengaged, starting with the costly amphibious foothold near Karachi. Only in the northern glaciers were the Indians able to hold on to some of their gains. Compared with the 1971 War, Pakistan had done well in combat.

Yet the impact of the war was soon to overshadow the euphoria of having staved off battlefield defeat. Pakistan realized that India had been defeated more by its failure to adapt fully to Soviet-style *Blitzkrieg* operations than by Pakistan's military power. The Soviets had made their point about Afghanistan, and Pakistan's support for the Afghan resistance remained at a constrained level, following the destruction of many of the camps and much of the support infrastructure in the border areas— though the Soviet invaders never managed to take Quetta or Peshawar. Pakistan saw that the damage done to its nuclear program had been considerable—there would now be no bomb for at least a decade—and that the next time the Indians might rely on nuclear blackmail to achieve their policy options.

Pakistan also realized how little it could count on the US to support it in a crisis. Following the events of 1980, however, this was hardly news. To Pakistan, it appeared that its future was linked to accommodation with the Soviet presence in Afghanistan and in greater links to the increasingly radicalized elements of the Islamic world. Pakistan realized that another conflict, after India had worked out its command of the operational art, might well result in its destruction as an effective nation before it had a nuclear deterrent. While the Soviet attempts to inspire division between Pakistan's diverse and divided ethnic and economic groups had not led to collapse during the war, the shared Islamic religion was seen as one thing that could keep them together for the future. An Islamicized Pakistan would also serve as a "poison pill" that India dare not decisively defeat and annex—for fear that radical Islam would spread to India's own Moslem population.

Sputtering Out

The Carter second term did not undo its 1980 decisions overnight. Rather than reversing them, it changed their context. Rather than being elements of a strategy of confronting the Soviets, they became impediments to achieving better relations. The INF decisions were incrementally reversed, with first the new weapons to be kept in the US and deployed only in times of a crisis and, finally, replaced by "earmarked" ballistic missile submarines, which had been used for this mission in the 1970s.

The US kept the Afghan resistance supported at a level of about $20 million annually through the second Carter administration. This kept the conflict going but—because the distribution of the aid reflected Pakistani policy concerns—this was not enough to change the dynamic on the battlefield, even though the Soviets were having little success in legitimizing the rule of their Afghan clients.

One of the key issues in determining the ultimate failure of the Afghan resistance was the US refusal to supply high-technology weapons. This had support, especially in the Congress, but was strongly opposed by the State Department, the Joint Chiefs of Staff, and the CIA.[35] Any president would have had difficulty in overcoming such opposition. The second Carter administration was unwilling to expend the political capital needed to win this fight. The president's political appointees were not likely to fight for issues such as the supply of Stinger SAMs to the Afghans when this was strongly opposed by the bureaucracy. So the situation rested when Jimmy Carter left the White House in January 1985.

The conflict continued in Afghanistan. When Gorbachev succeeded to the Soviet leadership, he escalated the conflict in 1985–86 as part of his goal to "have both reform and Afghanistan." While it would never be peaceful, after that, the Soviets were able to adapt to Afghan conditions and settle in. They were in occupation rather than in control and the body counts remained considerable, but the Soviets were able to meet their policy goals.

The Impact

The failure of the US to support the Afghan resistance against the Soviet Union beyond the continued flow of covert aid was critical because it went to the heart of the nature of Cold War competition. Because of the primacy of the nuclear balance, military confrontation between superpowers was not feasible. Winston Churchill, who had been first to identify the Iron Curtain in 1946, three years later prophesied that: "Safety will become the sturdy child of terror and survival the twin brother of annihilation."[36] Because war between superpowers became too costly, proxy wars became more important. Regarding Afghanistan, Carter decreed that, like Woodrow Wilson in the opening years of the Great War: "there was such a thing as being too proud to fight." Carter would persist in his claim that he was "the first American president in 50 years who has never sent troops into combat" and that no US personnel had died in combat during his administration. He was also practical. There did not appear to be any votes in supporting a distant and alien people. This was reflected also in his refusal to intervene in insurgencies in Central America.

The Soviet success in Afghanistan did not solve the fundamental problems of governance and the economy that were beginning to become apparent in the final senescent years of Brezhnev's rule. It did, however, suggest ways that his successors could use Soviet strengths to avoid dealing with them. It also meant that reform could be directed primarily in terms of state maintenance rather than meeting challenges by the US and the West, expressed either in terms of a military response or support for human and economic rights.

The success in Afghanistan had shown the Soviet leadership that they had backed the right horse in investing in military strength rather than in modernizing the economy or in broadening the base of the government or in expanding its legitimacy among many people who still saw themselves as under military occupation from Moscow. The Soviet Union would not extract much of value from Afghanistan, either in terms of natural resources nor even in having a base for future military operations adjacent to two key regions: Iran and the Gulf, Pakistan and the subcontinent. What it did take away of value was the lesson that military power, if effectively used, could solve Soviet problems. It also realized that, as long as the threat of Soviet military force kept foreign countries from providing aid and support, internal challenges to Moscow-approved rule could be defeated by the traditional application of stick and carrot. The promises of the Helsinki "Third Basket" on human rights were overshadowed by the reality of the KGB taking care of anyone too interested in these rights.

Internally, the success in Afghanistan strengthened the hand of the military and the security services. They had demonstrated that in return for the large-scale investment made in them throughout the Brezhnev years, they could deliver the goods in the form of imposing and maintaining Soviet policy objectives. They also demonstrated that, with strategic nuclear parity to back up the Soviet Union's long-standing numerical superiority in conventional forces, the West could be subjected to a form of nuclear blackmail. It might be as crude and intended for a mass audience as that which was directed at Western Europe following the 1956 Suez crisis, but its ability to deter the West from supporting Afghanistan or modernizing theater nuclear weapons showed its effectiveness.

The weakness of the Western response to the invasion also demonstrated that, as long as the Soviets did not attempt to redraw the map of Europe by the direct use of force of arms, they would be unlikely to be met by force of arms. The Soviet Union was able to concentrate on imposing a solution in Afghanistan—one that emphasized force of arms rather than building a legitimate government—because it was not straining to meet US challenges. By the time Gorbachev assumed power in 1985, the cost of the continuing conflict in Afghanistan was low enough that it did not stress either the economy or the internal will of the Soviet state, however unpopular it might be. Gorbachev's policy—enabled by the second Carter administration—was that he could have both reform and Afghanistan, and there had been four years of US policy that did not dissuade him by escalating the costs of Moscow's war. Gorbachev apparently remembered his mentor Yuri Andropov's words to the Politburo back on March 17, 1979: "We will be labeled as an aggressor but in spite of that, under no circumstances can we lose Afghanistan."[37]

The message of the Soviets' ability to impose a military solution on Afghanistan was unmistakable. To the critics of Soviet rule in Eastern Europe, such as Solidarity in Poland (under a harsh martial law regime) it became apparent that, as long as the Brezhnev doctrine would be backed up by force, the fundamental fact of rule from Moscow could not be challenged. It could be modified or obviated around the edges, but it became apparent that, if there would be no strong Western support to a challenge of the Soviet-dominated *status quo* where it was marginal and recent, as in Afghanistan, there certainly could not be one where it was long-standing and presumably vital to Soviet national interests, as was Poland. As a result, the opposition throughout Eastern Europe and the Soviet Union was marginalized

The West's failure to provide effective help to Afghanistan was key in the future of relations with the Islamic world. The West's unwillingness to provide effective support for the Afghan resistance made it apparent tha the West would rather have a pro-Moscow regime in Afghanistan than an Islamic one. Indeed, they saw informed opinion in the West stating that an Islamic regime would certainly lead to instability and likely to the export of terrorism. The failure to stand up for Afghanistan by the West diminished its influence throughout the Islamic world. Egypt, Saudi Arabia and others realized that they could not look to the US as a counter to threats in the region. This meant that the Camp David Accords, signed in March 1979, were not expanded. The rejectionist bloc was soon seen as dominant, with an increasingly embittered post-war Pakistan as a member.

As a result, Soviet influence in the Middle East reversed trends and increased. In the early 1980s, fuelled by reaction to Israel's incursions into Lebanon, the Soviet military presence in Egypt and Syria exceeded that of a decade before. While Jordan and Saudi Arabia still resisted more than a minimal Soviet presence, South Yemen (facing a conflict with North Yemen) and Iraq saw a strong security relationship with the Soviet Union as their best assurance against neighboring threats. To the east India, depending on increasing Soviet arms shipments to remedy the defects in its military seen in 1984, became closer to Russia.

Yet none of this helped the Soviet Union improve its economy or deal with the fundamental problem of paying for the Brezhnev era military build-up. However, the West's policy desire to maintain good relations with the Soviet Union—as seen in the failure to sustain sanctions post-Afghanistan—showed the Soviets how they might have access to the West's technology. With the Middle East's oil exporters increasingly undercut by instability and anti-Western engineered oil shortages, the West—especially Western Europe—became increasingly dependent on the Soviets for energy needs.

Slowly, through the 1980s, the Soviet military led the way towards modernization, with both overt (and covert) imports of computer technology. As in the mid-19th century, the military was the locomotive of reform. The microchip revolution spread to the command economy by the end of the decade. The Soviets were able to buy as much of the new technology as they wished from a demoralized West and so avoided any need to reform their society to meet the challenge.[38]

None of this solved fundamental problems of legitimacy or addressed economic failures, but it enabled any crisis in Eastern Europe, as in the Soviet Union, to be met with armed force and repression. The leadership in Moscow had seen that the use of military force to solve the problems of resistance in their sphere of influence would have no more than a temporary impact on relations with the West. Gorbachev proved, with the Afghan lesson in mind, to be willing to use repression to keep the Soviet empire together with the objective of what he saw as buying time for his reforms to work and so addressing the root causes of discontent. Gorbachev might have grave misgivings about the use of armed force to maintain Soviet control, but he could not rebut the apparent effectiveness of its use in Afghanistan, nor could he overcome the insistence of the Soviet military and KGB—their prestige undiminished by battlefield defeat—that this was an effective response. The use of force against East Europeans would certainly lead to a cooling in East–West relations and delay the "self-Finlandization" of Europe for some years. But in the end, detente was too precious to be disturbed by dead Poles or East Germans, any more than it was disturbed by dead Afghans.

The Reality

In assessing what might have happened, I have tried to abide by Geoffrey Parker's "minimal rewrite rule."[39] With the exception of the aborted Iran raid, all is factual until the "October surprise." In setting out a course of events that is reasonable as well as thinkable, the policies carried out by the US and the West in the 1980s in this scenario are basically those of the late 1970s carried forward. The changes are those that could be expected from a re-elected Carter administration in which Cyrus Vance became the leading foreign policy voice. Such an administration might well have aided the Afghan resistance not one dollar less than the real-world Reagan administration did. While in this scenario, it proved unable to supply Stinger SAMs to the Afghans, in reality the first Reagan administration was equally held in check by the bureaucracy.

The difference in this scenario is that Afghanistan becomes the salvation of the Soviet Union where, in reality, it was one of the key factors that doomed it to irrelevance and destruction. It is in the absence of the strong leadership historically provided by the Reagan administration (and which meshed well with that exerted, in different ways, by Prime Minister Thatcher and Pope John Paul II) and in the existence of a US strategy aimed not at keeping the Cold War going at decreasing levels of tension, but in winning it. That the Cold War ended when and how it did was by no means pre-determined. Indeed, those named above—and, in the early 1980s, Zbigniew Brzezinski—were among the few contemporaries who considered the eventual result possible, let alone likely.

The scenario differs from reality in that Carter confronts the Soviets in 1979–80 but backs away from this in his second term. The policies ascribed to the Carter administration are all those advocated at the time by elements within it, mostly by Vance and the State Department. The turning away from Afghanistan after the 1980 elections projected for a second Carter term certainly had many predecessors in the first term, such as the neutron bomb policy turn-around. Indeed, in 1980-81, in appeared as if none of the earlier Carter-era policies had succeeded. However, they did provide the groundwork for the more effective policies that slowly emerged under the Reagan administration. However, under a second Carter administration the policies would likely have perished in more "flip-flops." Under Reagan, they were integrated in a larger US strategy.

This is a key point. There is a difference between decisions made as problem-solving and decisions made as part of an integrated strategy, even when they are the same decisions. Carter and Reagan both decided to aid the Afghan resistance. The dollar amount of the aid to the Afghans supplied in this scenario's second Carter administration was at the same level as that actually supplied during the first Reagan administration. Both decisions had the same limitations (Pakistani intransigence, US bureaucratic reluctance) but here it is seen that Reagan succeeded and Carter failed in dealing with Afghanistan not because of decisions made with Afghanistan alone, but because Carter never integrated his Afghanistan-related decisions into part of a larger strategy to win the Cold War. Indeed, he never thought such a strategy was feasible or even, in the light of the nuclear risks, desirable. Some, such as Brzezinski, see this as no failing. He has accurately pointed out that the Carter policies— emphasizing human rights, support for the Afghan resistance, increasing defense spending—were those used by the Reagan administration to conclude the Cold War successfully.

In reality, US support for the Afghan resistance was crucial for its eventual success. With US support, Pakistan, China, Saudi Arabia, Britain, France and others could join in the effort. This scenario shows that, without strong US leadership, without a strong build-up of US strategic and conventional forces, there would not have been such a broad response. The Afghans developed the largest national rising of the 20th century without foreign support. But it was only the higher level of foreign support— especially that emerging in the second Reagan administration—that allowed them to overcome their lack of political development and make enough of an impact on the Soviets that Gorbachev realized he could not have both Afghanistan and reform. Reform needed better relations with the West, and the first Reagan term, for all its limits in supporting the Afghans, had demonstrated that this would remain a barrier to such relations.

The Soviets were unable to sustain the challenge Afghanistan posed to their system because they were being pressed on so many different fronts. Had accommodation with the Soviets been the US goal, Afghanistan would never have contributed to presenting Soviet power with a situation it could not handle. In different contexts, the same US actions could have had very different results.

Bibliography

Allin, Dana, *Cold War Illusions,* St Martin's, New York, 1994.

Calrey, Demetrios James, ed., *The New American Interventionism,* Columbia University Press New York, 1999.

Cogan, Charles G., "Partners in Time: The CIA and Afghanistan since 1978," *World Policy Journal,* v. 10 n.2 1993, pp. 73–98.

Friedman, Norman, *The Fifty Year War: Conflict and Strategy in the Cold War,* Naval Institute Press, Annapolis, 2000.

Gaddis, John Lewis, *Strategies of Containment,* Oxford University Press, Oxford, 1982.

Gates, Robert M., *From the Shadows,* Simon & Schuster, New York, 1996.

Hayward, Steven E, *The Age of Reagan,* Random House, New York, 2001.

Kaufman, Burton I., *The Presidency of James Earl Carter Jr.,* University of Kansas Press, Lawrence, 1993.

Kaufman, Robert G., *Henry M. Jackson: A Life in Politics,* University of Washington Press, Seattle, 2000.

Morris, Kenneth E., *Jimmy Carter: American Moralist,* University of Georgia Press, Athens, 1996.

Muravchik, Joshua, *The Uncertain Crusade: Jimmy Carter and the Dilemmas of Human Rights,* Hamilton Press, Lanham, MD, 1986.

Ranney, Austin, ed., *The American Elections of 1980,* AEI, Washington, 1981.

Rikhye, Ravi, *The Fourth Round, Indo-Pak War 1984,* ABC Publishing House, New Delhi, 1982.

Rikhye, Ravi, *The War That Never Was,* Chankaya Publications, Delhi, 1988.

Thomas, Raju G.C., *Indian Security Policy,* Princeton University Press, Princeton, 1986.

Vance, Cyrus, *Hard Choices,* Simon & Schuster, New York, 1987.

Westhold, Arne, ed., Meeting of the Politburo, March 17, 1979," *Cold War International History Project Bulletin,* issues 8–9, Winter 1996–97 (internet edition).

Notes

1. In his poem "September 1, 1939"-
2. Morris, *Jimmy Carter: American Moralist,* p. 320.
3. Gaddis, *Strategies of Containment,* p. 345.
4. Morris, *Jimmy Carter: American Moralist,* p. 263.
5. Muravchik, *The Uncertain Crusade,* p. 202.
6. Burton I. Kaufman, *The Presidency of James Earl Carter,* p. 365.
7. Hayward, *The Age of Reagan,* p. 537.
8. Hayward, *The Age of Reagan,* p. 537.
9. Burton I. Kaufman, *The Presidency of James Earl Carter,* p. 365.
10. Friedman, *The Fifty Year War,* p. 422.
11. Vance, *Hard Choices,* p. 387.
12. Cogan, "Partners in Time," p. 76
13. Gates, *From the Shadows,* p. 113 details the Vance-Brzezinski battle on this issue.

14. Nelson Polsby: "The Democratic Nomination," in Ranney, *The American Elections of 1980*, p. 45.

15. Robert G. Kaufman, *Henry M. Jackson: A Life in Politics*, p. 397.

16. Friedman, *The Fifty Year War*, p. 439.

17. *Ibid.*, p. 439.

18. Allin, *Cold War Illusions*, p. 146.

19. Friedman, *The Fifty Year War*, pp. 438–9.

20. Allin, p. 146.

21. This comment appeared in *The New Republic*, October 25, 1980, p.9.

22. Hayward, *The Age of Reagan*, p. 609.

23. Hayward, *The Age of Reagan*, p. 498.

24. Thomas, *Indian Security Policy*, p. 286.

25. On thinking on the India–Pakistan military balance and potential war plans in the early 1980s generally, see Rikhye, *The Fourth Round, Indo-Pak War 1984-* The author can attest that this work of "future history" was widely read by senior military and government officials in Pakistan at the time.

26. Rikhye, *The War That Never Was*, p. 165.

27. Rikhye, *The War That Never Was*, p. 87.

28. This was the rationale behind the Brass Tacks exercise (actually conducted in 1987). Rikhye, *The War That Never Was*, p. 154.

29. 29- Rikhye, *The War That Never Was*, pp. 156–57. The Indian plan is from Brass Tacks.

30. On Trident, see Rikhye, *The War That Never Was*, pp. 192–202.

31. On the potential problems of an advance on Hyderabad, see Rikhye, *The War That Never Was*, pp. 154–76.

32. On potential Pakistani countermoves, see Rikhye, *The War That Never Was*, pp. 180–85.

33. The potential risks to an Indian invasion are in Rikhye, *The War That Never Was*, pp. 177–80.

34. On Trident limitations, see Rikhye, *The War That Never Was*, pp. 195–97.

35. See generally Cogan, also Alan J. Kuperman: "The Stinger Missile and US Intervention in Afghanistan," in Calrey, *The New American Interventionism*, pp. 159–203.

36. Winston S. Churchill, *In the Balance: Speeches 1949–50* (Houghton Mifflin, Boston, 1951), p. 356.

37. Westhold, "Meeting of the Politburo, March 17, 1979," p. 139.

38. Friedman, *The Fifty Year War*, p. 486, sees this as a possible alternative.

39. Ferguson, Niall, ed., *Virtual History: Alternatives and Counterfactuals* (Basic Books, New York, 1999), p. xii.

10
RED LIGHTNING
The Collapse of the Red Army

Peter G. Tsouras

Svechin General Staff Academy: Moscow, December 2, 2007[1]
Marshal of Russia, Prince Ivan Vaselevich Chonkin mounted the rostrum of the lecture hall of the Aleksandr Svechin Academy of the Great Russian General Staff.[2] Two hundred pairs of eyes fixed themselves on the spare old man in the plain gray uniform, relieved only by the glitter of the Saint George Cross and two Hero of Russia medals. It was rumored that the very wrinkles of the uniform fell out in awe of the wearer. Behind him, the great wall of the auditorium was almost filled with Konstantinov's famous portrait of the historic meeting of Chonkin and the tsar-to-be, Piotr III. Some regarded Konstantinov's work more as an icon than a historical painting. There was an unearthly aura to the scene as the two soldiers received the blessings of the Patriarch at the St Sergeiv Monastery on that fateful day in September 1989. The three would march across the ruins of an empire to save Russia.[3]

Behind the ascetic face that had been compared to a Rublyev saint, a glint of carefully-disciplined mirth flickered. Chonkin began to speak:

> "Gentlemen, the seed of disaster that befell the former Soviet Union germinated in the US Army Center of Military History. Let me emphasize that this section represented some of the finest minds to have studied military history in any age. Their fertile, collective efforts were carefully directed and encouraged by a command structure that valued the lessons of the past more highly than the introduction of new technological toys."

They hung on his every word, of course. He allowed himself the luxury of admiring his own polished logic and his exquisite delivery. Well, he was good. Why deny it? What made it all so delicious, though, was that it was a lie... a beautiful, logical lie, but it was a lie nonetheless. Chonkin was one of the few who really knew what happened 20 years ago.

Center of Military History: Washington, June 15,1987

Major John T. Moran had poured his first cup of coffee that morning hoping to be able to read the new Greenhill translation of de Saxe's *Mes Reveries* in peace. The book was a gem, a rare reprint of the racy memoirs of a great captain of the early 18th century. Moran was hoping to write an analysis of de Saxe's techniques for the Army's professional journal, *Military Review,* but it did not seem possible. His in-box was always full. It had been made clear to him in his first week on the job that reading de Saxe was extracurricular. His job was to prepare biographies of generals about to retire. If he did well, he might even be allowed to join the team writing the section's pride and joy, a history of Army word processing.

Moran was savoring both the coffee aroma and the prospect of enjoying the forbidden fruit of his new book when Fate rushed through the door flailing its arms and reeking of panic.

"Your briefing, your briefing for the Vice... Is it ready?" Fate bleated. The annoying thing about Fate was that it always came in disguise. Today it appeared as his boss, Colonel "Wild Bill" Benson.

"What briefing?" Moran asked.

Benson then shifted from a bleat to a shriek. "What briefing! What briefing! The one we talked about last week, that briefing! You do have it ready, don't you, Major?"

Moran's puzzled look turned Benson's face beet red. He racked his brain and took a stab at it, "You mean my study on the Indirect Approach, Sir?"

"YES! That's it! You have only 30 minutes to get there. HURRY!"

Unfortunately, the colonel's appreciation of the Indirect Approach meant taking the wrong exit from the Capitol beltway to the Pentagon. Like a drowning man, he clutched at the thin assurance in Moran's voice as if it were a life preserver.

Moran had no time to wonder how a five minute conversation in the hall over a month ago could turn into a briefing for the Vice Chief so soon. At least he had the study finished and grabbed a copy on the way out of the office. As they dashed out the door, Major John Morgan, who shared a cubicle with Moran wondered why "Wild Bill" had run off with Moran. It must be very important, he thought, to cancel the briefing he was supposed to give the Vice shortly. What could be more important than briefing the Vice on his retirement biography?

"The Little Bedroom," the Pentagon

It is not a good omen when the Vice Chief of Staff of the US Army arrives at a briefing before the briefer, especially when the Vice's name is General Oscar "Razor" Rauch. The stench of sacrilege filled the Little Bedroom,[4] as the private briefing room of the Army Vice Chief was called. Moran was too intent on his subject to notice when he arrived. He pulled out his cold pipe, settled it in the corner of his mouth from where it would pass back and forth to his left hand, and began.   ,

"On the battlefield, NATO is at a permanent disadvantage in light of the vast Soviet preponderance in weight of numbers of personnel and equipment, especially when this is enhanced by rough techno-logical equivalence and an acceptable level of operational efficiency."

The slash of a permanent frown across Rauch's face deepened as he surveyed this officer. The man's whole manner was an affront to him as Vice Chief of Staff. He was so... so casual and at ease. Rauch felt cheated of the palpable tremor of fear and apprehension that he had come to expect as his due. It was a soothing, gratifying feeling, and now he missed it.

"To oppose the Soviet steamroller on its own terms is doomed. Rather, the solution is the classic use of the concept of the Indirect Approach. Do not aim to strike the armed might of the Soviet Union. Strike its greatest weakness, a facet of the national character of the Russians.

It is the Russians who are the imperial race among the many Soviet peoples. Strike the national weakness of the Russians, and you strike directly at their imperial control of the subject peoples."

Moran was enjoying himself. He was a natural teacher. The Vice, who long ago stopped being a natural learner, was not enjoying himself at all. He was being slighted, insulted. Where were all the accoutre-ments of a suitable briefing? Where were the graphs, the charts, the slides, and above all, the viewgraphs. He loved viewgraphs. What was a briefing without viewgraphs? Those who did not share his stamina or taste muttered about "Death by Viewgraph," or "Death of a Thousand Viewgraphs." Oblivious, Moran happily went on.[5]

"Such an approach will yield the most immediate and dramatic results at the very onset of war. The effect will be collapse of the intri-cate invasion plan on itself, resulting in chaos along the entire Central Front as each Soviet echelon crashes into the one ahead of it. NATO is then presented with the option of attacking on its own terms with immensely more favorable odds. A military victory against the War-saw Pact then falls within the realm of possibility."

The Vice was seething now. Each new discovery of affronted dignity stoked him hotter and hotter. It was not Moran's lucid exposition of a revolutionary approach in the art of war. Rauch really had not heard a word of it. Rather, it was the loose tie, the coffee-stained blouse adorned with sweet roll crumbs, and worst of all, the tell-tale outward pressure on the uniform seams that identified Moran as "overweight."

The explosion was not pretty, but then none of the Vice's carnivorous tirades were. Moran remembered leading a babbling Benson by the arm through the rings and corridors of the Pentagon, through the acres of parking lot, and finally driving into the colonel's slot in front of the Center of Military History. The next day was worse. "Wild Bill" had recovered enough to drink in every word of his personal interview with the Vice, an experience that left him looking for revenge.

If looks could have killed, Moran would have been a smoking cinder. As it turned out, the colonel's first sentence was the most positive note of the whole meeting. "I have just been ordered to retire, MAJOR. The only reason I was not relieved is so I can write your efficiency report myself, my last official act. Let me begin with your manifest failure to meet the Army's Weight Control Program standards."

The Patton Officers' Club, Fort Meyer, Virginia

Annie, the barmaid, did not mind providing an audience to the walking wounded who sought refuge there from the trench warfare of staff duty at the Pentagon. Tonight it was a chubby major she had rarely seen before. She recognized the look of a broken career.

"I just don't get it, Annie. It really was such a good concept. I'm sure it would have worked. Look, the Russians have such a horrendous alcoholism problem. It's a weakness that's begging to be exploited. Why, a study of military history is full of ways the Russians' inability to control themselves has screwed them up."

"Want another Diet Coke, honey?" Annie deftly interjected. "Sure sounds like an interesting idea," she purred, thinking of the tip. It was a slow night.

Rummaging through his briefcase at this mistaken sign of interest, Moran pulled out a thick bundle of papers. "Listen, Annie, this was written by a fellow named Vladimir A. Antonov-Ovesyenko, a leading Bolshevik who led the attack on the Winter Palace in 1917."

Annie's eyes glazed over at this point, but Moran did not notice as he read aloud,

> "The Preobrazhensky regiment got completely drunk while guarding the wine cellars of the Palace... The Pavlovksy regiment did not withstand the temptation either... Mixed picked guards were sent; they too got drunk. Members of the regimental committees were assigned... These succumbed, too. Men of the armored brigades were ordered to disperse the crowds—they paraded up and down and then began to sway suspiciously... An attempt was made to flood the cellars. The fire brigades got drunk... The Council of People's Commissars appointed a special commissar with emergency powers... But the commissar too proved unreliable."[6]

Moran looked up to find Annie wiping off the other end of the bar. Not to be deterred when on a hot military history topic, he moved down to continue his lecture. "You see, Annie, the Russians have a drinking culture in which the idea is to get blown away as quickly as possible. When the booze is available, they drink it all. Did you know that their liquor bottles don't have corks or screw-on caps but only foil tops; when the bottle is opened, it has to be finished."

Annie leaned on the bar to listen; professional curiosity had been aroused.

"Did you know that the single biggest source of revenue for the Soviet budget is the manufacture and sale of booze? No kidding! It was the same under the tsar, but they drink a lot more now under the communists.[7] Thanks to Castro and all that cheap sugar the Soviets have had to take off his hands, everybody is into making moonshine called Samogan or Kerosinka. Annie, they test the stuff by dipping a piece of paper into it and setting it on fire to see how cleanly it burns. They even sing a little ditty about it:

> "Thank you, thank you, Cuba
> All Russia does proclaim
> Ten ounces per kilo of sugar
> And it burns with a bright blue flame!"

"Well, that got me thinking of something I read years ago about the Eastern Front in World War II. When the Germans were retreating after the Battle of Kursk in 1943, they were forced to abandon a huge depot in the Kharkov area at the Feski Collective Farm which had been designed to support an entire army group with food and booze. Talk about being well-stocked, Annie! They had the looted booze of Europe. The depot had the entire production of the French spirits industry for one year, not to mention Spanish port and Italian Chianti. They had so much Russian vodka that it was stored in carboys, you know, those huge glass containers. Well, the quartermaster threw it open to any German unit that could haul anything away. Remember, this was an army in fast retreat. There was a traffic jam in every direction. They cleaned everything out—except the vodka—did not touch one carboy.

"No sooner did they leave than the spearhead of the Soviet pursuit runs right into the depot—the *5th Guards Tank Army,* the victors of the great tank battle of Prokhorovka. They did not move for three days as they drained every drop of vodka. A couple of days later, still hung-over, they were smashed up by one SS division.[8]

"It just struck me that we could do on purpose what the Germans did by accident. So I wrote up this plan. It was gorgeous. Then I brief the Vice, and it blows up in my face. Talk about driving a wooden stake through the heart of a new idea. Well, I guess I can always teach high school."

Svechin General Staff Academy: December 2, 2007

Chonkin theatrically straightened his notes, upon which he had not once glanced, pausing for the desired effect.

> "Of course, gentlemen, Red Lightning was instantly recognized as a work of genius by the American Army. With the highest of priorities, the Army's operations, logistics, and training staffs were set to work to prepare the plan for action."

Office of the Vice Chief of Staff, the Pentagon: July 15,1987

They used to say that the gods were perverse. Whether through perversity or just a misunderstood sense of humor, Fate was pleased to intervene when General Rauch retired on schedule. The normal administrative confusion attendant on such a momentous event was roiled even more by the short temper of the Vice's administrative officer, a disciple of his boss' leadership style. He barked through his office door: "Sergeant Parker, I don't want to tell you again to get those studies in here for signature."

Sergeant Parker swore under her breath: "Of course, you want to tell me again; you enjoy being an asshole." She tried to balance the two piles of studies, of cursed and of blessed briefing papers. They slipped and cascaded to the floor all in a heap. "Now that's all he needs to see," she muttered as she scooped them back into two neat piles approximately the same thickness as the original two piles. "Here we are, Sir." The major gave her a what-took-you-so-long glare and pulled over the pile with the approved cover sheets. He deftly began applying perfect facsimiles of the signatures of the series of officers whose responsibility it was to ensure that the particular documents had been properly approved at each stage of the staffing process. His final flourish was for the Vice's signature.

To the amused flutter of Fate's wings, Moran's plan left the Vice's office in the blessed pile. Safe in the hands of the military bureaucracy, the breath of immortal life was blown into it, and it received its name, Operation Red Lightning.

Army project that it was, it could find no godfather among the other services. Neither the Navy nor the Air Force showed the sUghtest sign of interest in its application. At a joint planning conference, Admiral "Reef" Callaghan warily sniffed at it, laughed, and said: "The Marines can have it when the Army wears it out." The Air Force representative, General "Wind Shear" Windham, was about to chime in with the condescension reserved for Army projects. It was easy to make fools of the Army. The Navy and Air Force were so much more adept at manipulating the system to get their way. The put down was on the tip of his tongue when a staff officer whispered: "General, this plan, as bizarre as it sounds, may represent a whole new strategic spectrum that the Air Force cannot afford to get frozen out of. I suggest we look at it more closely." Condescension became restrained interest.

Within a week, it was all the Army could do to keep the Air Force from wresting the lead role for Red Lightning away from it. Still, the Air Force grab had alerted the Army that it was on to something. If the Air Force wanted the project, it must be hot.[9]

Office of the Vice Chief of Staff, the Pentagon: January 7,1988

The new Vice Chief was noting with satisfaction the progress that Red Lightning had already made. The melodic voice of his favorite briefing officer was giving him good news, accompanied by full color slides. He must remember to send a note of acknowledgment to the graphics shop for its wonderful work.

"The Air Force reports its contracts for special munitions are 'on time and on target.' Our similar contracts for the small, unbreakable, plastic containers are also on track. You will see on this slide one of the labels being prepared in Russian for this type container.

Purchase of spirits through several CIA affiliated wholesalers has not caused any suspicious shortages or price increases in the domestic market. The strategic location of members of the Kentucky and Tennessee delegations on both intelligence and appropriations committees in both houses of Congress continues to assure strong support on the Hill. Purchasing of half the Soviet export of Stolychnaya brand vodka, considered the best in the world, is proving to be more difficult than expected. The Soviets appear to be having trouble increasing exports to meet the sudden new demand. CIA informs us that they expect the KGB to be sniffing around soon.

The most difficult element of Red Lightning has been the reorganization of 50 percent of the Utah National Guard and selected Alabama and Mississippi Guard units into multiple rocket launcher battalions. The high incidence in these units of Mormons and Baptists who are teetotalers will keep tampering with munitions to a minimum. Training has been behind schedule."

The Vice winced to himself. Utah's Adjutant General had had to be pulled down off the ceiling when the state's part in Red Lightning had been explained. The governor had gone to the President. That had been very unpleasant, but the Vice had not earned his nickname of "Tapdance" Tom Rollins for nothing. In the end, Utah had come around, but it had been at the price of a promise for a new depot and a pledge written in blood that Fort Douglas in Salt Lake City would *never* be closed. Alabama and Mississippi had also extracted their pound of flesh. The Vice's thoughts returned to the briefing as a brilliant new slide appeared.[10]

"The studies by the Surgeon General of the United States and the Judge Advocate General of the Army have both been positive. We are assured Red Lightning contains no violations of the Geneva Convention, the Laws of War, or chemical warfare treaties and protocols. That concludes my briefing, sir. Are there any questions?"

The Vice had none. The briefing had been polished, he thought. That was just like Major Massingale, a splendid officer, athletically trim, immaculate tailored uniform, perfect delivery, and always a bearer of good news.[11]

Svechin General Staff Academy: December 2, 2007

"The American planning process was complicated by the fact that Red Lightning could only be a success if employed by the entire NATO force structure. This resulted in the requirement to brief carefully the other members of the Alliance and integrate them into the planning. The manifest brilliance of the plan was sufficient to convince the Europeans, and their efforts soon worked hand-in-hand with the Americans. I must say that the subtlety of the plan found immediate resonance with the military intellectual traditions of the European members of NATO."

NATO Headquarters, Brussels: May 14,1988

The SACEUR (Supreme Allied Commander, Europe) was brought in to the planning late. His response was explosive. "Have they forgotten to nail down the booby hatch on the Army Staff again?" But "Iron Mike" Meyer was not one to rock the boat when subtler methods could be used. A back-channel call to the Vice ensued.

"Tom, this is Mike. How're Agnes and the kids? Great. And how's young Agnes doing at the Point? Great! Say, John, about this Red Lightning thing, has your staff really thought this one through? No, I did not know this was a pet project of Oscar's before he retired. That puts a different light on it. Oscar always knew what he was doing. I can't imagine him letting something like this out without some mighty fine staff work.[12] Of course, we can handle our end here in Europe, Tom. I've got a real CAN DO team here... Reservations? No, none at all now—well, one little one maybe. How the hell am I going to sell this to the Allies, Tom? Gee, thanks. Well, that's what I have a staff for. You can depend on us to hold up our end. Linda sends her love."

Pandemonium broke out at the NATO Defense Ministers conference when the Americans briefed Red Lightning. It was difficult to tell whether the ministers or their senior military staffs were more aghast. Here were men who had made careers out of fending off American military

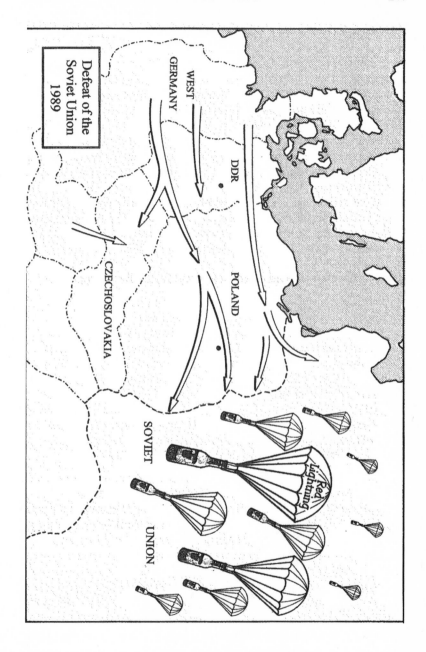

amateurishness, but this was too much. The descendants of Caesar, Marlborough, Napoleon, and Clausewitz, men capable of infinite disdain, were thoroughly mortified.

But again, Fate's wings fluttered. The Greek minister had been an island of calm amid all the shouting. During lunch, he dropped his bomb. "Gentlemen, I am going to recommend that Greece supports the plan— enthusiastically!" Now that he had their attention, he continued: "The wine produced for export in Greece has been so bountiful these last few years that even the French are unable to buy it all and slap their labels on it." The reminder that for two years the grape had been blessed from Lisbon to Izmir guaranteed the interest of the Italian, French, Spanish, and Portuguese ministers. Even the Turkish minister made signs of interest, albeit very slight; after all, it was a Greek proposal. The British minister thought of all the unused distillery plant in Scotland now that Scotch had hit an export slump. The lunch ended on a decidedly mellow note.[13]

Svechin General Staff Academy: December 2, 2007

"It would be appropriate at this time to consider what the Soviet intelligence services had learned of Red Lightning. All this time the KGB and the GRU were busy gathering information. Their problem was they had could not piece it into anything coherent. They had even picked up the name Red Lightning, but the relationship to the Utah National Guard, Soviet vodka exports, strange plastic containers, and sudden market for the lake of surplus Common Market wine eluded them.

I must say that it was an act of unpardonable incompetence for the intelligence services to fail to pass these findings to the Military History Institute for proper evaluation of the historical connections."

Military History Institute, Moscow, June 27, 1988

To Lieutenant-Colonel Ivan V Chonkin, Chief of the Correlation of Forces Analytical Staff, Military History Institute, these intelligence gatherings were intriguing. The holder of innumerable degrees in history, including one from Harvard, and a master in the Marxist-Leninist science of war, Chonkin could smell something interesting.

The steaming tea glass that would have scalded an American did not even distract him from his musings. He sipped it absent-mindedly as he stared out of the high, old-fashioned windows. His favorite staff historian, Major Vasili Dragomirov, listened attentively. "There is the delicious aroma of British special operations in the last war, Vasili. But that is just the problem. This Red Lightning is an American project. Their style is too high-tech, too straightforward, too unimaginative."

Chonkin was uneasy, like a man with an itch he could not scratch. Were the Americans doing something out of character? Impossible! Still? He stood up quickly and put down the tea. "Vasili, get me the historical probability study your team did." The study was the definitive Marx-ist-Leninist scientific analysis that had reduced the possibility of certain types of conduct by certain opponents, based upon history and national characteristics, into precise mathematical equations.

Dragomirov flipped to the heading: "Indirect Approach," and said: "Comrade Colonel, the Americans are at the bottom of the table with a probability ratio that was not listed as zero solely for the sake of math-ematical precision." He flipped to the table on "Military Historical Consciousness and Resultant Utilizations." Here the figure was indeed zero. The poor little circle even seemed to quiver under Dragomirov's smirk. So why was Chonkin not more comforted?

The Kremlin: July 3,1988

The KGB briefing to the Politburo finally had the answer to the mystery of Red Lightning. The briefer was interrupted by the Party First Secretary as the opening Vu-Graph went up. "I understand the Americans are using more advanced full-color slides. Why is the KGB behind the Americans? We must address this Slide Gap at our next meeting, comrades. Proceed, Comrade Briefer."[14]

For once the geriatric ward that doubled as the Politburo listened attentively. Hearing aids were set at max so as not to miss a word. "In summation, comrades, we believe the American government is attempt-ing to control the alcoholic beverage market in order to increase state revenues to relieve their public deficit."

The conclusion generated a good deal of smug satisfaction. Ancient Gregorii "Gulag" Grishin, spoke for the group: "This only shows the back-wardness of the entire capitalist system. It is incredible that they have only just discovered what an invaluable source of state revenue this can be. Under socialism, we have known this from the beginning!"[15]

Svechin General Staff Academy: December 2, 2007

"The origin of the war that began on the morning of May 15, 1989 is not germane to this lecture. Suffice it to say, that strategic deception had been successfully employed by the Soviet High Com-mand. NATO had mobilized but far too late. By that morning in May, the only American reinforcements that had reached Europe and deployed were National Guard rocket launcher battalions. The General Staff considered that as proof of the collapse of the Reforger reinforcement plan."

Just inside West Germany: May 15,1989

Major Yuri Vinnogradov was having a very bad night as the T-80 tanks of his battalion exploded one by one. His recollection of the regimental intelligence officer's briefing was becoming increasingly hostile. Major Andrei Golitsyn was all polish and effect, so elegantly nonchalant that he almost purred his Moscow accent.

> "Your mission is very simple, Major. You just take your battalion from A to B and brush off the trash in your path. That consists of barely a platoon, I expect, of the American 11 th Armored Cavalry Regiment, a notorious collection of cutthroats and assassins with no fighting value to speak of. Of course, you must not let the exaggerations of our fraternal Vietnamese allies concern you. Well, they call themselves, of all things 'The Black Horse.' Really, Major, you DO have the easy job, and certainly all the glory in all this; you should see what we on the staff must go through."

Regrettably, Vinnogradov thought, the Black Horse troops in his path had not heard Golitsyn's briefing. After two hours of combat, the advance march security detachment had already been wiped out twice; the third replacement unit was not going to last much longer, and regiment was screaming about keeping to the timetable in the plan. While it was not much comfort to Vinnogradov, he knew that his battalion and even the regiment could be wiped out by the American cavalry unit in front of him, but the enemy would be overrun sooner or later by the locust-like echelons stacked up all the way to the Soviet border. That was allowed for in the plan.

A fireball lit up the head of the column. Vinnogradov was not thinking happy thoughts as he yelled into the radio to douse the woodline to the left with fire. "Another tank gone," he said to himself. "I had 31 this morning; now I'm down to 15, no 14, counting the steel pyre up ahead. What was the name of that American cavalry in this sector? The Black Horse, that was it." He promised himself the first thing he was going to do if he made it through this night was to punch Golitsyn in the mouth.

The last tank hit had been Pol'shin's, the second company commander to buy it. The tank had been struck at the curve in the road that blocked the whole column; the fire that was roasting poor Timofey Pol'shin and his crew had illuminated other vehicles struggling to pass the wreck on the narrow, hilly shoulder of the road. They too died under the marksmanship of the Black Horse. One of those hit in due course was Yuri Vinnogradov's own tank. As he leapt from the exploding vehicle, he saw in the firelight piles of cardboard cases and the gleam of glass along the road and under the trees.

By dawn new battalions were clogging the roads trying to pass through the wreckage of the first echelon's lead elements like Vinnogradov's. All along the front, NATO screening forces had done their best to keep the Soviet torrent confined to a manageable depth. They had been successful. In the British sector, the bloodied Soviet advance elements reported over and over again strange bugle calls and shouts of "Tally Ho!"

With the morning's light what Vinnogradov had seen only in the reflection of a burning tank, the back-up Soviet columns could see in the plain light of day. Lining the roads were tens of thousands of cases of bottles of all shapes and sizes. The tops of the cases had been opened to reveal their contents. Millions of bottles were strewn in heaps throughout the well-cropped grass that bordered the German roads and along the myriad logging trails through the forests.

Gradually, across the whole front, from Austria to the Baltic, these displays were gaining the fixed attention of the tens of thousands of vehicle crewmen passing by. If it took longer than expected for someone actually to examine the curiosity, it was not because of iron discipline. It was simple incredulity. Men who should have been examining the terrain ahead or spotting for enemy aircraft found their attention focused along the road as certain brain synapses were activated that transmitted the sensation of great thirst.

Svechin General Staff Academy: December 2, 2007

"Yes, gentlemen, unbeknownst to the KGB and the GRU, the Allies had already executed the first and passive phase of Red Lightning. Although the successful *Maskirovka* measures of the Soviet Armed Forces had succeeded in delaying NATO's full mobilization until it would have been too late, it was soon enough to put Red Lightning into effect. Upon warning, the Allies relocated the liquor stocks of Western Europe to a ten kilometer belt along the inter-German border."

American Sector, Bavaria: May 16,1989

A scholarly post-war study among veterans of both sides determined that the time elapsing between sighting the booze and physical examination by the first member of each unit never exceeded 7 minutes and 35 seconds. The average time, however, was much closer to a flat 3 minutes. Once the cry went up, entire columns of armored vehicles emptied of their crewmen. It was never revealed, though, that the bulk of the data was found in the meticulously detailed ledger of a betting pool maintained by a member of the Black Horse. They were given the drama of real events by Czech intercepts of the actual betting pool reporting over the air.[16]

"Booze Bet One, this is Red Claw Four. I have a positive sighting at 0615, a motorized rifle battalion backed-up on the road at KL 763432. Some little guy jumped out of the hatch of his BMP and grabbed a bottle. Thirty seconds later the whole battalion un-asses. Man, this is the first a.m. happy hour I've ever seen."

"Booze Bet One, this is Blue Hammer Three. Got one for ya at KM 759466 at 0621. This ZSU-23-4 battery just drives off the road into the woods. I thought they were going to set up, but they just circled the biggest pile of the stuff they saw. Then they all jumped out at once."

"Booze Bet One, this is Gold Arrow Six. I gotta have the winner of the special event category. Time 0711 at the road junction in KL 743453. A tank company and an artillery battery show up at the same time by the same booze pile. Two officers jump out and start waving their arms at each other. Then, so help me, one hauls off and pops the other. And everybody joined in. I haven't seen anything like this since those guys from the 101st tried to take Kelley's new black beret. I think the Red Legs down there might win this one."[17]

Labeling the bottles in Russian had been a good idea because it had made for an instantaneous, reflex action by the Russians which cut down the chance of second thoughts while trying to remember secondary school English.

VODKA
100 Proof
GIFT OF THE AMERICAN PEOPLE

The contents of this bottle have been certified fit for human consumption by the Surgeon General of the United States.

The gift of the contents of this bottle does not constitute any violation of the Geneva Convention, the Laws of War, or of any Treaty or Protocol dealing with the ban of Chemical Weapons.

The United States is not liable for any damages resulting

from the use of this gift, or for any disciplinary action taken by second party armed forces as a result of its use.

Product of Blue Grass Distilleries
Lexington, Kentucky

The legal warnings may have been the pride and joy of the Army lawyers, but they were incomprehensible to the Soviet soldier. Not that the Russian was bad, rather Soviet legal tradition simply did not breed the Philadelphia lawyer mentality expressed here. Being sued was not a big problem in the Soviet Union; being hauled off to the *gulag* was.

Svechin General Staff Academy: December 2, 2007

Now Chonkin roused himself.

"In this supreme crisis, the leadership style of the Russian officer asserted itself. The selfless and heroic efforts of thousands of officers wearing the Soviet uniform nearly defeated the American plan. Countless stories exist of officers setting a courageous example to their men in the face of this unbearable provocation. However, it was the iron habit of drunkenness, forced upon our people by the Soviet system, that proved the stronger force, one immune to higher moral values."

Westphalia, West Germany: May 17,1989

Guards Colonel Vladimir Lushin leaped out of his command car, roaring like the god of war he was. The column had been halted, and he wanted to know why. A young lieutenant stood, legs apart, in front of a pile of crates and bottles, his AK-74 still smoking. Two dead soldiers lay in front of the lieutenant. "Comrade colonel," he reported, "These men violated Soviet discipline and were swilling this vodka. They refused to stop. It could have destroyed discipline in the entire unit. I shot them."

"Very good, lieutenant!" He paused long enough to see that the lieutenant had not shot up all the cases as well. "Have a squad load up the remaining cases into my vehicle. We must examine this filthy capitalist trick more closely to see what poisons or mind-altering drugs the enemy has filled them with." As the colonel drove away, the lieutenant gave him his best salute, elated at having done his duty so well. The hand that quivered along the lip of his helmet went limp and fell to his side as he watched the colonel waving a newly opened bottle from the hatch as his command car turned around the bend.

Here and there a "real" communist, usually a junior officer but rarely a political officer, tried to stem the breakdown.

"Comrade Warrant Officer Bulyagin, what are you doing? Stop this at once! How can you, a Party member, act so unlike a communist?" Junior Lieutenant Aleksander "By the Plan" "Vegorov stood his ground in front of the warrant officer, pistol drawn, ready to impose the ultimate sanction of Soviet military justice in the field. The older man looked up from the pile of crates he was loading into his BMP and defiantly broke the neck off the bottle against the steel armored door. The sharp smell of the vodka filled the air between them. Bulyagin decided it was time to explain the facts of life.

"Listen, Sasha," he said, using the diminutive of the lad's name. He was not a bad officer; he took better care of his men than most, so Bulyagin thought he was worth the trouble. "My card says I'm a Party member, but God knows I'm not a communist, and it's about time you knew the difference."[18]

Soviet Headquarters, Zossen, East Germany: May 18,1989

When thousands of vehicles in the first echelon had been loaded to the limit with bottles, the men bravely attempted to consume what was left strewn about. Thousands of liters of alcohol entered the bloodstream of the fighting elements of three Soviet fronts.

It did not take the headquarters of the 25 first echelon divisions long to notice a growing sluggishness in the movement of their regiments as well as a definite frivolity and slurred speech in their radio transmissions. Needless to say, COMSEC (communications security) went right to hell. It was Christmas for NATO signals intercept units. Stern inquiries from Soviet higher headquarters only increased the apprehension; frantic visits by commanders and staff followed. It is recorded that the commanders of the *51th* and *201th Guards Motorized Rifle Divisions* and the *6th Guards Tank Division* all died for the Motherland at this time.

Late in the day the extent and nature of the situation began to filter up through Army and Front headquarters. Lieutenant-Colonel Chonkin was present as a General Staff observer at the main Soviet headquarters at Zossen outside Berlin when the situation finally began to clarify. He immediately requisitioned a secure telephone line back to his office in Moscow.

"Vasili, find every copy of that probability study and burn it! What's wrong? I'll tell you what's wrong. We're supposed to be 60 kilometers inside West Germany by now, and the furthest we've gone anywhere is 15. The first echelon divisions have been stopped dead. Stopped dead drunk is more precise. Instead of massing their divisions along the border, they've massed vodka. I tell you, Vasili, it must be that Red Lightning business. Who would ever have thought the Americans could have... No, I have not been near the front!"

Svechin General Staff Academy: December 2, 2007

"Exhaustive planning and wargaming by the Americans had predicted this crisis of the Soviet offensive quite accurately. They were fully prepared to take deadly advantage of the disaster overtaking the Soviet first echelon armies."

NATO Headquarters, Brussels: May 19,1989

"What the hell?" Iron Mike kept muttering to himself as his increasingly euphoric staff put together from intelligence reports the stark picture of the collapse of the Soviet offensive. He had expected little from Red Lightning, at most some confusion in the Soviet advance, but this?

Whatever else you could say about Iron Mike, he was not slow on the uptake. He could see that the Soviet second echelon armies were going to be crashing into that mess along the border soon. His most pressing problem now was logistics. All the war plans had worked on the assumption that NATO forces would have to back-pedal west and thus fall back upon their supplies. Such was the nature of his call to his chief of logistics, General Sir Nigel Smith-Wilson.[19]

"Bunny!" he yelled over the phone. "What are you doing now?"

Smith-Wilson flinched. Bunny was his school nickname and a privileged one among a few friends. He hated this Yankee informality. Damn whoever had betrayed him to the crass American. Still, he managed a cool tone and answered: "Why, sir, we are displacing west and are even ahead of schedule."

"Put that on hold! Be prepared to support a static defense all along the front for an indefinite period."

Bunny clutched at his dignity. Every professional logistician lived in terror that the operations types would do something like this. "But, sir, you just can't turn this sort of thing around at a moment's notice. Why, the planning time alone..."

"General Smith-Wilson, I don't want excuses. I want to see a CAN DO attitude."

Smith-Wilson later pouted to his sympathetic staff: "And if I hear another American say CAN DO, I shall throw up." It was only just beginning to dawn on him exactly how things had changed as he discovered he had over 250,000 Soviet prisoners dropped into his officious care. And the war was not even a week old.

To Smith-Wilson, they were not really people, just so many rations, so many guards, so many camps to set up. If he could have seen...

Trudging west, the column of Soviet prisoners had to get off the road to let the French truck convoy continue east. Warrant Officer Bulyagin put his arm around the dejected shoulders of young Yegorov. "Sasha, perk up! The world is turning over. Just think of the possibilities. You did tear up that Party card, didn't you?"[20]

Further to the south in another column, the German reservist guards had to break up a rather one-sided fight between two Soviet officers. A smoke-blackened tank major had to have his fingers pried off the throat of a thoroughly thrashed staff officer.

Svechin General Staff Academy: December 2, 2007

"The crucial phase of the battle now arrived with the Soviet second echelon armies. The Allies had exhausted their prepositioned stocks of alcohol. Now would be the time to see if their alcoholic munitions could create a similar effect on a forewarned enemy."

The Front: May 20,1989

The passive phase of Red Lightning was over. Prepositioning booze along the enemy's path of advance was not feasible now that the war had become fluid. Iron Mike ordered the execution of the active phase. This phase was essentially a joint operation between US National Guard multiple rocket launcher units and NATO tactical fighter-bombers.

The MRL battalions were issued their tightly controlled munitions once they had arrived in Germany—KICAS-AMs (Kinetic Controlled Air Scatterable Alcoholic Munitions). Maximum reliability was expected from the Mormon and Deep South Baptist Guardsmen. It was hoped they would not be sampling their own ordnance. At the same time, the NATO fighter-bomber squadrons were issued the air munitions variant of the KICAS-AM. It was from this acronym for the special munition that the soldier's term for the war was born—Operation Kickass.

Priority targets for the KICAS-AMs would be in the path of attacking Soviet units. Each exploding rocket would scatter hundreds of florescent orange round plastic miniatures, each with its own little parachute. The targets for fighter-bombers would be assembly areas, river-crossing sites, and headquarters. For headquarters targets a special subcategory of the KICAS-AM was developed, the DEBOCALL or Delayed Effect Bomb Cluster, Alcoholic, Leadership, because its content was the exquisite Stolychnaya vodka that most Russians never saw because supplies were reserved for the elite or for export. It was felt that the special target population in headquarters with its more "refined tastes" required a special munition.[21]

The new weapons were quickly employed. The *Rogachev Motorized Rifle Division* attacked on a narrow ten kilometer breakthrough front through the Lower Saxon countryside determined to sweep aside the British armored cavalry screen and come to grips with the British Army of the Rhine. They made an impressive sight, four regiments attacking in waves of tanks and infantry fighting vehicles. In one of those IFVs, nine infantrymen rattled around its cramped interior just like thousands more on both sides. They collectively flinched as airbursts cracked overhead. Instead of rending steel, an orange ball on a parachute floated through an open hatch. When the command to dismount for the assault was given, the squad rushed out with an enthusiasm their platoon leader had never noticed before. Instead of shaking out into an assault line, they were running all over the field chasing those little orange balls.

Colonel-General Valeri Odinstov was about to climb into his staff car outside the field headquarters of his *13th Combined Arms Army* when the Luftwaffe Tornado fighter-bombers swung in low. A groan escaped from the terrified driver as the Tornados dispensed their canisters. Visions of a fiery death shot through Odinstov's mind as the canisters peeled open. His mouth gaped. A mass of little orange balls, like garish dandelion fluff, floated out on tiny parachutes. One of the parachutes failed and its cargo shot earthward to strike Odinstov right in his open mouth. Despite the subsequent hell of Soviet dental reconstruction, he could count the event a blessing. He could rightly claim at his court-martial that he was not responsible for the utter breakdown of good order and discipline that followed at his headquarters.

Svechin General Staff Academy: December 2, 2007

"It has been argued that it could have been simpler and more effective to have taken out headquarters with conventional munitions. However, as pointed out in the original study from the American Center of Military History upon which this strategy was based, destroyed headquarters are automatically replaced by lower echelon staffs. A headquarters still physically intact but attempting to function through a thickening alcoholic fog cripples its subordinate elements more surely than unending combat."

The Kremlin: July 19,1989

The disaster that overcame the first echelon was repeated on a greater scale with the second echelon. The third echelon armies halted in Poland and Slovakia to dig in, but Red Lightning's ethnic selectiveness factor was on the point of paying off.

The members of the Defense Council of the Politburo had not slept in three days. The Chief of the General Staff envied them. He had not slept in a week. His briefing on the mobilization of reserve formations was acting as a depressant on everyone. There was no good news.

"The loss of over 50 of our best divisions and the defection of all the Warsaw Pact armies except Bulgaria's puts us on the horns of a dilemma, comrades. The front will collapse without reinforcement by newly mobilized formations. Unfortunately, the majority of such formations are from the non-Slavic republics of the Transcaucasus and Central Asia. They either don't drink at all or are more moderate in their habits.

While they are inherently less vulnerable to NATO's secret weapon, these peoples are historically and politically unreliable. They continue to resist the leadership of their Russian big brother and openly resent the reality of Soviet power. We are taking a great chance on placing these formations at the front, but we have no choice."

The Front, June-July 1989

Privates Yusef Sultanov and Mohammed Ulsanbekov were not happy about manning a machine-gun position in the dank oak forest outside Lodz in Poland. The dry cleanliness of their oasis near Samarkand in Uzbekistan was an all too recent memory. They were reservists, as was the fat Russian captain who commanded their company. He had come from Tashkent, some administrator in the Ministry of Agriculture. He had actually been born in Uzbekistan but had not bothered to learn a word of Uzbek other than an impressive collection of curse words.

Captain Petrov's tight uniform tortured his pudgy body. It was so much easier to be a boss behind a desk with all these swarthy *Churkas* properly bowing and scraping. But now he was afraid. There had been a subtle yet noticeable decline in the alacrity of their obedience the closer they came to the front.

He approached their position for the third time that morning on his ceaseless round of inspections. He muttered to himself: "And what am I supposed to do with 112 men of whom 83 are Uzbeks, 12 Turkmen, 2 Tajiks, 8 Tatars, 3 Ukrainians, an Estonian, a Mongol, one Greek, and only four Russians?" Looking down at the two privates in their position, he thought to himself: "And these two yellow dogs are not even the worst. At least, these two understand Russian, I think."

"You two," he barked in Russian in his best colonial apparatchik tone: "Have you seen anything to your front?" The Uzbeks smiled back, their black eyes blank of understanding. Petrov had that sinking feeling. He shrugged and trudged off to the next position along the muddy trail. The Uzbeks' laughter followed him through the trees and seemed to strike between his shoulder blades. Did they really call him that? .. .in Russian?— "Captain Orange Balls."

Field Headquarters, SACEUR, Location Undisclosed

General Smith-Wilson paled when he was told Iron Mike was on the secure phone. He did not need any more surprises. He already had in excess of 1,300,000 Warsaw Pact prisoners he had never planned for, and they were still pouring in. He did not even want to think about all the East Germans, Poles, and Czechs. He was appalled at the thought that the greatest contribution of his career would be the operation of the world's largest drunk tank.

"Bunny! Change TWO!" Meyer shouted over the phone.

Smith-Wilson felt faint. "Yes, sir, we are still prepared to begin displacing west."

"Dammit, Bunny, will you forget that crap. We're moving EAST!"[22]

Svechin General Staff Academy: December 2, 2007

"Therefore, shorn of its military forces, Soviet power collapsed quickly. Who could have foreseen the changes, gentlemen? The secession of the Union republics, the introduction of capitalism, and the re-establishment of the monarchy—at least we were spared the imposition of a liberal democracy and a continued border with

Poland. Only I am not sure I wouldn't trade it for our new border with the Ukraine!"

The last line brought the expected chuckle from the audience. He always tried to end with a joke.

That evening Chonkin worked late. He dismissed his aides and surveyed the clean expanse of an uncluttered desk. From a small drawer, he drew out a box of his personal stationery. He took out several sheets and briefly admired the quality of the vellum paper and the black and gold two-headed eagle engraving of his coat of arms, the gift of his grateful sovereign. Dipping an ancient pen into a gilt inkwell, he wrote in English,

"Dear John,
I must thank you for your kindness in reviewing the manuscript of my latest book.[23] I particularly liked your comments on how the art of the indirect approach is actually a variation on asymmetrical warfare. There is one point, however, that I wish to discuss further on the human element in war..."

Several hours and two dozen sheets of paper later, he finished. He personally addressed the envelope, enjoying the smooth flow of the ink across the rich paper. It read:

> Mr. John Moran
> c/o The History Department
> Jeb Stuart High School
> Falls Church, Virginia

The Reality

The sad reality of this chapter is that the alcoholism culture of the Russians was worsened by the moral bankruptcy of the Soviet experiment until it became a major source of concern to the reformist First Party Secretary, Mikhail Gorbachev, in the 1980s. Deaths of young fathers due to alcoholism had become a common social phenomenon and the major cause of the rapid decline of the lifespan of the average Russian male. The Soviet Union was the only country to be conducting research into infant retardation due to intoxication of the father at the moment of conception at this time and the only country that needed to. Within the Soviet armed forces, drunkenness remained an enormous problem to the end. To Western observers the appearance in public of drunken Soviet officers was not an infrequent occurrence. Nor is it a problem that disappeared with the Soviet Union.

Would the use of alcohol as a weapon have worked to a useful degree? We will never know. We do know that it was a glaring cultural weakness and that the epitome of the art of war is to strike weakness. We also know that there is enough historical evidence to show that it did work on occasion in the past. What is more important than this particular *deus ex machina* is that the technological armies of the West increasingly are blind to the human element in war. "Men are nothing. Man is everything," Napoleon has been quoted as saying. We neglect the study of man in war at our peril.

Bibliography

Barron, John, *MiG Pilot: The Final Escape of Lt. Belenko,* Avon Books, New York, 1981.

Carrell, Paul, *Scorched Earth: The Russo-German War 1943–1944,* Little Brown, Boston, 1970.

Gabriel, Richard A., *The New Red Legions: An Attitudinal Portrait of the Soviet Soldier,* Greenwood Press, Newport, CT, 1980.

Goldhammer, Herbert, *The Soviet Soldier: Soviet Military Management at the Troop Level,* Crane Russak, New York, 1975.

Seaton, Albert, *Battles: Moscow 1941–1942,* Jove Books, New York, 1971.

Notes

*1. I.V. Chonkin, *The Masterpiece of War: Red Lightning and the Fall of the Soviet Union (The Chonkin Lectures)* (Moscow, 2009), p. 12.

2. Aleksander Andreyevich Svechin (1878–1938), General, Imperial Russian Army, during World War I and chief of staff to General Brusilov, then Chief of Staff of the Army. Along with Brusilov, he went over to the Reds during the Russian Civil War. Served finally as chief of the General Staff Academy and made great contributions as a historian and theorist to the art of war. He was murdered by Stalin during the purges. His ideas were resurrected after the collapse of the Soviet Union and became an important theoretical underpinning of the new Russian Army.

*3. Piotr III, born Piotr Dmitrivich Suvorov, had been a young airborne forces colonel whose charisma and leadership skills made him a magnet for all those who wanted to save Russia in the death throes of the Soviet Union. The fact that he had been a descendant of Russia's most famous and revered soldier, Aleksander V Suvorov, was a great help. Chonkin's organizational brilliance was a perfect match. They served as a faithful team that saw Russia through the terrible civil war of 1990-92. The third member of the team was the young priest, Father Pavel, who blessed them on the same spot where St Sergei had blessed Dmitri Donskoi as he led the Russian hosts to defeat the Mongols and save Russia in 1380. Father Pavel was the spiritual inspiration of the Piotrist movement. More than a few miracles were attributed to him. Piotr was acclaimed tsar of the new Suvorov Dynasty in the Kremlin's St George's Hall in December 1991. A few years later, after the death of the old, KGB-tainted patriarch, Piotr made it known to the Holy Synod that he favored Pavel for the job. Russia rejoiced in its young Patriarch, and the Russian Orthodox Church marked its new flowering from that triptych scene at the St Sergeiv Monastery.

4. "The Big Bedroom" is the nickname given to the official briefing room of the US Army's Chief of Staff.

*5. After retirement, Rauch was hired by a computer software development company and successfully marketed the new Powerpoint briefing system to the Army. He was responsible for the golden age of Army briefing in the late 1990s. Because of him, learning to manipulate Powerpoint was considered the most important skill a captain could acquire. Of course, there was a terrible breach of decorum when a certain captain asked him how George Patton got across northwest Europe without Powerpoint. A few words to some old friends and the captain finished his career early after a stint in the Recruiting Command.

6. V.A. Antonov-Ovesyenko, *Zapiski o grazhdanskoi voine* (Moscow, 1924), pp. 19–20. In this context "armored brigades" refers to units equipped with armored cars.

7. Gabriel, *The New Red Legions,* pp. 152–59. A survey among former Soviet military personnel showed that 55.8 percent of the respondents had seen officers drunk on duty and 64.6 percent had seen NCOs in a similar condition. Over 30 percent thought that combat capabilities were degraded by alcoholism in their units. See also *Krasnaya Zvezda,* November 23, 1972, p. 2. Over one-third of all law violations by military personnel were also said to be committed in a state of drunkenness; cited in Goldhammer, *The Soviet Soldier,* p. 152.

8. Carrell, *Scorched Earth,* pp. 305–06.

*9. *Red Lightning: Conception and Planning* (Center of Military History, Washington, DC, 1995), pp. 39–43.

*10. Utah's role in Red Lightning was immortalized in a downtown Salt Lake City monument and a major float in the annual Pioneer Day parade.

*11. Interview with Lieutenant General (ret) Courtney Massingale.

*12. Oscar S. Rauch, *Godfather to Red Lightning: A Memoir* (New York, 1997), p. 145.

*13. Panayiotis Koriopoulos, *How Greece Won World War III* (Athens, 1993), p. 173.

*14. The Slide Gap was indeed at the head of the next meeting's agenda. The Politburo ordered GOSPLAN to include upgrading the Soviet Union's entire briefing technology to full color slides. Within weeks plans were drafted to build a network of factories to produce slides at three locations for the entire Soviet Union—Talinn, Moscow, and Khabarovsk. Looking back on the Soviet threat, one is amazed that so much of what the Politburo did seemed to be conceived in the midst of an opiate dream. The best history so far of the post-Stalin Politburo was the recent book by Vladimir Luzhkov *Dreamland and Other Fantasies of the Radiant Future* (Moscow, 2003), see especially pp. 334–35.

15. Both under the tsar and the communists, the sale of alcohol was a state monopoly and the primary source of state income, exceeding all others.

*16. Edward Colliers, *Black Horse Bookies* (New York, 1997), p. 211.

*17. Red Legs is a nickname for US Army artillerymen who in the 19th century wore a red strip down the uniform trouser leg. The black beret was the object of the heart's desire for the men of the US Army's armor branch, but the dominance of the infantry ensured it would never ever be issued to the Army. Many men, however, bought the beret and wore it in defiance. In officers' clubs, young armor officers were known to make grandiloquent vows to introduce the black beret should any of them become chief of staff. Of course, the introduction of the blue beret after the war killed any hope of that.

*18. Bulyagin and Yegorov, *How We Brought Walmart to Russia* (New York, 2002), pp. 34–36.

*19.   Michael L. Meyers, *How I Wielded the Red Lightning: Command in World War III* (Boston, 1991), p. 245.

*20.   Bulyagin and Yegorov, *How We Brought Walmart to Russia*, p. 45.

*21.   *Proceedings of the Committee on the Conduct of the War, US House of Representatives, July 23, 2002*; the Committee concluded that the expense of buying Stolychnaya for this special purpose had been wholly unnecessary; it accused the Army of mirror-imaging its Soviet opponent in assuming more refined tastes when the Committee's research showed that Soviet generals were just as happy with grain alcohol.

*22.   Nigel Smith-Wilson, *How Logistics Won World War III* (London, 1992), p. 221.

*23.   I. V Chonkin, *The Human Factor in Asymmetrical Warfare* (Moscow, 2008), p. 311.

Index